Social History i

General Editor:

Social History in Perspective is a new
many topics in social, cultural and re. ˷ ˷˷ ...ˑˑˑˑy ıor students. They
will give the student clear surveys of the subject and present the most
recent research in an accessible way.

PUBLISHED

John Belchem *Popular Radicalism in Nineteenth-Century Britain*
Simon Dentith *Culture and Society in Nineteenth-Century England*
Harry Goulbourne *Race Relations in Britain since 1945*
Tim Hitchcock *English Sexualities, 1700–1800*
Sybil Jack *Towns in Tudor and Stuart Britain*
Helen Jewell *Education in Early Modern England*
Christopher Marsh *Popular Religion in the Sixteenth Century*
Hugh McLeod *Religion and Society in England, 1850–1914*
Michael A. Mullett *Catholics in Britain and Ireland, 1558–1829*
John Spurr *English Puritanism, 1603–1689*
W. B. Stephens *Education in Britain, 1750–1914*
David Taylor *Crime, Policing and Punishment in England, 1750–1914*
N. L. Tranter *British Population in the Twentieth Century*
Ian D. Whyte *Scotland's Society and Economy in Transition, c.1500–c.1760*

FORTHCOMING

Eric Acheson *Late Medieval Economy and Society*
Ian Archer *Rebellion and Riot in England, 1360–1660*
Jonathan Barry *Religion and Society in England, 1603–1760*
A. L. Beier *Early Modern London*
Sue Bruley *Women's Century of Change*
Andrew Charlesworth *Popular Protest in Britain and Ireland, 1650–1870*
Richard Connors *The Growth of Welfare in Hanoverian England, 1723–1793*
Geoffrey Crossick *A History of London from 1800–1939*
Alistair Davies *Culture and Society, 1900–1995*
Martin Durham *The Permissive Society*
Peter Fleming *Medieval Family and Household in England*
David Fowler *Youth Culture in the Twentieth Century*
Malcolm Gaskill *Witchcraft in England, 1560–1760*

Titles continued overleaf

Please note that a sister series, *British History in Perspective*, is available which covers all the key topics in British political history.

CRIME, POLICING AND PUNISHMENT IN ENGLAND, 1750–1914

David Taylor

Principal Lecturer in History
University of Huddersfield

First published in 1998 by
MACMILLAN PRESS LTD
Houndmills, Basingstoke, Hampshire RG21 6XS
and London
Companies and representatives throughout the world

ISBN 0–333–64198–1 hardcover
ISBN 0–333–64199–X paperback

A catalogue record for this book is available from the British Library.

This book is printed on paper suitable for recycling and made from
fully managed and sustained forest sources.

10   9   8   7   6   5   4   3   2   1
07   06   05   04   03   02   01   00   99   98

Printed in Hong Kong

Typeset by Aarontype Limited, Easton, Bristol, Great Britain

 Published in the United States of America 1998 by
ST. MARTIN'S PRESS INC.,
Scholarly and Reference Division
175 Fifth Avenue, New York, N.Y. 10010

ISBN 0–312–21396–4

*To Thelma and the memories
of holidays in Spain and Tunisia*

CONTENTS

ACKNOWLEDGEMENTS

In writing this book I have become indebted to many people. As will be clear from the Notes and References section, I owe a great deal to a wide range of scholars upon whose works I have drawn. I trust I have represented them accurately and treated them fairly. I am particularly grateful to those colleagues and former students who have listened to my strange views and sought to keep me from straying too far into error. Dr Richard Lewis of Teesside University provided much useful comment and encouragement at a critical time, Dr Bertrand Taithe of the University of Huddersfield ensured that certain sections did not become Foucault-free zones, while Dr Philip Woodfine, also of the University of Huddersfield, not only commented in great detail on an earlier draft but also provided perceptive observations on the overall structure and argument. The book is better for their contributions. Errors of fact and questionable interpretations are my responsibility. My thanks also go to the various libraries and record offices in which I have worked. In particular, I would like to thank the staff of Huddersfield University library, who have been cheerful and efficient throughout.

Finally, my warmest thanks go to my wife, Thelma, who has contributed greatly to the book's evolution, having read and commented on every draft, and offered much advice and encouragement, as well as injecting a sense of realism into the whole venture. The book is dedicated to her as a small token of my gratitude.

DAVID TAYLOR

INTRODUCTION

'The administration of criminal justice is the commonest, the most striking, and the most interesting, shape in which the sovereign power of the state manifests itself to the great bulk of its subjects.' (J. F. Stephen, *A General View of the Criminal Law of England*, 1863, pp. 99–100)

Over the course of the long nineteenth century, that is from about 1780 to 1914, a distinctive disciplinary state – the policeman-state, to use Gatrell's telling phrase – developed, and the growth of the criminal justice system was a central aspect of state formation in this period.[1] Power in nineteenth-century society lay primarily in the hands of property-owning Anglo-Saxon males who had substantially more influence than other groups such as women, the poor, vagrants or gypsies. Society, seemingly unequal to a greater degree than before, also appeared to be more fissiparous. The 'threat to order' was a recurring theme. The need to preserve order was couched in terms of protecting an essentially law-abiding majority against the depredations of a law-breaking minority. Despite the rhetoric, maintaining order was more than a question of upholding an abstract concept of justice; it was also one of finding a balance between coercion and consent that would ensure the preservation of a complex property-based and patriarchal socioeconomic and political society. The evolution of the criminal justice system, the emergence of the policeman-state, can only be understood in this wider context. This book seeks to provide an overview of the existing literature and an interpretation of the development and significance of the criminal justice system.

The first major argument is that the evolution of the 'modern' criminal justice system was a two-phased process, centred, firstly, on the late eighteenth and early nineteenth centuries and, secondly, on the decades around the turn of the twentieth century. In both of these phases significant and interrelated changes took place in the perception of crime and the criminal, the theory and practice of policing, court procedures and the punishment of offenders. Changes in perception and practice were not completely synchronized in either transitional period and the break between 'old' and 'new' was never complete.

The process of change can be characterized in the following broad schematic fashion. Society in the mid-eighteenth century was still largely rural and small-scale. Face-to-face communities and informal sanctions, legitimized in part by religion and custom, meant that the legal system was often used as a last resort. The courts, dominated by amateurs, dealt with the cases that came before them with breathtaking rapidity and operated in a highly personalized manner, but with little protection for the accused. Punishments were severe but, despite an increase in the number of capital offences, relatively few people were actually executed. Crime, as an abstract concept, was rarely discussed and the criminal, though a problem, was seen as a naturally sinful figure but not one that posed a major threat to the stability of society. Parish-based policing touched but lightly on everyday life. Protection, to use an analogy made by Lord Carnarvon in the 1860s, came, as it were, from a variety of defensive works. At the outer line were the old workhouses and bridewells which had a welfare as much as a disciplinary role. Their role was to sift out and cater for those who might otherwise succumb to temptation and be driven to crime. The next line of defence took the form of a moat: transportation carried away some of the more dangerous criminal elements. Finally, behind this was a legal Maginot line: the gallows, that highly visible last line of defence, dealing with those whose actions threatened the health of the body politic.

By the mid-nineteenth century, significant changes had taken place. A more urbanized, more mobile and impersonal society, more reliant upon formal sanctions, had come into being. Reform of the criminal law and the expansion of summary justice, coupled with a greater willingness to use the courts, meant that the law, in a formal sense, was a more immediate presence in the lives of ordinary men and women. The courts had also changed as the administration of justice, at all levels, became more professional. Trial procedures were significantly different following the 'invasion of the lawyers'. In addition, crime had been invested with far greater significance and more attention was paid to the causes of criminal behaviour. The fear of disorder was such that society's protection had been greatly increased. The outer line of poor-law 'bastilles' were clearly located in a disciplinary, rather than welfare, regime. Society was now patrolled by a paid and bureaucratically organized police force which was more organized and more intrusive than before. A further line of defence was provided by the state penitentiaries and enhanced local prisons which had taken over from the gallows and transportation as the dominant form of punishment and deterrence.

This was the first transition from an old order to a more 'modern' one; but further changes took place by the early twentieth century. Now society was not only more urbanized and impersonal but was also more scientific in its understanding. Crime and the criminal, particularly the habitual criminal, remained a major source of concern but explanations and answers were couched in the language of the administrative and scientific expert. The basic structure of the 'defence system' inherited from the early and mid-nineteenth century remained in place but significant refinements had taken place. The workhouse retained its disciplinary function but the role of the police had increased markedly, partly because of the consolidation and pro-fessionalization of the new forces and partly because of the extension of their powers, especially over working-class life. A stronger defensive wall was pro-vided by the rationalization of local prisons, under central control after 1877, and by the creation of convict prisons developed after the abolition of transportation. Furthermore, the prison system was bolstered, not so much by the gallows, as by a series of new institutions – reformatory and industrial schools, and borstal for the young offender, and specialist institutions for the criminally insane, the feeble-minded and the habitual drunkard – each directed at a specific target group. Thus a more complex and sophisticated system of control, based on a more scientific understanding of crime and the criminal, and recognizably 'modern' in most respects, had come into being.[2]

The second major argument is that this two-phase development of the criminal justice system has to be set in a wider context of socioeconomic, political and cultural change, while at the same time recognizing its internal dynamics. Adequate explanation and evaluation can only be given by recognizing the criminal justice system as a complex social institution with a variety of not necessarily compatible objectives. For many years the devel-opment of the legal system, changes in the pattern of punishment and the evolution of the police were seen to be problem free. Change was character-ized in terms of progress, representing both a legitimate and widely-desired response to the threat of criminality, and a transition from irrational and inefficient to rational and efficient methods of crime control. This self-confident view can no longer be sustained. The late eighteenth and early nineteenth centuries did not witness a 'golden age of gangsterdom' in which the law-abiding majority was threatened by a lawless minority. In the more recent writings of Hay, Storch and Ignatieff, emphasis has been placed on class divisions as the propertied elites, old and new, in a rapidly industrializing and urbanizing country, sought to protect their interests via an extended criminal code, the new police and the new prison regime. Further, the harshness of the new practices has been seized upon, not least by Foucault, as evidence to undermine the idea of humanitarian progress. Social control has replaced crime control in analyses of the criminal justice system. However, the developments of the late eighteenth and early nineteenth centuries, let alone those of the late nineteenth and early twentieth, cannot be explained simply in terms of the changing economic order and the ideological and political consequences that flowed from it. Rather, the criminal justice system of 'the old order' contained within itself the means of adaptation and development. There were internally driven administrative and bureaucratic developments which helped shape the process of change.[3] In this way significant, though not necessarily rapid, adjustment took place under a variety of interrelated pressures which, in the long run, had the effect of transforming the criminal justice system.

In the first phase of change identified above, the external pressures were partly social and economic, reflecting the gathering pace of urbanization and commercialization; partly political, reflecting the changing composition of local – and to a much lesser extent national – elites; and partly intellectual, reflecting both the new rationalism and the evangelical revival of the late eighteenth century, which predated the crisis of order of the 1820s and 1830s. In addition, there were internal pressures for change which grew out of the practical experience of law enforcement, especially in the more rapidly changing cities and towns. In the second phase, a similar complex of factors interacted. Internal pressures for reform again grew out of experience, most notably in the prison system, and combined with external factors. In particular, concerns for the continuing economic well-being of 'the first industrial nation' in the face of competition from younger rivals co-existed, indeed were inextricably linked, with worries about the international standing of the world's greatest imperial power. At the same time the gradual democratization of politics aroused fears, in some quarters, of the dangers posed by 'the great unwashed'. And underpinning both sets of anxiety was an even greater fear of racial degeneration. New and pessimistic scientific theories were reinforced by the development of new statistical techniques and seemingly proved by a growing body of empirical evidence from the broad social surveys of Mayhew, Booth and Rowntree and the narrower, specialist information generated by police and prison records and inspections. As in the earlier period, new forms of discipline were developed. Problem groups were more precisely defined, in both popular and scientific discourse, and more specialized institutions developed. At the same time, the identification and marginalization of these 'threats' to society helped to legitimize the state and its increasingly visible agents, the police.

Thirdly, precisely because of the complex genesis of change, the criminal justice system was subject to varied and conflicting claims which it was never able to meet fully. The evolution of the disciplinary state is a history of the growing power of the state, but it is also a history of failure, of exaggerated fears that never fully materialized and of ambitious aims that were only partly realized. Crime was to be controlled and new codes of public behaviour enforced while maintaining social stability and political order. Criminals, at one and the same time, were to be punished, deterred and reformed. Justice was to be dispensed speedily, efficiently and humanely but also inexpensively. At every stage (that is, detection, trial and punishment) there were differing expectations of what the criminal justice system could and should deliver. The debates were about the appropriate balance to be struck. To what extent were individual liberties to be infringed by the extension of police powers to guarantee the well-being of society as a whole? What was the balance between punishment and reform in the prison system? How could justice be delivered without involving unacceptable delays and costs? There was, however, a broader dimension. What part was the criminal justice system to play in the maintenance of social order and political order? What role did it have to play in the creation and preservation of a physically and economically strong nation?

The present volume falls into three sections. The first looks at the incidence of crime and explanations for the criminal. Chapter 1 deals with the way in which the law developed and the problems of measuring crime. This is followed in Chapter 2 by a closer inspection of the nature of crime, which acts as the backcloth to the discussion of the changing image of the criminal in Chapter 3. The second section focuses on the development of the new police and their role in society. Chapter 4 concentrates on the advent of the 'new police', their initial impact and the popular response, while Chapter 5 looks at the period of consolidation in late Victorian and Edwardian England and challenges the popularly held view that police legitimacy was widely established by 1914. The third section is devoted to changes in trial procedure (Chapter 6) and punishment. Chapter 7 discusses the question of capital punishment and Chapter 8 the development of secondary punishments, notably imprisonment. Thus it will be possible to explore the development of the criminal justice system over the course of the long nineteenth century, the motives and aspirations surrounding the changes that took place and the extent to which these changes achieved their purposes. Finally, the criminal justice system will be evaluated as a product of and causal factor in the modernization of the country.

1

CRIME AND CRIME STATISTICS

The Law and Society

In a formal sense, the law derives from a variety of sources including custom, court precedents, royal prerogative and legislation. Acts of Parliament, and judicial interpretations of those acts, along with the common law are the major formative influences. However, such an approach leaves much unanswered about the evolution of the criminal law and the relationship between the law and society. It is tempting to argue that the law is grounded in an absolute morality that transcends time and place. There are a number of acts, notably murder but also including certain forms of theft, which have been condemned throughout time and across widely differing societies. This suggests that certain actions are seen to be intrinsically wrong and, as such, are universally criminalized. Thus Durkheim, in *The Division of Labour in Society*, argued that 'the totality of beliefs and sentiment common to average citizens of the same society forms a determinate system . . . one may call it the *collective* or *common conscience*'. He continued that 'an act is criminal when it offends strong and defined states of the collective conscience'.[1]

This consensus view of crime as clear and unambiguous wrongdoing has a powerful appeal. Right/moral and wrong/immoral are clearly demarcated and actions in the latter category are rightly labelled criminal and dealt with accordingly. This belief, comforting to the individual, is also a powerful legitimizing argument for the legal system, and its proponents and practitioners, and is neatly summed up in J. F. Stephen's comment that 'the moral sentiment of law' was expressed by 'the sentence of law'.[2] On closer inspection, such clear-cut distinctions quickly break down and moral consensus proves to be very elusive. Even a cursory consideration shows that definitions of crime vary between different societies at any given period in time, as well as varying over time in any given society. Furthermore, there is a not a consensus within, let alone between, societies on many matters. This is well illustrated by the conflicting attitudes, and legal responses, to questions of sexuality. The issue of birth control has given rise to fierce debate in which the conflicting sides have claimed that morality was on their side and that the law should reflect their belief. In similar vein, attempts to control 'deviant' sexual behaviour, male and female, has given rise to equally bitter conflict that highlights the absence of any consensus and, furthermore, illustrates how the law is the product of a specific political process that is rooted in an equally specific socioeconomic and cultural context. Rather than a Durkheimian *conscience collective*, it is more convincing to think in terms of a dominant moral order, albeit one subject to challenge and change. However, there is a way in which a general sense of morality is retained within the law. This is enshrined in the idea of blameworthiness, encapsulated in the principle of liability, *actus non facit nisi mens sit rea*, roughly translated as 'the act is not blameworthy unless the mind is guilty'.[3] By focusing upon intent and arguing that the sanctions of the law should be applied only to the blameworthy, a sense of generalized morality is retained at the heart of the system.

Finally, even where there is common ground on certain issues of morality, it is evident that not all immoral acts are criminal. Adultery, for example, though much condemned as immoral by many in the nineteenth century, was not a criminal offence. Further, it is not always clear that a criminal act is immoral. Footballing youths in the streets of early nineteenth-century towns did not see themselves as acting immorally, nor did the men and women of Hampshire and Wiltshire who appeared in large numbers before the courts charged with stealing wood from forests. Indeed, in these cases – and also in some instances of poaching – there existed a popular sense of justice which rejected both the illegality and immorality that had been assigned to these acts. In other words, crime, far from being absolute and moral, is both a relative concept and a social and political construct, varying with time and place. Despite the circularity of the definition, crime is most simply but most satisfactorily thought of as an action (or in certain circumstances inaction) that has been criminalized by the state and which involves criminal prosecution and, on conviction, some form of sanction. While such a definition, as *The Times* once noted, rejects the distinction drawn by the ordinary person between 'acts that are wrong in themselves and others that are wrong because the law has forbidden them', it has the considerable merit of focusing attention upon the criminal law as the product of a political process which itself is intimately linked to the distribution of social and economic power and influence.[4]

Given the existence of a plurality of values in society, the enshrining of some and not others into law has to be seen in political terms. However complex the process may be, its essence is the possession and effective use of political power, though reform of the law was not sought simply for narrow sectional or class interests. There was widespread acceptance of the idea that the law was concerned with social stability, even justice, which required the recognition of a common good that led to limitations on the powerful. Undoubtedly the law was also used to protect narrower elite interests, but not necessarily in a uniform or blatantly self-interested manner. For example, the interests of industry were important but so were restrictions on unfettered industrialization. Few members of parliament in the late eighteenth century would have disputed that property had to be protected, but all property owners could not automatically expect to enjoy this protection.[5] In fact the extension of the law was piecemeal. There was a plethora of property laws and no single, all-embracing piece of legislation. This reflected 'a restrictive, libertarian approach'[6] which was of a piece with the unwillingness of the political elites to introduce new forms of policing. In similar vein, nineteenth-century parliaments passed a number of acts which limited, in theory at least, the actions of factory owners. Such legislation is doubly significant, reflecting a willingness to curb the excesses of capitalism in the interest of preserving social stability and a patriarchal order.

These examples highlight the problematic issue of the relationship between the state and dominant social and economic groups in society. Douglas Hay has argued powerfully that the criminal law was one of the 'chief ideological instruments' of the ruling class in the eighteenth century.[7] In certain respects this argument cannot be denied, though it needs to be refined to recognize the complexities of eighteenth-century society and of the actual workings of the law. Attitudes towards the law did not fit simple class divisions. Some laws were welcomed and supported by substantial parts of the working classes as much as the middle classes while others were disliked as much by elements of the middle classes, as by the working classes. This is perhaps most clearly seen in the attempts to legislate on moral issues. Policing morals aroused strong feelings, both for and against, that cut across class lines.[8]

Nonetheless, the fact remains that property and its protection was seen to be central and the law as a 'multi-use right' was enjoyed by property owners, albeit drawn from a wider range of society than has sometimes been conceded. The desire to preserve order, including patriarchal order as well as civil order, and to defend property specifically, recurs constantly and reflects the well-founded fear that consensus did not extend to all sections of society and was shallow-rooted in others. However, the rhetoric of 'the fight against crime' served a further purpose. It was a powerful cry that gave legitimacy to the extension of the power of the state through legislative change and the growth of policing.

Legal Distinctions and Definitions

While it is important to see the law in its wider political context and to appreciate the social definition of crime, we must not lose sight of narrower but equally important legal distinctions and definitions. First, there was the distinction between indictable and summary offences. The latter were less serious and were dealt with by magistrates in petty sessions. The scope of summary justice was greatly expanded in the early nineteenth century and again in the mid-century, notably through the 1847 and 1850 Juvenile Offenders Acts and the 1855 Criminal Justice Act. The latter allowed minor larcenies, though still indictable offences, to be tried summarily. The 1879 Prevention of Crime Act brought a further extension when the value of goods for which those accused of theft or embezzlement could be tried summarily was raised from 5s to £2. Offences such as common assault, minor affrays, drunk and disorderly behaviour, breaches of the peace, vagrancy and breaches of local by-laws were also dealt with in this way. The former, indictable offences, comprised more serious offences and were tried on indictment either at quarter session before magistrates or at assize before a judge. Within this category were distinctions which were observed in practice and formally recognized by an act in 1842 whereby at quarter sessions all offences were dealt with except those for which the death penalty or transportation for life for a first offender could be imposed, or for a range of specified offences – bigamy, blasphemy, bribery, forgery, perjury and libel – which were restricted to assize. In other words, the most serious crimes of murder, burglary, rape, robbery with violence and assaults accompanied by wounding were tried at assize.

The situation is complicated by the legal distinction between felonies and misdemeanours which dates from the Middle Ages. Both were indictable offences, but misdemeanours did not amount to felony and were generally punished by imprisonment or fine. Felonies were generally capital offences and were distinguished as crimes which occasioned at common law a total forfeiture of lands or goods, or both.[9] Forfeiture for felony was not abolished until the 1870 Forfeiture Act. Significantly, this distinction affected legal procedures, including the right of an accused's counsel to address the jury, and the degree of force that could be used in arresting a suspect.[10] However, any meaningful distinction between more and less serious offences had largely disappeared. While the theft of 6*d* worth of goods was a felony in the early nineteenth century, serious assault and obtaining goods by false pretences were misdemeanours.[11]

Furthermore, the two distinctions between indictable and summary offences and felony and misdemeanour did not necessarily coincide. While all felonies were indictable offences, some could be tried summarily and a number of misdemeanours, such as assaults, riots and obtaining goods by false pretences, were also indictable offences and tried on indictment.

Finally, we need to consider briefly the technical elements of a crime. All crimes comprise two parts, both of which had to be proved before the accused was found guilty.[12] The first element, the *actus rea* of the offence, is the action proscribed in law; the second, the *mens rea*, is the state of mind regarding the *actus rea*. The concept of *mens rea*, which should not be confused with motive, was problematic in that it was difficult to define precisely and was interpreted differently as attitudes towards crime changed. The difficulty of precise definition is well illustrated by the advice given by Blackstone, quoting Hale:

> In cases of larceny [*sic*] the variety of circumstances is so great, and the complications thereof so mingled, that it is impossible to prescribe all the circumstances evidencing a felonious intention, or the contrary; but the same must be left to the due and attentive consideration of the judge and jury, wherein the best rule is *in dubiis* to incline rather to acquit than convict.[13]

The law commissioners spent much time considering the question of theft in their first report of 1834.[14] Conflicting rulings and 'imperfect and uncertain rules' created an unsatisfactory situation but this was compounded by the fact that changing circumstances had rendered many older judgments of dubious validity. Anomalies abounded. A carrier stealing a whole package entrusted to him was not guilty of an offence, whereas if he broke open the package and stole part of it he was guilty of a felony.

The problem surrounding *mens rea* was compounded by the belief that certain unlawful actions should be punished as criminal, even though the defendant lacked any clear intention to commit the crime in question. The question of murder, which much exercised the minds of the law commissioners in the 1830s, is a case in point. Where there was clear proof that the defendant intended to kill the victim there was no problem, but what if the victim had been accidentally killed by the defendant during the commission of another crime? By the doctrine of constructive or implied malice a person might be guilty of murder even though he or she had intended only to commit another felony, had not intended to harm another individual and had done so by pure accident. In a famous ruling, Coke had determined that, if a person, meaning to steal a deer from the park of another, shot at a deer and the arrow, being deflected, killed a boy hidden in a bush, unbeknown to the defendant, that was murder, because the act was unlawful, even though there had been no intention to hurt the boy. This was later modified by Foster so that, if the intention was to commit a trespass, the offence could be no more than manslaughter.

The fourth report of the law commissioners in 1839 dealt at length with this problem. As they noted: 'implied malice, according to the law of England, is loosely defined, or rather is not defined at all'.[15] In an attempt to clarify the situation, they considered a variety of circumstances from which they were able to distinguish between an accidental killing that occurred during the commission of a non-violent crime and an accidental killing that occurred as the result of a violent crime; the death could be seen as purely accidental and unconnected with the criminal intent in the former case, but not in the latter.[16] Although their recommendation was not implemented, they were not alone in thinking the law to be unsatisfactory and disquiet with the felony murder question continued well into the twentieth century. The Report on the Homicide Law Amendment Bill in 1874 contained a familiar complaint:

> The existing definition of murder, which may be roughly stated as killing with malice aforethought, is far too narrow, and the defect has been supplied, not by re-defining the crime, but by subtle intendments of law, by which malice is presumed to exist in some cases where the action is unpremeditated, and even in some cases where death is caused by accident. It is most desirable that a state of the law under which people are condemned and executed by means of a legal fiction should cease.[17]

It is important to recognize the legal distinctions that existed and the changing and problematic nature of fundamental aspects of the criminal law. Nonetheless, there was a body of law which defined criminal behaviour and a legal system that dealt with breaches of the law. From the early nineteenth century onwards, annual criminal statistics, recording those crimes brought to court, were published. Unfortunately, these crime statistics are themselves problematic and do not provide a simple measure of the incidence of crime.

The Official Crime Statistics and the Incidence of Crime

Fears about increases in criminal activity in the late eighteenth century led to demands for the collection of national statistics which were finally heeded in 1810, as the debate on capital punishment gathered momentum. In addition, the preoccupation with the moral and physical well-being of the nation led to the creation of local statistical societies which sought to explore the extent, nature and causes of crime. Increasingly, the contemporary debate was shaped by perceptions of the threat of crime which were drawn from such statistics.

In 1810, clerks of court or circuit were instructed to make annual returns, related to a list of some 50 offences and backdated to 1805, of the number of people in each county of England and Wales under the following headings: (a) committals for trial for indictable offences, (b) discharges on 'no true bill', (c) acquittals and (d) convictions.[18] In 1833, important changes took place. The old list of serious crimes was extended in number, from roughly 50 to 75, and a new sixfold classification, which remained largely constant thereafter, was introduced by the Criminal Registrar, Samuel Redgrave. Crimes were now categorized as follows: (a) offences against the person, (b) offences against property involving violence, (c) offences against property not involving violence, (d) malicious offences against property, (e) offences against the currency and (f) miscellaneous offences. The addition of new offences, for example simple assaults and assaults on police officers under the general heading of offences against the person, would clearly give an artificial inflation to the recorded crime figures. However, this change does not entirely invalidate comparisons with the earlier period. In addition, after 1833 the criminal returns contained information on the age, sex and degree of instruction of those committed for indictable offences for the years 1834–49, while from 1836 the appendix to the annual report of the inspector of prisons included similar biographical data as well as previous gaol records, distinguishing between indictable and summary offences.

A further and more far-reaching reorganization of the official statistics, again conducted by Samuel Redgrave, took place after the passing of the 1856 County and Borough Police Act. In addition to the court and prison returns, the new statistics included the number of people tried summarily by offence and also the number of indictable offences known to the police. From 1859 the Criminal Registrar provided a commentary and review as part of the annual report. Existing information was refined. Data on juvenile offenders sent to industrial and reformatory schools were tabulated separately and information on the birthplace and occupation of prisoners was also included. Finally, a further reorganization in 1893 saw returns standardized on the calendar year and figures given as ratios per 100 000 of the population for ease of comparison, but the underlying structure remained largely unchanged.

The statistics of committals, convictions, discharges and acquittals can be seen as the end product of a complex and changing filtering process. This is shown in Figure 1.1. Critical decisions had to be taken at a number of points and these decisions had the effect of filtering out a large number of criminal (or allegedly criminal) acts. The initial decision, whether or not to start proceedings, was the most important one. For much of the period the onus for initiating a prosecution rested with the individual. The police increasingly took over this role in the latter part of the nineteenth century and the Office of the Director of Public Prosecutions was created in 1879, though its role was essentially advisory until the early twentieth century. Having recognized that he or she had been the victim of a criminal act and decided that it would be appropriate to take formal action through the legal system, the individual would have to weigh up the various costs of taking action. It is impossible to say how many people were deterred by such considerations, but it was felt by many observers, particularly in the early years of the nineteenth century, that there was a serious problem of non-prosecution.

The next set of decisions rested with the local justice of the peace. It was for him to decide whether the case should be proceeded with or not and, if the former, whether it could be dealt with summarily or at quarter session or assize. In the late eighteenth and early nineteenth centuries, the role of the magistrate was more inquisitional but Jervis's Act of 1848 confirmed his developing role that made him akin to a preliminary judge, evaluating the strength of the cases put before him and rejecting those deemed to be inadequate for whatever reason. The number of cases thrown out at this stage is unknown, but magistrates undoubtedly sought informal settlement between the disputing parties or refused to take further action in cases where the allegation seemed frivolous or malicious. But even if the justice was convinced of the need to proceed further, a decision had to be taken as to where the case would be tried. Generally, this was a relatively straightforward matter, but in some cases of both assaults and thefts a judgment had to be made as to whether an indictable offence had been committed.

Figure 1.1   From crime to court

If the case was deemed to be sufficiently serious to warrant trial by jury at the quarter session or assize, there were further hurdles to be overcome. Initially the case would go to the grand jury, which was charged with the responsibility of determining the validity of the prosecution case. Only if a true bill was found would the case proceed to trial. A case could also collapse if, for example, the prosecutor was unwilling or unable to continue. However, once the case was brought the decision rested with the jury to find the defendant guilty or not. Thus, at a number of points in the process, the exercise of discretion was an important element in the actual working of the law.

Furthermore, changes in attitude – a growing intolerance of certain forms of activity, a greater faith in the courts, or even a belief in the need to make an example in a time of trouble – had an effect on the recorded crime rate without any change in the incidence of 'real' crime.

There are those, notably J. J. Tobias, who argue that the crime statistics are so flawed as to be valueless in historical analysis. Quoting the celebrated debate in the columns of *Nineteenth Century* in 1892, in which experienced figures such as W. D. Morrison, Wandsworth Prison Chaplain, Edmund Du Cane, the chairman of the Prison Commissioners, and G. A. Anson, the Chief Constable of Staffordshire, argued that crime was, respectively, increasing, decreasing and largely unchanged, Tobias concludes that 'criminal statistics have little to tell us about crime and criminals in the nineteenth century'[19] and expresses a clear preference for literary sources, including novels, arguing that

> when they [the nineteenth-century statistics] point to a conclusion opposed to that based on contemporary description they can perhaps be discarded without much anxiety. This is even more the case when the conclusion to which they point conflicts with plain common sense.[20]

Ignoring the problems of defining 'plain common sense', it is not self-evident that literary evidence provides a more accurate indication of the extent of crime and the nature of the criminal. Sensationalism aside, contemporary descriptions are as likely to reflect contemporary prejudices and misconceptions as they are to reveal the truth. Furthermore, many literary sources reflected, wittingly or otherwise, the statistical information available at the time. While conceding these points, Rob Sindall has reiterated trenchantly the sceptics' case.[21] Quoting with approval the Recorder of Birmingham's observation in 1868 that 'crime in Sheffield, Leeds and Birmingham was taken to have a very different meaning from what it had in the minds of those who made the returns for Liverpool and Manchester', he takes to task certain historians, notably Gatrell and Hadden, for the pointlessness of admitting the deficiencies of the statistics as a measure of actual crime but then proceeding as if 'the admission has neutralized its own import'. The upshot, he argues, is to produce 'an image of crime which is comfortingly based on numbers [but which] allows the fact that the numbers are almost irrelevant to the state of crime to fade into the background'. In other words, 'these people know with perfect accuracy a past that has never existed'.[22] There is much force in Sindall's argument. Criminal statistics are important as an indicator 'of what people believed was happening.' However, to see them as no more than this is to lose much of the value that can be derived from them if used sensitively and in conjunction with other evidence.

The sceptical argument centres on two key observations. First, the crime figures do not measure the totality of criminal activity; that is, there is a dark area of unrecorded and unknown crime. Second, the relationship between real and recorded crime is likely to vary over time because of a variety of factors affecting attitudes towards the law and its administration. Both points are clearly correct, but it does not necessarily follow that this renders useless the crime figures. Such is the nature of crime, in almost any society, that the totality of crime is both immense and unknowable. Even if it were possible to count every infraction of the law, however petty, this would not automatically generate useful knowledge. The crucial consideration is not so much the overall total of criminal behaviour, and its changing composition, but the nature and level of what is deemed to be unacceptable crime and the effectiveness with which it is dealt. All societies tolerate certain levels of crime and inefficiency on the part of their law-enforcement agencies. The historian's interest lies in the way in which levels of toleration towards crimes (including the creation of new criminal activities) have changed over time and how society has dealt with this changing problem. This is not to deny the imperfections of the data. Clearly, there are real problems relating to the classification and recording of criminal behaviour which result in a degree of inaccurate and misleading information but it is not clear that these subjectivities are sufficiently widespread or damaging to invalidate the use of the material as a measure of society's ability to deal with what it deems unacceptable criminal behaviour. Furthermore, by examining those factors which might change the willingness and ability to prosecute (that is, broad factors such as changes in values that bring new definitions of 'acceptable' behaviour, changes in attitude towards the legal system as a means of seeking redress or narrower considerations such as changes in the cost of prosecution) the historian is able to comment on likely changes in the underlying incidence of 'real' crime.[23] However, it is only by appreciating how the crime figures were generated that one can hope to arrive at a sensible interpretation of them.[24]

There are several factors which influence the recorded crime rate. First, there were a number of changes in the definition of crime. The list of serious crimes was extended in 1834 and new ones were created. The criminalizing of certain work practices, notably the taking of certain perquisites, and the assault on public leisure activities in the late eighteenth century are well known. Similarly, the creation of 'gross indecency' as an offence resulted from Labouchere's amendment to the 1888 Criminal Justice Amendment

Act, while the criminal offence of incest was created in 1908. The increase in sexual offences in the years before the First World War was not a reflection of a sudden increase in illicit sexual behaviour but the product of a new concern with certain forms of behaviour and a formal recognition of them as criminal activities.

There was also a redefinition of existing crimes. There was a steady and significant increase in the scope of summary justice, concerning juveniles initially but extended to adults later, during the course of the nineteenth century. The Wilful and Malicious Trespass Act of 1820 saw the start of the process. Peel's Larceny Act of 1827 dealt with such matters as the theft of deer, hares and dogs and damage to trees and fences. The following year saw further legislation making common assault a summary offence. The Juvenile Offenders Acts of 1847 and 1850 extended summary justice to simple larcenies committed by those under 14 and 16 years of age, respectively, while in 1853 aggravated assaults on women and children were the subject of legislation. The two most important pieces of legislation were the 1855 Criminal Justice Act and the 1879 Summary Jurisdiction Act, both of which were motivated by a desire to deal more expeditiously with crimes that were no longer viewed so seriously. The former allowed for summary trial in larceny cases under the value of 5s, with the agreement of the accused, and for larceny cases over the value of 5s where the accused pleaded guilty. This led to a significant increase in the work of magistrates, as some three-fifths of larceny cases at quarter sessions involved property valued at less than 5s. The latter act extended the principle to all children under the age of 12, except for cases of murder and manslaughter; to all juveniles under the age of 16, if they consented, for larceny, embezzlement and receiving stolen goods; and to all adults pleading guilty or consenting to being tried summarily for similar offences to the value of £2. Subsequent acts of 1899 and 1914 built on this breakthrough.[25] This extension of summary jurisdiction, and particularly the acts of 1855 and 1879, had a profound effect on the official statistics which makes long-term analyses problematic.

Other legislation had an impact on the recorded crime rate. Concern with the deterrent effect of the costs of prosecution led to a series of acts intended to encourage people to bring cases to court. Bennet's Act of 1818 permitted courts to award an allowance for loss of time and trouble to all prosecutors and witnesses in felony cases and to pay the expenses in carrying out a prosecution, while the payment of expenses in the case of certain misdemeanours was provided for by the 1826 Criminal Justice Act. However, fears remained that the burden was still too great, though further legislation in 1855 went some way towards assuaging these misgivings.

Prosecutions were eased in a number of other ways. The growth in the number of associations for the prosecution of felons in the late eighteenth and early nineteenth centuries, followed by the gradual creation of a legislative framework for policing in the second quarter of the nineteenth century, had a cumulative effect on the number of people brought before the courts. Similarly, if contemporary fears of the Bloody Code are to be believed, the reduction in the number of capital offences increased the willingness both to prosecute and to return guilty verdicts.

The selective nature of the technicalities of the legal process cannot be divorced from the wider socioeconomic and political context with its deeply rooted inequalities. Stephen Box's observation on the twentieth century holds good for the nineteenth: 'Our criminal justice system is . . . a selective process in which the powerful are unlikely to be criminalized, whilst the powerless are more likely to end up behind the walls of crumbling, overcrowded Victorian prisons'.[26] As he concludes, the selection process does not draw a representative sample of the offending population at large but is greatly influenced by criteria such as 'class, race, religion, sex and sexuality'.[27] Such observations apply with comparable force to the nineteenth century. The inequalities of class and ethnicity were reproduced, if not magnified, by the criminal justice system. The criminal statistics can be seen as a form of self-fulfilling prophecy. Members of parliament, often working from a preconceived notion of deviants and deviant behaviour that was shared by many of their constituents, criminalized certain forms of behaviour, associated predominantly with the working classes. The police, seeking to utilize their limited resources to the best effect, enforced the law according to 'commonsense' assumptions about the criminal and his whereabouts. In this way, the criminal statistics reflect popular perceptions of criminality as much as criminality itself. Intentionally or otherwise, the statistics played an important role in shaping and legitimizing the policies of politicians and the practices of the police. They also influenced subsequent debates about crime and ensured that the force of the law continued to fall unevenly upon society. In this respect, the criminal statistics have a historical value independent of their accuracy.

Long-term Trends in the Incidence of Crime, c.1800–1855[28]

In this and the following section, the statistics of recorded crime will be analysed to provide a general framework for the more detailed discussions of specific crimes and criminals that will take place in the following chapters.

First, it is important to comment briefly on the state of crime in the late eighteenth century. In the absence of national statistics, the qualitative evidence of contemporary commentators has to be judged against the quantitative evidence drawn from detailed local studies.[29] Many contemporaries, more so in the last decades of the eighteenth century, believed they were witnessing a crime wave. It is not clear that such fears were well founded. The total incidence of crime increased simply as a result of the hitherto unprecedented increase in population. Moreover, certain crimes may have become, if not more common, more visible as parts of England and Wales became more urbanized. Concern with crime in and around London certainly figured very largely in contemporary analyses. However, if one discounts contemporary fears and attempts to discuss the crime figures in terms of rates, rather than global totals, then a less dramatic picture emerges. Interpersonal behaviour had changed and there was less tolerance of violence in society. Even London was a safer place in which to live and work in the late eighteenth century than in the previous century. Similarly, the increase in prosecutions for various forms of theft reflects partly an increase in population, partly an increase in the number of items that could be stolen and the ease with which this could be done, but also a growing concern with property rights that led to a greater determination to prosecute. Establishing the existence of a long-term increase in the rate of thefts is not easy, but in the short run there were sharp increases which, broadly speaking, were related to the level of food prices and the state of the labour market.[30]

Turning to the recorded crime figures for the first half of the nineteenth century, which largely coincides with the classic 'Industrial Revolution' but is also set apart by the discontinuities in the crime statistics created by the legislation of 1855 and 1856, we appear to see a dramatic growth in recorded crime. The numbers committed for trial in superior courts, the overwhelming majority of which were offences against property, rose from around 4500 a year in the early nineteenth century to almost 30 000 a year by the early 1840s. The number of those convicted increased at a greater rate. Averaging about 2700 in the early nineteenth century, the figure had risen to over 20 000 by the early 1840s. Even allowing for the doubling of population that took place at the same time, this was still a substantial increase and one which alarmed many contemporaries. Urbanization and industrialization seemed to have created the conditions for a spectacular increase in criminal behaviour – a view echoed by some later historians, including such influential figures as Harold Perkin, who had no doubt of the reality of a 'vast increase in crime and prostitution' in the first half of the nineteenth century.[31]

However, the crime statistics cannot be seen simply as a direct measure of changes in offending behaviour. Rather, the figures tell us more about the willingness and ability to prosecute. The upward trend in recorded crime was well under way before reforms in the criminal law and the advent of the new police, which suggests that attitudinal changes were of paramount importance. However, other factors played their part. The establishment of the new police is likely to have had an upward effect on the numbers apprehended and the reduction in the number of capital offences may well have increased the willingness to take legal action. Establishing the precise link is altogether more difficult. Indeed, national figures, aggregating all serious crimes from all parts of the country, will necessarily obscure the impact of changes which, by their nature, affected either a specific area (as with the piecemeal development of the new police) or a specific crime (as with the reduction of capital offences). Thus it is likely that there was no significant long-term increase in serious crime during the 'Industrial Revolution'. This is not to say that were no real increases, especially in the short run. The sharp rise in the number of committals after the end of the Napoleonic wars reflects, in part, a real increase. The demobilization of a relatively large number of men, drawn from those sectors of society which produced the highest number of criminals, and an overstocked and dislocated job market created considerable suffering. Not for the first time, there was a sharp increase in the number of cases brought to trial.[32] But even in these circumstances it is likely that postwar concerns about the threats to stability amplified the real increase in crime. Similarly, it is not entirely coincidental that some of the sharpest downturns in economic activity were accompanied by a sharp increase in the number of committals in the early 1840s and especially the peak years of 1842 and 1848. If one looks specifically at crimes against property there is a clear and inverse correlation between fluctuations in economic activity and the number of crimes against property. However, crimes of violence increased in times of relative prosperity. The reasons for this are not immediately clear but the prevalence of drink-related assaults may provide one important explanation. The likelihood of drink-related incidents was increased as more alcohol was purchased in relatively good times.

Long-term Trends in the Incidence of Crime, c.1855–1914[33]

The range of statistics available to the historian for the second half of the nineteenth century is much wider. In particular, the collection of information on summary offences and indictable offences known to the police greatly add to our knowledge of the period. That said, the figures still have to be handled with care. Nonetheless, it is clearly the case that there was a steady decline in the recorded serious crime rate during the period from c.1860 to 1914. The rate for all indictable offences shows a long-term decline, with a slight blip in the early 1880s, from its peak in the early 1860s until the second half of the 1890s, when the decline is in excess of 40 per cent. Thereafter, there is a slight upturn but even in the Edwardian years the rate is still a third lower than it had been in the mid-Victorian years.

Unsurprisingly, given their preponderance in the overall total, the pattern for larceny offences is almost identical to the general pattern. The figures for assaults and burglaries follow different patterns. The long-term trend for the assault rate is clearly downward. At its trough, in 1906–10, it is 35 per cent below the level of the early 1860s. However, the greatest falls took place in the late 1860s/early 1870s and again in the first decade of the twentieth century. The figures for the 1870s and 1880s are somewhat sticky. Moreover, there was an increase in the immediate prewar years that leaves the assault rate at a level 25 per cent below its peak. The burglary figures are even more distinctive. Having dropped to a level 35 per cent below the early-1860s peak within a decade, the figures stay at roughly the same level until the turn of the century when they started to rise, slightly exceeding the mid-Victorian peak by the eve of the First World War.

The Criminal Registrar, writing in 1896, was confident that, from the 'steady diminution in the number of prosecutions, we may infer with tolerable safety that there has been, at least, a corresponding diminution in crime',[34] but in a powerfully written article drawing on the experience of London, Jennifer Davis argues that 'declining official crime rates in the second half of the nineteenth century were not necessarily a reflection of a real decrease in law-breaking behaviour'.[35] Her detailed analysis shows that, despite widespread pilfering and fraud in a variety of occupations, prosecutions by employers remained relatively rare. Furthermore, they were used as one of a range of sanctions. An increase in employer prosecutions was as much related to periods of prosperity, when the sanction of dismissal was less powerful, as to real levels of employee theft.[36] In similar vein, Davis points to the large amount of crime that was known to but not prosecuted by the police. The points are well made and act as a useful reminder of the complex way in which criminal statistics are socially constructed. However, the case for a real decline in the latter part of the nineteenth century has not been demolished by these observations. If the level of real crime did not change over the course of the nineteenth century, there would have to have been a significant reduction in the willingness of the various groups of prosecutors to take formal action after 1850 or 1870 to explain the changes in the official crime statistics. While it may well be the case that the greater prosperity of late-Victorian England brought with it a greater tolerance of relatively small-scale thefts, there is little firm evidence to suggest that this took place on a sufficient scale to explain away the differences in the crime figures. Indeed, with the growth of police forces, the greater ease of bringing prosecutions and a gradual move away from the use of informal sanctions, one would expect, *ceteris paribus*, the recorded crime rate to have increased. The fact that it fell suggests this was a real phenomenon and there is indeed good reason for agreeing with the Criminal Registrar. Improving working-class living standards, for some at least until the early twentieth century, diminished the pressure to steal or defraud for survival, while the steady diffusion of ideas of respectability brought a greater determination to prosecute criminal behaviour.

The situation is complicated by the extension of summary justice, especially in 1855 and 1879. The first act resulted in something like 75 per cent of offences against property without violence being tried summarily, but this figure had risen to almost 90 per cent by the end of the nineteenth century, largely as the result of the second act. By redefining certain forms of larceny as summary offences, the changes in the law had the effect of reducing the serious crime figures. In addition, the relative speed and cheapness with which cases were dispatched in petty sessions and police courts brought an increase (of about 10 per cent) in the number of cases brought to trial immediately after the 1879 act. Thereafter the figures for offences against property without violence show a steady fall after the early 1880s.

The figures relating to crimes of violence are more varied and more problematic. However, certain generalizations can be made. Looking first at the very rare cases of homicide, there was a significant reduction. The rate for murder and manslaughter stood at around 1.6 per 100 000 of population in the late 1850s and early 1860s. Thereafter it declined steadily and by the eve of the First World War the figure had fallen to 0.8 per 100 000. A less dramatic decline took place in the incidence of felonious and malicious wounding, from a rate of 4.8 per 100 000 in the peak years of the early 1870s to 3.3 in the prewar years. The pattern of decline is stepped rather than gradual. After a drop from the high levels of the 1860s and 1870s, rates stagnated at about 4.2 per 100 000 for the next two decades before dropping slightly again in the early twentieth century.

Notwithstanding the problems of underrecording, notably in cases of domestic violence, these figures reflect genuine changes in behaviour. Arrest rates for murder were very high and there is no reason to believe that the late Victorians were significantly more tolerant of, and therefore less willing to prosecute in, cases of serious assault involving shooting, stabbing and wounding to maim. Indeed, it is more likely that the figures were inflated in the short term by 'moral panics' such as the garrotting panic of the early 1860s.[37] However, there may have been an artificially deflationary effect stemming from a downgrading of the seriousness of certain wounding offences to assaults.

The other figures for assaults are less clear cut. The decline in the rate for all assaults (that is, common assault, aggravated assault and assault on the police) is dramatic. From an 1860s peak of around 420 per 100 000 of population it had plummeted to around 120 by the prewar years. As one might expect, the figures are dominated by cases of common assault which were non-indictable. The figures may exaggerate the actual change in the level of violence in society during these years. The Criminal Registrar noted in the 1890s that there was a growing disinclination to prosecute trivial cases of assault. In contrast to the more tense and socially divided years of the mid-nineteenth century, the latter decades saw a more relaxed, more confident attitude which led to a greater tolerance of acts of petty violence. Responses to late nineteenth-century football hooligans illustrate the point well. The growth of football as an organized spectator sport brought with it, or revitalized, parochial rivalries in a manner that appalled those who had seen in an amateur participatory sport a means of civilizing the masses. Adolescent gangs of supporters, such as the Peaky Blinders from Birmingham, came into conflict in a variety of predictable places – around football grounds and at railway stations. Serious assaults sometimes occurred and in extreme cases there were fatalities. Legal action was taken at times but there is little evidence of any widespread 'moral panic'. Indeed, local press coverage suggests that such acts of violence were to be expected, and not to be worried over, when large groups of working-class men were gathered together.[38] The figures relating to assaults on the police also give an exaggerated impression. Outright hostility towards the police may well have declined in the last third of the nineteenth century as they were recognized to be a permanent feature. This was probably reinforced by the deterrent effect of the provision under the 1869 Habitual Criminal Act which stipulated a penalty of a maximum £20 fine or six months' imprisonment for assaulting a police officer. However, it is also likely that the police themselves were no longer so keen to prosecute for minor cases of assault.

In stark contrast to the declines recorded elsewhere are the figures relating to sexual assaults. The rate of sexual assaults known to the police increased from 2.5 per 100 000, or less, in the third quarter of the nineteenth century to

almost 5.0 by the second decade of the twentieth, with a dramatic and sustained increase dating from the period 1886–90. However, these figures
are almost entirely the result of significant changes in attitude which were
translated into important pieces of legislation. As was recognized by contemporary observers, the 1885 Criminal Law Amendment Act created a
range of new sexual offences and this, coupled with the determination that
existed to prosecute in such cases, greatly inflated the official statistics. The
act, which was primarily intended to provide a means of suppressing broth-
els, also raised the age of consent for girls to 16 and, in the notorious Labouchere amendment, criminalized male homosexual behaviour both in public
and in private. Subsequent legislation, notably the 1898 Vagrancy Act and
the 1912 Criminal Law Amendment Act, further strengthened the sanctions
against prostitution and homosexuality. The 1908 Children Act provided
for the summary trial of indecent assaults on children under the age of 16,
while the Prevention of Incest Act of the same year made incest by men, previously an ecclesiastical offence, a criminal offence punishable by imprisonment for a period of between three and seven years.[39] The rise in sexual
offences coming before the criminal courts is important to note, but it does
not invalidate the overall argument that there was a real decline in violence
during these years. Attitudes towards male violence were changing and this
was reflected in the volume of critical material condemning assaults on
women and children. There was greater awareness and less tolerance of
such behaviour. Attitudes and actions were changing and many contemporary observers certainly felt that their world was a safer place and that violence had declined since the mid-nineteenth century.

Conclusion

Bringing together the various discussions of the level of crime, we can offer
the following broad conclusions. First, the fear of crime and a belief that serious crime particularly was on the increase characterized the period from the
late eighteenth to the mid-nineteenth century. However, from about the
1860s there was a growing sense of confidence about the stability of society,
though the fear of criminality and the criminal never went away. Second,
the statistical evidence suggests a gradual increase in the totality of criminal
behaviour in the late eighteenth century followed by a much sharper
increase in the first half of the nineteenth. Levels of recorded crime began
to decline from the 1860s onwards, although subject to short-term fluctuations and important variations between different categories of offences.

Third, the overall increase in recorded crime, particularly in the period c.1805–50, does not necessarily mean that there was a corresponding increase in 'real' criminal behaviour. These years saw not only a substantial growth in population, which in itself would have led to an increase in recorded crime, but also the increase in prosecutions. More people were being brought to trial, which boosted further the overall level of recorded crime, irrespective of any changes in the rate of offending behaviour. Thus the period experienced, at most, a modest long-term increase in the overall crime rate, albeit punctuated by some sharp peaks, notably after the Napoleonic wars and during the years of severe economic hardship in the 1840s. Fourth, the decline in the rate of recorded crime in late Victorian and Edwardian England and Wales almost certainly reflects 'real' changes, albeit magnified by a greater tolerance of petty crimes.

2

THE PATTERN OF CRIME

The writing of 'history from below' has led to a highly selective view of criminal behaviour, emphasizing riots and protest crimes, but from which 'the multitudes of petty thefts and minor assaults which account for the bulk of the business of the courts are conspicuous by their absence'.[1] Lurid images, drawing heavily if uncritically upon Dickens and Mayhew, depicting a world, urban rather than rural, in which both property and person were threatened with violence by a distinct race of criminals, living in a world apart from the rest of society, are a commonplace of the popular imagination. Such views have been given greater substance by writers such as Chesney and Tobias.[2] In fact, these images bear little relation to the true nature of most crimes. This chapter will give a more realistic picture of criminality, bringing out variations in geography, gender and class.

Crimes of Violence against the Person

The Ratcliffe Highway murders of 1811 and the Jack the Ripper murders of 1888 are the best known of a number of high-profile murders that often shaped the perceptions of and debates about crime in the nineteenth century. Often much publicized, the stuff of sensationalist popular literature, such cases have given a misleading impression of the nature and extent of violent crime. Even London, which had a higher than average rate of violent crimes, was not the hotbed of crime depicted by Dickens and his imitators. An analysis of the crimes tried at the Old Bailey between 1810 and 1850 shows that murder and manslaughter accounted for less than 2 per cent of the total. Indeed, all violent crimes only accounted for 15 per cent of the total in 1810, dropping to around 10 per cent for the years 1830 to 1850.[3]

A similar picture emerges from the Black Country where, between 1835 and 1860, violent crimes accounted for about 15 per cent of all of committals. Homicides, that is murder, manslaughter and infanticide, accounted for only 11 per cent of these offences and for less than 2 per cent of all offences. In these 25 years only 56 people in the Black Country were indicted for murder, of whom eight were convicted.[4] The situation was not uniform across the country, but even in those towns with reputations for violence, charges of murder, attempted murder and manslaughter were not common. Of over 400 Middlesbrough cases tried at the York Assizes between 1855 and 1914, 62, or 15 per cent of the total, fell into this category. Some years were exceptional: there were 11 such cases in 1865 and 1866 and six in each of 1909 and 1913. Yet in at least half of these years no such cases were brought to trial and there were only one or two cases in a further 15 years.[5]

In national terms, the incidence of homicide was declining in the long run, albeit with some interesting local variations. Cockburn's study of Kent reveals a fluctuating pattern, as can be seen from Table 2.1. The well-publicized murders achieved their notoriety precisely because they were exceptional and as a consequence they create a misleading picture of the nature of violent death. Most homicides tended to be more mundane, usually involving close members of the family or friends and often carried out on the spur of the moment. As the pages of the national and local press reveal, many more deaths were caused by parents – more often mothers than fathers – killing very young children or by husbands killing wives than by strangers. The evidence from Kent illustrates the point well. Between the late eighteenth and early twentieth century, a time during which the overall homicide rate there fell by over 50 per cent, the proportion of victims from within the extended family increased from about 20 per cent to 55 per cent. The percentage of infant victims remained largely

Table 2.1   The homicide rate in Kent, 1771–1911 (per cent)

1771	3.7	1821	5.5	1871	8.3
1781	4.5	1831	3.7	1881	6.1
1791	5.3	1841	5.4	1891	8.4
1801	4.8	1851	4.6	1901	5.7
1811	5.7	1861	5.4	1911	7.3

Source: Adapted from J. S. Cockburn, 'Patterns of Violence in English Society: Homicide in Kent 1560–1985', *Past & Present*, vol. 130, 1991, table 1, p. 78.

unchanged, but there was a marked increase in the percentage of victims who were adult family members.[6] Shorter-term analyses from different time periods provide supporting evidence. In eighteenth-century Surrey, as in late nineteenth-century Middlesbrough, some 30 per cent of murders, attempted murders and manslaughters were perpetrated on family members. Belief in the sanctity and safety of the family made it attractive to believe in the unknown murderer from outside, but he (and to a much lesser extent she) was a less common figure whose alleged existence shored up domestic ideology rather than illuminated the nature of this particular crime.

Murder was characterized by the presence of malice aforethought. In its absence, cases were treated as manslaughter or justifiable homicide. Consequently, many domestic killings were treated as manslaughter because the crime was committed (or was presented as having been committed) on the spur of the moment or when the accused was not in full control of his or her reason. The former was common in wife-killing cases; the latter in cases of infanticide.[7] Similarly, in many other cases the participants were known to each other and the death was treated as manslaughter. One of the most common occurrences was a fight between male friends and acquaintances, often after a drink, that led to the fatal incident. The absence of malice aforethought ensured that such cases were manslaughter. The steady number of cases of men killed in brawls emphasizes the persistence and acceptance of interpersonal violence, often as an informal means of resolving disputes, well into the nineteenth century, though this was probably declining in the last quarter. As late as the mid-eighteenth century swords, knives and cudgels were common instruments of death. Although firearms added to the repertoire of killing instruments in the early nineteenth century, there was a declining proportion of killings that involved weapons routinely carried on the person. The use of fists and boots became a more common cause of death.

Manslaughter cases also involved recklessness or gross negligence. Careless riding or driving of horses and horse-drawn vehicles resulting in death gave rise to prosecution from the mid-seventeenth century. Thereafter, a small but increasing number of cases was brought. However, there was little strong popular feeling concerning such incidents. More contentious was the increasing number of accidental deaths due to negligence at work and which resulted in court action as industrialization proceeded apace. Prosecution tended to take place only in cases of blatant or persistent disregard for the safety of the employee, as the predominant view remained that safety at work was the responsibility of the individual. Perhaps unsurprisingly, relatively few of these cases led to a successful prosecution.[8]

The homicide rate does not necessarily reflect accurately changes in the incidence of other forms of interpersonal violence. It is necessary, therefore, to consider the most common crime of violence brought before the courts, that is assault in its various forms. However, there are difficulties with the evidence. First, because violence was accepted and often seen as a legitimate way of resolving a dispute, not all incidents became legal cases. This was particularly true of domestic violence. The widely-held belief in a husband's right to chastise his wife and the economic and legal weaknesses of most women meant that many incidents of assault were never reported or were dealt with by mediation before coming to formal trial. Attitudes were not unchanging. In their different ways, people like J. S. Mill and Frances Power Cobbe drew attention to the scandal of wife beating.[9] However, despite the passing of the Aggravated Assaults on Women and Children Act in 1853 and the Matrimonial Causes Act of 1878, relatively little was done in practical terms to improve the position of women. Moreover, on closer examination, the debate about wife beating reveals much about class and gender assumptions. Domestic violence was seen to be an overwhelmingly working-class problem with certain northern districts achieving particular notoriety. Such 'barbarous behaviour' had a wider political significance and was seen as proof positive, by some at least, of the uncivilized nature of the ordinary working man and the folly of contemplating the extension of the franchise to such a person. Further, in condemning this behaviour and seeking to criminalize it, parliament showed itself to be more concerned with redefining acceptable masculine behaviour than with extending protection for women. The legal fiction of marital unity was a powerful force and led to the rejection of anything that suggested spousal equality.[10] Furthermore, sexual harassment, in a wide variety of forms, was a major problem, particularly for working-class women, and yet few cases ever reached the courts.[11]

Second, the vast majority of common assaults, that is those with no aggravating circumstances, were misdemeanours tried at petty sessions, and were not included in the yearly statistics until 1856. Third, the extension of summary justice resulted in certain types of assault being removed from quarter sessions, which makes long-term comparisons problematic. Fourth, the distinction between various forms of assault is less clear-cut than the legal definitions would suggest. Much depended upon the discretion of the individual prosecutor and/or the police and magistrates involved in the case. For example, it is unclear why David Richardson was charged with assault at the Middlesbrough Petty Sessions in 1860 when his attack on Samuel Crompton resulted in the loss of an eye.[12] Even more surprising was the decision of a

Maidstone magistrate in 1868 to sentence a local labourer, James Walter, to four months' imprisonment for cutting the throat of his wife.[13]

Nonetheless, various local studies suggest that there was a decline in the incidence of violence. For example, in north Lincolnshire between 1740 and 1780, assaults accounted for just under a quarter of all cases at the Lindsey Quarter Sessions. However, the total number of such cases brought to court fell by some 20 per cent during this period. Although the larger centres of population produced the majority of cases, the actual rate of assaults was not significantly lower in the smaller villages and in some cases was actually higher. In the North Riding of Yorkshire from the mid-1830s to the mid-1850s, assaults accounted for just under 5 per cent of all cases that came before the Northallerton Quarter Sessions – a figure that was only slightly inflated by the violent propensities of the men of Middlesbrough – with a decline over the 20-year period. In the Black Country, at about the same time, the figure for assaults was just over 2 per cent of all committals.[14] A large percentage of serious assaults, such as unlawful wounding and inflicting (or intending to inflict) grievous bodily harm, were perpetrated on family, but more so upon friends and acquaintances. Once again, drink-related incidents, in which boots and fists were used, were commonplace. Nonetheless, taking a broad perspective, there was a long-term decline in various forms of interpersonal violence.

Property Crimes

Property offences (burglary, housebreaking and robbery, as well as various forms of larceny) dominated the overall criminal statistics throughout the nineteenth century, though the more serious crimes against property, that is those involving violence, were in a clear minority. Broadly speaking, non-violent offences against property accounted for four out of every five indictable committals.[15] This pattern appears to hold throughout the country, in rural areas as much as urban, even though there were differences in the level of recorded crime from district to district.

Yet, despite this, spectacular crimes of violence, with the fascination and fears that they arouse, seized popular attention. This was particularly true of highway robbery. In the late eighteenth and early nineteenth centuries there was considerable concern about the incidence of this offence, especially in the environs of London. Although the crime statistics do not reveal a large-scale problem, contemporary fears were not totally ill-founded, as large numbers of these offences went unprosecuted.[16] Nonetheless, the highwayman, invariably smartly dressed and astride a magnificent horse in popular accounts, achieved something of a cult status despite the seriousness with which his crime was viewed by the authorities. McLynn paints a rosy picture of cultured and courteous 'gentlemen of the road', indulging in wit and repartee as they went about a task that they regretted having to do.[17] Figures such as John Rann, better known as '16-string Jack' and Richard 'Galloping Dick' Ferguson could easily be transformed into folk heroes, especially if their escapades made fools of the authorities, but not all highwaymen were chivalrous gentlemen. Violence, including death and rape, could and did accompany robbery on the highway and there was an often squalid selfishness and self-interest lurking beneath the 'gentlemanly' veneer.

However, the highwayman was less associated with violence than the footpad, whose *modus operandi* brought him into more direct contact with his victim and carried with it a much higher risk of violence if things were to go wrong. Highway robbery was a declining activity, the last case being recorded in 1831, but robbery on foot remained a frightening crime and one that continued to arouse considerable concern. Perceptions were dominated by the problems of London, graphically described by reformists such as the Fieldings and Colquhoun in the eighteenth century and continued later by Mayhew and Dickens. Although there was an element of exaggeration in popular accounts, the harsh underlying realities cannot be denied, as the following incidents from the early to mid-nineteenth century illustrate. Jane Cox was violently robbed in Angel Alley on her way to the laundry, Thomas Allerson was robbed of a watch and chain, valued at £3, by a mob almost in front of Lord Castlereagh's house, while John Morgan was hit about the head before having his watch stolen in the notorious Wentworth Street, Whitechapel.[18] However, such incidents have to be put into perspective. Between 1810 and 1850, robbery declined from 3.5 per cent to less than half a per cent of all crimes tried at the Old Bailey.[19] Nor should London's reputation blind the historian to what was happening elsewhere. In the Black Country between 1835 and 1860, there were just under 500 cases of robbery. Typically, the offence took place at night when the victim was returning home, often after spending some time drinking in a local public house. John Roahan, for example, was attacked by three men in Caribee Island, the Irish quarter of Wolverhampton. He was knocked down by one and held down by another while his pockets were searched by the third, who stole his purse, containing 5s 6d. James Beddow was robbed in similar fashion when leaving a public house in Walsall after he had been paid. Although his assailants had been in the same pub, they were not known to him but John Clough was attacked and robbed by two men whom he knew well.[20] Nor was robbery simply an urban phenomenon. On 17 January 1866, Arthur Battley was attacked and robbed of a watch, various items of jewellery and money as he walked from Fornham All Saints to Bury St Edmunds.[21]

The statistical evidence shows that there was a relatively low level of violent thefts. However, popular perceptions could be quite different, especially as the popular press developed in the second half of the nineteenth century. Moral panics surrounding street robbery were a recurring feature, but it is the events of the 1850s and 1860s that attracted most attention, with two panics identified in 1856 and 1862.[22] Prison reform and the treatment of the criminal were a major cause of concern at the time. Press coverage of a 'New System of Robbery' gradually built up from early 1851, with accounts of garrotte attacks in a variety of provincial centres including Manchester, Birmingham and Leeds, and reached its height in 1856, with attention increasingly focused on London.[23] The number of people charged with robbery and attempted robbery increased sharply, but it is unlikely that this reflected a real increase in violent street robbery. Rather, the growing public concern led to a greater number of cases being sent to the higher courts. However, the very fact of increased committals for these offences gave further substance to the fears. The 1850s panic finally blew itself out, but not without long-term effect. The debate on penal servitude and the legislation of 1853 and 1857 were shaped by public perceptions of the 'ticket-of-leave' man turned garrotter.

A further panic broke out, as if afresh, in 1862. This panic was precipitated when Hugh Pilkington, the MP for Blackburn, was robbed at night of his watch and £10. Public concern, already sensitized by the continuing debate on the treatment of criminals, was further heightened by the press coverage of this and similar attacks. With little hard evidence to support the assertion, elements of the press could claim that 'highway robbery is becoming an institution in London, and roads like the Bayswater Road are as unsafe as Naples'.[24] Fears led to more arrests by the police and more prosecutions, while the courts also took a tougher line. Thus, as in 1856, a crime wave was created by the popular panic. Such was the extent of the panic that parliament passed an exceptional measure, the Security Against Violence Act, which reintroduced flogging for robbery with violence. Equally, the fears aroused had an important part to play in the evolution of the Penal Servitude Act of 1864 and the Prisons Act of 1865. The panics of 1856 and 1862 were firmly centred on London. This may explain why the concern with provincial juvenile gangs, notably the Scuttlers in Manchester and

Salford in the 1870s and the Cornermen and the High Rip Gang in Liverpool in the 1870s and 1880s, did not develop into full-scale panics. Similarly, the absence of a more general sense of insecurity and fear may explain why the attack in 1874, near Marble Arch, upon a high court judge, Chief Baron Kelly, did not precipitate a moral panic.

Yet more serious were the crimes of breaking and entering and burglary. Although intrinsically the same offence, that is breaking into a property and stealing, burglary was made a distinct and more serious offence in law by virtue of the action taking place during the hours of darkness, which brought the additional element of fear. After Peel's Act of 1827, burglary was restricted to breaking into a dwelling-house and remained a capital offence until 1837, though it had become commonplace to commute the sentence to transportation before this. The death penalty for burglary when accompanied by an attempt to wound or murder the occupants of the house was retained until 1861.

The offences in this category varied widely in their scale and nature. Particularly in London, certain burglaries and housebreakings were committed by organized gangs and involved substantial sums of money. In exceptional cases, members of the aristocracy found themselves victims of audacious thefts. The house of the Earl of Ilchester in Old Burlington Street was stripped of plate and silver in January 1772, and £1200 of silver plate was stolen from the Archbishop of Canterbury's Palace in 1788, while in 1791, Buckingham Palace was broken into.[25] Most crimes were less spectacular. When the Reverend Father Johnson, of Skipton, was burgled in December 1866, he lost two sovereigns, five or six shillings and small quantities of sugar and tea, while Robert Holt, of Fishponds, Gloucestershire, lost five sheets, some towels and miscellaneous items of clothing when his cottage was burgled, also in December 1866.[26] Some crimes involved considerable violence and conformed to the popular image. Thus, for example, Samuel Thompson, a Black Country publican, was burgled in 1836 by three men, armed with iron-tipped bludgeons, who assaulted his two sons. This was exceptional. More were relatively small-scale affairs and said more about harsh economic conditions than innate depravity. In 1842, the house of Mr and Mrs Reynolds was broken into in the early morning and some beef, pork, bread and cheese stolen. It was the eagle-eyed Mrs Reynolds who was able to identify the stolen piece of beef and marrow bone, thus bringing the culprit to book![27]

An analysis of housebreaking cases tried at quarter session in the North Riding of Yorkshire during the same period confirms this picture of relatively mundane crime involving money or goods of limited value.

The largest theft of property involved two men's shirts, one woman's chemise, four children's shifts and five nightcaps, but more common were sums of around £1.[28] Some thieves took both money and goods. James Lee and William Leighton, transported for 15 years in 1844, took money to the value of 19s (95p), two pairs of stockings, two handkerchiefs and a piece of bread from a house in North Kilvington. The majority of housebreaking charges involved the theft of relatively small quantities of goods. Robert Scott was charged with the theft of a white loaf, an apple pie and two geese. Nor does the situation appear to have changed significantly in the latter part of the century. Burglary cases tried at the York Assizes, for example, reveal a catalogue of stolen watches, teaspoons, small pieces of jewellery and relatively small sums of money or quantities of goods. Typical was Thomas Wade, who stole a purse and the sum of £1.5s (£1.25) or Patrick Marron, who stole an overcoat, a cloak and a pair of boots.

Unsurprisingly, housebreaking cases followed a similar pattern. On occasions, the items stolen could be quite considerable in number, if not value. Two hawkers, Christopher Brown and Andrew Quinn, broke into the house of William Ryder in Ellington and took over 20 items of clothing. The relatively wealthy were obvious targets. William Thompson, a labourer, broke into the house of Blanchard Ringrose at Thirkleby and helped himself to two loaves of bread, a pound of bacon, a pound of sugar and a quarter-pound of coffee. Servants, with their knowledge of the geography and possessions of a house, appear frequently in the records. Bessy Eccles, a servant, pleaded guilty in 1874 to the theft of six silver teaspoons, a pair of silver sugar tongs, a petticoat, a worsted scarf and a handkerchief from Jesse Eccles of Ampleforth. But not all victims were in this position. John Brooks, a sawyer, broke into a house in Middlesbrough, stealing shoes and clothing from two Irish labourers who lodged in the house.

There were certain crimes against property, never large in number, most notably arson and machine breaking, which aroused considerable fear and condemnation. Fears aroused by the often extensive destruction of property were compounded by the element of 'political' protest that accompanied such crimes. Arson, understandably, was much feared. The destruction that could be wrought by even a small fire could be considerable. Firefighting resources were scarce and in the countryside in particular it was difficult to get to the scene of a fire with the speed necessary to prevent widespread damage. Not surprisingly, arson remained a capital offence until the 1830s. Incidents of arson were to be found in town and country in the late eighteenth century. In many cases, the crime had much to do with personal revenge, often on the part of disgruntled domestic servants or dismissed employees. Other cases involved defrauding insurance companies.[29] However, in some cases there was a political dimension which could be quite explicit, as in the case of John the Painter, a supporter of the American Revolution, who was responsible for a series of fires in naval dockyards and along docksides in southern England and who was hanged in 1777.[30]

During the early nineteenth century, arson became associated predominantly with the countryside and with eastern England in particular. The novelty of arson was commented upon in 1816 and in subsequent years it became both endemic and epidemic in this part of the country. In Norfolk and Suffolk between 1815 and 1870, there was a total of almost 2000 recorded fires.[31] This is an underestimate, as not all fires were reported to insurance companies or recorded by the local press. Certain years stand out. In 1822, there was a sharp increase in the number of fires, particularly in Suffolk. From 1830 to 1834, particularly in Norfolk, fires raged on a larger scale, while the greatest numbers of fires were recorded in the years 1843–6 and 1849–51.[32] Although there was a diminution during the 1850s and 1860s the problem never disappeared and, as in 1868, could still assume large proportions. Nor were Norfolk and Suffolk exceptional in this respect. Lincolnshire, Cambridgeshire and Kent faced similar problems, as did, to a lesser extent, counties such as Bedfordshire and Essex. Indeed, during the widespread rural disturbances of 1830–3, commonly known as the Swing disturbances, acts of incendiarism were recorded the length and breadth of England. Kent was the worst affected, with 61 incidents of incendiarism, followed by Sussex (34), Lincolnshire (28) and Surrey (23). In a further five counties, Norfolk, Wiltshire, Hampshire, Berkshire and Dorset, there were between a dozen and 20 such incidents.[33] The number of fires is striking but so too was the damage. Properties to the value of £4000 and £5000 were destroyed and large tracts of land were laid waste.

Not all fires were the result of arson attacks. Sparks from a machine or an accidentally dropped lucifer match could start a conflagration. However, as the insurance companies well knew, a significant number of the fires were started deliberately. Pyromaniacs, insurance company fraudsters and embittered individuals pursuing private vendettas all played their part. But there was more to it than this. The frightening element for the propertied classes of rural England was the selectivity with which individuals were attacked – farmers known to pay low wages or to treat labourers badly, or poor-law officials – and the open animosity that was directed at the victims by labourers and their families who witnessed the conflagrations. What was worse, there appeared to be a wider degree of support from the community for the arsonist. The relationship is a complex one. Arson, by destroying crops and equipment as well as buildings, could destroy jobs. The arsonist was not a universally liked 'guerrilla fighter' acting on behalf of the community in which he lived. That said, there were incidents which demonstrate varying degrees of support. Refusal to help in the attempt to put out the fire, assaults on firemen and the cutting of hoses were very explicit actions. So was the rejoicing and frolicking which accompanied fires in some areas. As one appalled correspondent in the *Cambridge Chronicle* noted at Keysoe in 1830,

> The conduct of most of the labourers was most disgraceful; they not only refused to work, but indulged in the grossest language and jests, and appeared to delight in the calamity; many of them assembled at the public houses, and were drinking and singing during the raging of the fire.[34]

Arson was a cheap, quick, easy and effective weapon of vengeance and intimidation and, as such, aroused fears out of proportion to the actual incidence of the crime. Closely related and equally worrying for many nineteenth-century observers was the crime of animal maiming. If arson was seen as second only to murder, then animal maiming, which carried overtones of symbolic murder, also ranked highly in the catalogue of detestable offences, though not all were crimes of protest.[35] There were also fewer cases brought to court. The number of animal-maiming incidents in Norfolk and Suffolk was little more than one-tenth of the number of fires in these counties between 1815 and 1870. Only in three years, 1828, 1834 and 1849, did the number of incidents reach double figures and, while the level of attacks remained roughly constant from the 1820s to the 1840s, there was a clear decline after 1850. Nonetheless, this crime, less public than arson and involving a greater degree of intimacy between criminal and victim, still shocked. The killing of sheep, for example, and the display of the head and skin before the door of the owner's farmhouse was a macabre indication of feelings. More explicit was the note left by Edmund Botwright to his employer Mr Watling after he, Botwright, had strangled two of the farmer's bullocks.

> You bluddy farmer could not live it was not for the poore, tis them that keep you bluddy raskells alive, but their will be a slauter made amongst you verry soone. I should verry well like to hang you the same as I hanged your beastes. You bluddy rogue I will lite up a little fire for you this first opertunity.[36]

Botwright, who among other things was unhappy with the new equipment that Watling had introduced, was as good as his word, for two days later one barn, three stables and four animals were burnt. He himself was brought to court and tried in 1844. In cases such as these, few and far between as they were, social relations had reached their nadir.

Also indicative of deteriorating social relations was machine breaking. As an urban/industrial crime, particularly associated with the Luddite incidents in Nottinghamshire and the West Riding of Yorkshire in the early nineteenth century, it has been well treated by historians, but its rural counterpart tends to be less well known. Machine breaking in the countryside is often seen solely in terms of the destruction of threshing machines in the winter of 1830–1. While these were the most hated and most widely destroyed pieces of agricultural equipment, attacks were also directed at scuffling ploughs and even rakes, which were seen to pose a threat to jobs. The most dramatic examples of machine breaking took place during the Swing riots of 1830–1 and were more concentrated among the advanced arable districts of the south-west. Wiltshire, with 89 recorded incidents, and Berkshire with 86, head the list but there were 45 incidents in Hampshire and 49 in Kent. However, there were no machines broken in Cambridgeshire or Bedfordshire, only one in Suffolk and four in Lincolnshire, though 28 were destroyed in Norfolk.[37] Destruction of equipment was not always a large-scale affair. The precise dimensions of the crime will never be known, since many 'accidents' that befell 'new-fangled' machinery may well have been a form of industrial sabotage.

Many crimes of violence against property were preceded by the sending of threatening letters which, in itself, was a criminal offence carrying the death penalty until 1823. The surviving evidence is patchy, giving only an imprecise indication of the frequency of this offence. Indeed, the number of cases brought to court probably tells us more about changes in the pattern of prosecution, though it cannot be entirely coincidental that there was an increase in the number of letters concerned with social grievances in the late 1790s and early 1800s. Their nature is clear. Threats of death, mutilation, damage to or destruction of property (including animals) and of armed insurrection were of the essence. Charles Taylor, a Manchester calico printer, received a letter in 1786: 'If you dont discharge James Hobson from the House of Correction we will burn your House about your ears . . . we are determined to destroy all Sorts of Masheens for Printing in the Kingdom'.[38]

Swing letters were equally forthright:

this is to inform you what you have to undergo. Gentlemen if providing you Dont pull down your messhenes and rise the poor mens wages the married men give tow and six pence a day the singel tow shillings. or we will burn down your barns and you in them this is the last notis.[39]

In addition, many letters struck a moral tone and carried a defence of traditional rights. A letter pinned to the church door in Crediton, addressed to
the gentlemen of the parish, opened in the following manner: 'Know ye not
that the Lord of Life Liveth and that he will come again at the Last day to
judge the world in Righteousness?'[40] Thompson makes the distinction
between 'private' and 'social' grievances as the motive for sending threatening letters. As with incendiarism or animal maiming, personal animus was a
major motive for the sending of such letters, but fewer than 20 per cent of
Thompson's sample fell into the former category, though this does not necessarily give a correct indication of the true ratio between the two. The
remainder dealt with a variety of more general issues. Unsurprisingly, food
prices were the commonest source of complaint, with grievances relating to
work – the level of pay, the use of machinery or cheap labour and so forth –
occurring frequently. The letters also give an indication of the range of popular grievances, covering such issues as enclosures, the poor laws, turnpikes
and press gangs.

Food riots and, to a lesser extent, anti-enclosure riots were a recurring
and important feature of market town and village life in the late eighteenth
and early nineteenth centuries. Notions of a 'moral economy' in which a
person's labour as well as the necessities of life had a 'just price' were important. Food rioters did not usually steal flour and bread but tried to have
them sold at a fair price. Entrepreneurs, operating in an emergent national
market and responding to the seasonal fluctuations in prices, found themselves faced by angry protest. The availability of cheap grain after the
Napoleonic wars and improved transport helped undermine this form of
protest, though it continued in counties such as Cornwall and Cumberland
well into the nineteenth century.[41] Other features of the new agrarian capitalism, notably enclosures, also came under attack. In Northamptonshire,
protest against enclosure was more persistent and more varied than is
usually suggested.[42] Although violence was but a minor tactic, it still had a
part to play in local resistance.

However, it was non-violent crime against property that dominated the
work of the courts. Until the early nineteenth century all forms of larceny,
except petty larceny which involved goods under the value of 12d (5p), were
capital offences. Pickpocketing ceased to be a capital offence in 1808.
In 1827, the distinction between grand larceny and petty larceny was abolished and a new offence of simple larceny was created which could be punished by imprisonment or transportation. In 1832, the last two capital
larcenies – larceny in a dwelling house of goods valued at more than £5
and larceny of horses, sheep and cattle – disappeared from the statute

book.[43] A variety of local studies clearly show that the many larceny cases were concerned with relatively humdrum, everyday items of comparatively little value. The short-term fluctuations in the recorded crime figures for non-violent crimes against property show a correlation between economic activity and the incidence of theft. A closer examination of certain crimes strengthens this belief. In many cases where the stolen goods comprised small quantities of food, fuel or clothing, as well as money, there was a close link between necessity and criminality, though the relationship was not always simple.

In Sussex and Gloucestershire, non-violent thefts from shops, houses and farms, as well as from the person, were the most common offences tried at quarter sessions, accounting for at least 60 per cent and sometimes more than 80 per cent of all cases.[44] This type of crime was not confined to towns. In 1840, there were 427 cases in Sussex, drawn from 127 different parishes, of varying sizes, while in the same year in Gloucestershire there were 456 cases, drawn from 144 parishes. The bulk of the stolen property took the form of food, clothing and money, or other valuables. In rural districts smaller farm animals were an obvious target. Poultry were particularly vulnerable. Potatoes, turnips, cabbages and other vegetables were stolen from field and garden, often on a very small scale, while grain and flour were also taken for human consumption.[45] Hay and firewood were also commonly stolen items, while poaching was a perennial problem that persisted well into the nineteenth century. In urban areas the pattern was necessarily different. It was still possible to steal poultry and small domesticated animals as they grazed on open land or in urban farms, but it was more common to steal food from shops or market stalls. Butchers and bakers were the most common victims of opportunist thefts. The theft of wood for fires was also to be found, but in many towns there was the additional opportunity of 'black gleaning', that is the taking of coal from railway companies and factories. The theft of relatively small quantities of food, or of firewood and coal, again suggests a close link between crime and poverty. Many of those brought to court came from the poorly and irregularly paid ranks of the unskilled, for whom life was both hard and precarious. Cases of extreme hardship are to be found, and particularly in the severe winter of 1841–2 several Black Country prisoners claimed hunger in mitigation. However, many thefts were carried out by people in employment who did not simply steal to assuage immediate hunger and who did not plead want in their defence.[46]

The theft of clothing was almost as common as the theft of food. In Sussex and Gloucestershire, between 1805 and 1850, clothing accounted for approximately 20 per cent of all stolen items. In the Black Country, between

1835 and 1860, the figure was slightly lower (17 per cent) while in Middlesbrough during roughly the same period it was significantly higher, at over 30 per cent. Clothes were stolen from employers, from the rooms of fellow-lodgers and from the washing lines of neighbours as well as from pawnshops, clothes shops and stalls. Such thefts were easy to carry out and the items stolen easy to dispose of in a pub or pawnshop. Some thefts were more acquisitive than necessitous. The Black Country police knew where to go to apprehend suspects and the courts gave severe punishments in certain cases. Both facts suggest the existence of known multiple offenders.

Theft from the person was largely opportunistic and unplanned and sometimes related to poverty. The most common situation involved men drinking in a pub. As one fell into a drunken stupor, another rifled his pockets or took unattended money. But other cases were more calculated. Stallholders haggling with would-be customers had to be careful that their attentions were not so distracted as to overlook the accomplice stealing the petty cash. Men buying sexual favours, or simply allowing themselves to be bought drinks by women, ran the risk of being robbed, and with no guarantee of a sympathetic hearing should they overcome their embarrassment and bring the case to court! And finally, there were the professional pickpockets, operating in a variety of ways, who quite clearly sought to make a living from theft.

There is a category of more contentious thefts which were the subject of dispute, particularly in the eighteenth and early nineteenth century. These cover a range of activities including some forms of poaching, the taking of firewood, coal, raw materials and manufactured goods and of tools. These activities stemmed from a clash of values that was particularly acute during the early phases of the 'Industrial Revolution' and which gave rise to a popular perception that rightful 'perks' were being denied and that customary rights were being criminalized. Nowhere is the social construction of crime more easily seen than in this contested area of occupational or industrial larceny.[47] The rapid expansion of outwork, which involved the putting out of expensive materials, and the recruitment of new workers increased the risks faced by entrepreneurs, but there were two other important and interrelated elements involved here. The first was the growing emphasis upon individual property rights; the second the move to a wholly monetarized wage. As employers in a growing range of industries moved away from the mixed wage, there was a decline in the practice of payment in kind. 'Perks' which had been an essential part of the mixed wage were now being withdrawn. The employer now saw himself as the sole owner of all the property and an employee rendered himself liable for prosecution for theft if he took property which was now seen to belong rightfully to his employer. One man's legitimate perk was another man's industrial larceny. This source of conflict has a long history. Legislation of the second quarter of the eighteenth century dealt with the question of industrial larceny in shoemaking, iron working, woollen manufacture, the leather and skin trades, and hat and watch making. The most famous legislation, however, was the Worsted Act of 1777. The extent to which change proceeded in one industry or one region in contrast to another is a matter for labour historians, but it is clear that there are important consequences for the historian of crime.

In the Black Country almost 30 per cent of committals for larceny between 1835 and 1860 fell into this category. Men were prosecuted for taking iron and selling it to dealers or other workshop masters, while women, more than men, fell foul of the law for taking coal. Jeremiah Cocklin was prosecuted for stealing a sledge hammer; Benjamin Scriven for stealing a bundle of iron for chain making which he sold to another workshop owner; Mary Ann Whatmore for the taking of coal. The number of such prosecutions increased with time. In the late 1830s, some 17 per cent of all theft prosecutions were for industrial larceny, but by the late 1850s the figure was 36 per cent. The link with industrialization seems obvious. However, this pattern was not repeated in all industrializing districts. In Middlesbrough between 1835 and 1855, only 13 per cent of thefts were industrial larcenies. The ironmasters, who dominated the local economy and played an important role in the political life of the town, showed little desire to make large-scale use of the law. Bolckow & Vaughan, the largest employer in the town, paid for their own constable at the works to prevent theft, but rarely prosecuted. Informal sanctions, such as dismissal, may well have been sufficiently effective, especially in a local economy dominated by relatively few manufacturers.[48]

The question of customary rights occurs most frequently with regard to coal stealing where the right of 'black gleaning' was claimed. With its clear allusion to agricultural gleaning, this was a commonly mounted defence and one which seems to have had some impact, as the chairman of the Staffordshire Quarter Sessions felt it necessary to remind the grand jury, on more than one occasion, that, 'however small the value, the party was equally guilty of stealing'. The authorities and local employers were aware of the strength of popular feeling and sought to dispel the belief that the taking of coal was not a criminal offence.

Ordinary gleaning was another customary activity to come under attack. Unlike the gathering of wood, which was subject to legislation in 1776, gleaning was not formally redefined by parliament as a criminal activity. However, in 1788, the Court of Common Pleas, in *Steel* v. *Houghton*, ruled that 'No person has at Common Law a right to glean in the harvest field'. Gleaning itself was not declared illegal – prosecutions had to be for trespass – and the decision did not necessarily override local custom. In Essex, there was no great rush to litigation on the part of farmers. Juries were unwilling to find against gleaners who continued their defiance of the wishes of farmers into the nineteenth century.[49] Wood gathering was the subject of parliamentary action. An act of 1776 sought to clarify the situation regarding the right to collect snap-wood and laid down stiff penalties for those found guilty. In many parts of southern England, notably Hampshire and Wiltshire, a bitter battle raged which generated more prosecutions than for any other offence.

However, it is the Game Laws that have attracted the most attention. The old Game Laws were strengthened by legislation passed in the late eighteenth and early nineteenth centuries and intended to preserve aristocratic privileges from the grasp of aspiring members of the bourgeoisie. By the early nineteenth century, poachers and gamekeepers were often organized into large gangs and a number of spectacular conflicts aroused fear and attention. Poaching offences rose dramatically. In Bedfordshire, they accounted for less than 4 per cent of prison commitments in the first decade of the nineteenth century, but by the 1840s the figure had risen to 36 per cent. Game Law convictions were four times greater than the national average in counties such as Bedfordshire and Buckinghamshire. The patchiness of the figures raises problems. While the very low prosecution figures in Cornwall, Cumberland and Westmorland might be explained in terms of non-detection, it is less easy to explain why there was so little recorded poaching in Cambridgeshire or why the level in Norfolk was some 50 per cent of that in Suffolk. The picture is further compounded by the complex motives involved. Undoubtedly there were poachers who stole for the pot – rural poverty was a major problem in many southern and eastern counties of England – but not all poachers were responding to economic privation, let alone fighting a class war against aristocratic privilege. Many of the poachers of Bedfordshire or Hertfordshire were involved in the lucrative, though illegal, trade in game with the poulterers and hoteliers of London. Poaching was as much an entrepreneurial enterprise in many southern counties as sheep rustling was around the northern industrial towns.[50]

Other Crimes

The law was also used to deal with forms of behaviour that were deemed, by elements of 'respectable' society at least, immoral or in some way unacceptable. Drunkenness, urinating in public places, swearing or otherwise causing a breach of the peace, as well as gambling and soliciting, were subject to periodic bouts of public condemnation and police prosecution. The significance of these crimes lies in the fact that the state, through the agencies of the law, sought to control and shape certain day-to-day aspects of working-class life. There was an attempt, never consistent and not always concerted, to create a new leisure ethic to go alongside the work ethic. The class bias of much of this legislation was clear at the time, as the attempts to curb prostitution and gambling clearly reveal. It was all too easy to elide working classes, criminal classes and dangerous classes. There was a continuing preoccupation with the crimes committed by the working classes and this has been reflected in much of the scholarly writing on the subject.[51] Class preoccupations of the past have distorted the picture of criminality created in the present and yet a strong case could be made for the proposition that the most serious and fastest growing area of crime in the nineteenth century was that of 'white collar' offences, ranging from breaches of the Factory Acts or Food Adulteration Acts to often spectacular cases of embezzlement and fraud.

One of the more important developments of Victorian England was the growth of the government responsibility for various aspects of health and safety. Legislation covering conditions of work in mines and factories or the quality of foodstuffs affords but the best known examples. On the surface, the success rate for the prosecution of such regulatory crimes was impressive, with figures in excess of 90 per cent being recorded.[52] However, on closer inspection the statistics are less impressive. The most important point was not the high level of successful prosecutions but the low level of cases actually brought to court.[53] Between 1834 and 1855, the number of offenders rarely exceeded 200 per annum and fell below 100 in 12 of the 21 years under review. An assiduous inspector, such as Leonard Horner, might bring as many as 20 cases per month in his busiest period, but this figure could fall to as little as two cases per month in slack times. Furthermore, many magistrates in the industrializing districts of south Lancashire and the West Riding of Yorkshire were not wholly impartial in their attitude towards this legislation, acting in ways that discouraged prosecutions. The real number of crimes committed under this legislation cannot be calculated, but the official statistics record but a small part of a much larger problem.

The shortcomings of the historical record are even more striking when one considers such crimes as embezzlement and fraud.[54] Nonetheless, very large sums were involved and the subsequent suffering could extend widely. The burden of the £1 million collapse of the Liberator Building Society in 1892 fell on the thousands of small investors in the company. Some 2600 individuals were reduced to 'total or semi-destitution'. Over half the victims were widows and spinsters, many over 60 years of age. Financial crimes were not unique to the nineteenth century but the dramatic growth of industry, and indeed of local and national government, the transformation of finance, the underdeveloped nature of accounting and auditing and the inadequate protection offered by the law meant that the opportunities for such activities increased dramatically, but with no corresponding increase in legal protection. As a consequence, large sums of money were illegally expropriated and thousands of often ordinary men and women suffered financial ruin, but only a few of the financial criminals ever appeared before the courts. The railway boom of the mid-nineteenth century led to numerous scandals. George Hudson of York, 'the railway king', was spectacularly involved in one such case, though the precise scale of his criminal activities is difficult to establish. In another case, Leopold Redpath, registrar of the Great Northern Railway, defrauded the company of some £240 000 over a period of ten years. Banking frauds could also involve large sums of money. In 1849, the manager of the Rochdale Saving Bank, George Haworth, was found to have embezzled £71 000 in the previous ten years, while in 1855 the manager and chief cashier of the Shropshire Banking Company were found to have embezzled some £200 000 over a 13-year period. The keeping of fictitious ledgers and books and fraudulent borrowing were major problems revealed in the banking crises of 1857 and 1866. But proof was not always easy to find. It is significant that the prosecution for fraud of the directors of the bank of Overend, Gurney & Company, which collapsed on 11 May 1866, failed. The law 'put few obstacles in the path of white-collar criminals [and] the depressing history of fraud and chicanery detailed before Parliamentary committees in 1867, 1875 and 1878 had little influence on resulting legislation'.[55] The growth of local government also opened up possibilities for financial crime as the rather melodramatic tale of the seemingly respectable town clerk of Middlesbrough in the 1860s shows.[56]

The failure of historians to highlight white-collar crime is quite staggering. Individual losses could lead to ruin, even suicide, while in a broader sense the loss to the nation's economy was considerable, not least given the vulnerability of new industries and new technologies to fraudulent promotions. William Pullinger, bank clerk and embezzler, was found guilty in 1860 of illegally obtaining some £260 000. In the same year, Henry Mayhew estimated the total value of goods stolen by thieves in London to be a mere £71 000. Literary evidence is not always an accurate guide but, in this instance, Victorian novelists were far more perceptive than many later historians in portraying crooked financiers as the villains of the day.[57]

Conclusion

There are four general points that deserve emphasis. The first has to do with the geography of crime. It is a commonplace to contrast the crime-ridden and socially divided town with the law-abiding and harmonious village. Even before Tonnies talked about the shift from *Gemeinschaft* to *Geselleschaft*, numerous Victorian writers and painters created a mythologized country-side that was both physically and morally superior. Despite the fact that such a distinction is supported by the official crime statistics, the contrast is overdrawn. At certain times, for example in the 1830s and 1840s, officially recorded crime rose more rapidly in rural counties such as Bedfordshire than in urban counties such as Middlesex.[58] There was not a uniform urban experience, any more than there was a uniform rural experience. Moreover, even in seemingly idyllic surroundings unpleasant things were to be found. As George Sturt, for one, was to discover when he retreated to his village around the turn of the twentieth century, there was a less attractive, but less publicized, side to rural life. Domestic violence was not confined to the kicking districts of Wigan or Liverpool; neither were drunkenness and immorality solely urban phenomena.[59] Undoubtedly towns offered greater opportunities for crime, particularly petty theft. There was also a greater chance of breaking the bounds of social conventions. To this extent the higher urban crime rates may reflect real differences. On the other hand, informal sanctions may well have been used less while the lower police/population ratios in towns increased the likelihood of apprehension. Such factors inflated the official statistics and gave a false impression of the con-trast in criminality between town and country.

Secondly, the overall timing of change is, in broad terms, relatively straightforward. Looked at more closely, the temporal pattern is more com-plex and more problematic. The local experience could vary considerably from the national, especially in the short run. Further, the temporal inci-dence of specific crimes is problematic. The relationship between crime and economic and social conditions was rarely simple. This is most clearly seen with crimes such as arson or cattle maiming where, on many occasions, there were no clear links between the outbreak of these crimes and the state of the local economy. Some years of prosperity saw an upsurge in the number of fires, while some years of depression did not. Individual motivation was complex, with rarely a simple cause-and-effect relationship between eco-nomic suffering and criminal behaviour. The arsonist's decision to fire his master's barn could well be triggered by a specific but random incident after years in which a sense of anger and injustice had built up. The fact that the final incident took place in a 'good' year does not make the act irrational. Rather, it should sensitize the historian to the need to recognize the complexities of human motivation and to reject the simplistic and mechanistic explanations of criminal behaviour.

The third point relates to the gender distribution of crime. Although crime was largely associated with adolescent and adult men, women played their part in the criminal history of the nation. Prostitution, habitual drunkenness, infanticide and receiving were the crimes most commonly associated with women, but they were to be found committing virtually all crimes. However, relatively speaking, their contribution diminished significantly from the late eighteenth to the early twentieth century. At the Old Bailey, for much of the eighteenth century, female defendants accounted for some 30 per cent of the total, and exceeded 40 per cent at certain times. Their share fell steadily over the course of the nineteenth century, so much so that by the 1890s they accounted for less than 10 per cent of the total.[60] The decline appears to be a real one whose explanation lies in the wider processes of social change, in which redefined gender roles restricted the opportunities for women to the domestic sphere, and of economic change which also reduced opportunities for women.

The fourth point concerns class. Crime was associated most strongly with the working classes, particularly of the non-respectable kind. Commentators, drawn overwhelmingly from the middle and upper classes, have written at length on these problem people; members of parliament, also from the elites of society, have enacted legislation focused on these groups; and policemen, for once coming from a similar background, have been called upon to enforce the legislation and to oversee difficult areas in the name of preserving the peace and security of society. Not surprisingly, the official statistics have confirmed the existence of the working-class criminal! Once again, there is an overdrawn contrast, this time between the respectable propertied classes and the rough propertyless. Despite the seriousness of the crimes concerned – endangering life and limb, defrauding large sums of money – white collar crimes have rarely been at the centre of official concern with criminality. All crimes are underrecorded, but perhaps none more so than certain white-collar crimes. And yet commentators, policy makers and, indeed, historians continue to discuss crime as if it were an almost exclusively working-class problem.

3

THE CRIMINAL: MYTH AND REALITY

The public concern with the threat of crime was accompanied by a growing desire to identify the type of person responsible for criminal activity and the reasons for his or her behaviour. This concern with the criminal led to a scapegoating of certain groups and to the creation of mythical types upon whom could be heaped the blame for the myriad ills of society. In this chapter we will explore the ways in which contemporaries perceived the criminal and the extent to which these perceptions matched the reality. For most commentators the criminal was adult and male. However, there was also an awareness of and concern with female crime and juvenile delinquency which, at times, dominated contemporary debate.

The Male Criminal

The most common image of the criminal was that of the anti-social outsider who threatened the health and well-being of the community. During the eighteenth century, and indeed into the nineteenth, the language of the 'body politic', the idea of an organic and harmonious society, allowed for a quasi-medical construction of the criminal. He was analogous to a diseased and malfunctioning organ that threatened the very life of the body (that is, society) as a whole. The criminal, if not actually outside the community, nonetheless was an unhealthy element set apart from the rest. It was, therefore, an easy step to portray the causes of crime as being essentially external. As the human body was infected by an outside disease, so the community was infected by extraneous elements. Nowhere was this more clear than at times of major civil disorder. Contemporary explanations of the Swing Riots of 1830–1, for example, abound with references to mysterious and sinister outsiders who were responsible for fomenting discontent among essentially loyal, if somewhat childlike and easily-led, labourers. The external threat came in a variety of forms. Ideally, the source of dissension was literally a foreigner. It was comforting to be able to ascribe machine breaking in Kent to the malicious work of Frenchmen. In the absence of such a figure, the 'foreign body' that had invaded and infected the local community could be identified as a politically motivated figure, such as William Cobbett in particular, or one of his acolytes. Either way the threat was presented as external, thereby preserving a comforting but nonetheless mythical view of an intrinsically healthy and harmonious community.

The image of the criminal as someone outside 'normal' society was not restricted simply to the 'political agitator'. Indeed, this figure was an exceptional variant of a more common type. There was a powerful and persistent belief that criminals constituted an outcast class, set apart from ordinary men and women in their disregard for the law. They inhabited a different world both morally and geographically. These were the people found in the rookeries and slums. Mostly hidden from view as they pursued their nefarious ways, they appeared periodically in a blaze of publicity when the social enquiries of Mayhew or the literary writings of Dickens, or Arthur Morrison, revealed them to a wider public. Fear and fascination surrounded these members of the dangerous classes from a nether world. However, the criminal underworld was, with the possible exception of London, a literary construction. The evidence of the courts does not reveal a distinct criminal class. Rather, it suggests that criminals were drawn from the more marginal and more vulnerable sectors of ordinary society. The unskilled and the illiterate were more likely to stray into crime, but illegal survival tactics were adopted by otherwise 'respectable' men (and women) in times of hardship.

Ethnicity also played a part in the construction of the criminal. The gypsy as thief or abductor and the Jew as fence were well-established stereotypes. Celts in general were viewed with suspicion by the English. Taffy, according to the old rhyme, was, after all, a thief! But it was the Irish who were most consistently associated with criminality, especially after the large-scale influx of the 1840s. The reputation for heavy drinking and violent behaviour resulted in Irish districts being more closely watched by the police. Not surprisingly, in a self-fulfilling prophecy, the Irish were disproportionately represented in the crime statistics as, in many towns in England, from London to Liverpool, from Manchester to Middlesbrough, they became the prime targets for the local police.[1]

If the belief in a distinct criminal class was a constant theme, the precise image of the criminal was more varied. In the early and mid-nineteenth century, the archetypal male criminal was not simply a threat to the moral welfare of the nation but was also a physically threatening figure. In the eighteenth century there was a romantic aura surrounding certain criminal figures, most notably the highwaymen, but this was soon to be replaced by a less sympathetic image. The romantic Dick Turpin had been replaced by the brutal Bill Sikes by the mid-nineteenth century. It was an image that aroused fear as much as revulsion.

The threatening image was never to disappear entirely. Indeed, spectacular incidents such as the Jack the Ripper murders of 1888 enhanced it. However, there was a significant shift in the popular image in the latter part of the century based, in part at least, on the popularization of the results of studies of actual prisoners. The criminal was no longer the physically imposing figure of earlier representation. Instead, he was seen to be a below-average rather than above-average figure. With his stunted growth, he was a product of physical degeneracy. He was also deficient in other respects. Below average physically, he was also below average mentally. Here was an image of a weak man. Thomas Holmes, a police court missionary of many years and secretary of the Howard Association, writing in 1908 (*Known to the Police*), looked back almost nostalgically on the sturdy prisoners of yesteryear who stood in marked contrast to the 'broken wretches' of Edwardian England:

> Time was when prisoners had character, grit, pluck, and personality, but now these qualities are not often met with . . . [prisoners now] are devoid of strong personality, and the mass of people in many respects resemble a flock of sheep. They have no desire to do wrong, but they constantly go wrong . . . weakness not wickedness is their great characteristic.

There is an element of romanticization, but Holmes' description of the late nineteenth-century criminal is borne out by the criminal and prison statistics. By the end of the century, the overlap between the criminal population and the rest of society had diminished considerably. Most criminals were drawn from the least educated and least skilled sections of society and, for a substantial number, involvement in petty crime had become a way of life. Legislation in 1869, revised in 1871, enshrined the notion of the habitual criminal in law. The operation of the law, however, gave rise to some striking regional variations. The habitual criminal was a more common figure in the northern industrial towns, particularly those of Lancashire. The explanation lies more in a labelling process that reflected the attitudes of local magistrates and police than in variations in local economic conditions.[2]

The late nineteenth-century criminal, and particularly the habitual criminal, aroused a mixture of not always consistent responses. On the one hand, he was a figure to be pitied for his weaknesses. Morally and physically deficient, he lacked the ability to control his own life. He was, in a sense, a victim of forces and circumstances that were beyond his control and, as such, deserving of sympathy and support. On the other hand, he was still a figure to be feared and needed to be controlled for the good of society at large. The reason for this fear had changed fundamentally. The fear engendered by a mid-century Bill Sikes stemmed from the fact that he was not only physically strong but also in control of his actions, however wrongful in the eyes of the law. He was the representative of a powerful 'evil empire' that threatened to overthrow respectable and law-abiding society. The concern created by the habitual criminal stemmed from the degeneracy which he literally embodied. At one level, physically and mentally weak, he was not a threat. At a deeper level, however, he – or what he embodied – posed a major threat that right-thinking people ignored at their peril. The habitual criminal was one manifestation of the racial degeneration that was taking place in the towns and cities of late Victorian England. Breeding prolifically, at a time when the elites in particular were limiting family size, the degenerate in society threatened to swamp respectable society, bringing physical deterioration as well as moral collapse.

Identifying the criminal was one thing; explaining his behaviour was another. A multitude of explanations are to be found in contemporary writings. There are a number of general interpretations, though they are best viewed as loose collections of ideas rather than rigorous schools of thought. For much of the early and mid-nineteenth century, explanations were couched in terms of the individual, rather than society, and emphasized his deficiencies and shortcomings. The belief that the criminal suffered from an inability to distinguish between right and wrong and/or an inability to choose right from wrong dominated discussion. Religious beliefs provided the basis of one of the most common explanations. Men (and, indeed, women) were born innately evil and the criminal, quite literally, lacked the saving grace of religion. That said, circumstances had their part to play in the creation of the criminal. The criminal was an individual who had not learnt the necessary religious and moral lessons. In this type of explanation of criminality, which was equally to be found in popular culture, great emphasis was placed upon the deleterious effects of not observing the Sabbath and neglecting parental advice. Almost equally serious was the failure of parents to provide the necessary guidance for their children without which the individual could easily be corrupted by the pernicious influence of cheap, sensationalist secular literature and succumb to the temptations of drink and luxury. Other factors, such as the disruption brought about by urban and industrial change, unemployment or the pressure of poverty, had little or no part to play in such an explanation. Thomas Plint summed up this point of view, stressing the importance of religion in shaping the moral character of the individual:

> Still less [than the manufacturing system] is absolute want, or the defi-ciency of the means of employment, the most efficient cause of the crim-inal class . . . [nor] is it the total absence, or the bad quality of education, which engenders the criminal class . . . There is neither in individuals, nor in nations, any solid basis of greatness apart from the pervading and con-trolling force of moral principle – and moral principle, in its proper and specific sense, is only another name for RELIGION.[3]

This type of argument could take a more secular and scientific form. Thus the physician and ethnologist, J. C. Prichard, explained criminal behaviour in terms of uncontrolled passions and 'moral insanity'. Passions themselves were a natural part of all men and women but the criminal lacked the reli-gious and moral teaching to hold them in check. As a consequence, 'the latent devil in the heart of the best of men' broke forth. Once again, popular literature was heavily criticized for allowing the young to see 'success and its reward attendant on action prompted by passion, without any intermediate stage of self-control'.[4]

Not all explanations were couched in terms of innate evil and inadequate religious training. Criminals, rather than being born such, were made. Moreover, the criminal as a rational and calculating individual played a central role in his own creation. His behaviour was the product of free will and the application of a Benthamite 'hedonistic calculus'. Drawing on Enlightenment thinking that saw the mind as a *tabula rasa* upon which both good and evil could be inscribed, people such as Jelinger Symons explained the creation of criminals in terms of inadequate training and inadequate role models, particularly in the teeming working-class districts of the towns where 'the communication of thought and the contagion of habit and exam-ple are more rife and rapid'.[5] The criminal was thus perceived as a rational and calculating individual but one who had made the wrong decisions, for himself and society as a whole, by faulty socialization in which crime was not associated with pain or loss. Once again, the pernicious effects of popular literature were condemned. John Gay's *Beggar's Opera* came in for continuing criticism precisely because the central character, Macheath, a highwayman, did not provide the appropriate role model. As well as being a gentleman and popular with women, Macheath was reprieved. This was not the message that was required. The impressionable might believe that crime did not bring an awful punishment but might actually pay! Thus the stage, instead of being used to disseminate a moral and uplifting message and to offer guidance, was seen to be corrupting the young in particular.

Similarly, people such as John Clay, the prison chaplain at Preston, and Mary Carpenter, the well-known social reformer, were convinced that cheap literature was at the root of much crime. Clay quoted numerous examples of prisoners who had been led astray by the published lives of Jack Sheppard and Dick Turpin and for whom the *Newgate Calendar* had become their catechism.[6] Closely related to this was another form of corruption which stemmed from 'the excitement and injurious tendency of low penny theatres, singing and dancing rooms'.[7] Carpenter noted with approval John Clay's melodramatic description of one such place of entertainment in Preston. The singing-room, which at one point had an audience of 700, was notable for its 'gross and open immorality' which pandered to depraved tastes, encouraged resistance to parental control and, through the repertoire of pieces which were 'full of gross innuendoes, "double entendres", heavy cursing, emphatic swearing, and incitement to illicit passion' was a veritable 'manufactory and rendezvous of thieves and prostitutes'.[8]

For both religious and rationalist thinkers, there was one thing worse than the various forms of 'corrupting' popular entertainment: the demon drink. John Clay presented a paper to the Statistical Society in 1856 which sought to give a statistical underpinning to his belief that 'BEERHOUSES and low ALE-HOUSES . . . [were] the chief direct causes of crime'.[9] Such views were shared by key figures in the judicial system. Justice Talfourd told the Stafford Grand Jury in 1854 that he had 'No doubt *the exciting cause* in the far larger number of these cases [is] . . . '*the greatest English vice*', the vice of drunkenness'.[10]

William Hoyle, while sympathetic to the pressures of want and harsh circumstances in the early nineteenth century had little doubt that by his day, the 1870s:

> the great expansion in our trade, the increase in the wages paid, coupled with the moderate price of food, have almost annihilated every possible excuse for the commission of crime on the plea of want. [Rather] . . . the greatest proportion of crime of the country results from the intemperance which is so fearfully prevalent.[11]

By emphasizing the moral causes of crime and highlighting 'the temptation of the profits of a career of depredation as compared with the profits of honest and even well paid industry', commentators were able to reach the conclusion that 'the notion that any considerable proportion of the crimes against property are caused by blameless poverty or destitution' is 'disproved at every step'.[12] Although in some senses fundamentally different in the nature of their explanations, all the early-Victorian constructions of the criminal shared a common belief, namely, the centrality of the absence of reason and 'civilized habits'. This lack of a civilized moral code, for whatever reason, set him apart from that emerging legal fiction of the age, the 'reasonable man'. There was an underlying optimism to these explanations of the criminal which derived from the belief that this defect could be remedied.

While many early Victorian commentators emphasized the moral deficiencies and lack of self-control that distinguished the members of the criminal classes, there were those who sought to explain criminal behaviour in terms of external, environmental factors rather than internal, moral ones. Despite the explicit and detailed denials in the dominant discourses that poverty was a cause of crime,[13] there were those, William Cobbett for example, who argued that there was a direct causal link between the circumstances in which many working-class people grew up and criminal behaviour. Low wages, under-employment, unemployment, harsh, unjust and uncertain working conditions could all contribute to otherwise 'inexplicable' criminal behaviour. During the Swing disturbances, *Punch*, with its cartoon depicting the impoverished home of the rick-burner, and the anonymous pamphlet, *Case of the Labourer truly stated*, rejected the conventional wisdom that blamed outsiders and subversives for the troubles and emphasized instead the harshness and injustice of the labourers' lot.[14] Similarly, when Thomas Campbell Foster toured the fire-stricken districts of the eastern counties of England in 1844 for *The Times*, he aroused considerable wrath by seeking to explain the upsurge in arson in terms of the poverty and desperation of people receiving inadequate wages, dependent upon a humiliating system of poor relief and subjected to what they saw as unjust treatment. But not just arson and machine breaking could be explained in this way. Robert Owen, like Engels later, saw 'sheer necessity' as a fundamental cause of certain crimes.

Such opinions were not confined to political radicals. There was, in fact, a greater awareness of the likely contribution of poverty to the incidence of crime than many historians have allowed. William Hoyle, looking back on the opening decades of the nineteenth century, conceded that 'the economic circumstances of the national life were ... pre-eminently favourable to the perpetration of crime', though he felt it necessary to add the qualification that in addition 'the educational position of the country was far from being satisfactory'.[15] Joseph Fletcher concluded that 'a great excess of crime is observed to follow every considerable excess to the price of food'.[16] In similar vein, *The Economist* noted in 1856 that 'the less there was amongst them [the lower classes] of poverty and pauperism – the less there would be of crime in the community . . . how desirable it is, in order to diminish crime, that the multitude should be as rich as possible'.[17]

Not the best known nor most influential writer of the time was Friedrich Engels, who offered a social-conflict explanation of criminality. While arguing that some thefts were the result of 'sheer necessity', he argued that in a society which he believed was visibly dissolving, in which 'social war' was well under way, crime against property was not simply an expression of 'contempt for the existing social order' in its 'most conspicuous [and] extreme form' but also the product of the tensions and conflict created by capitalist society. He had no doubt that capitalism and crime marched hand in hand: 'The extension of the factory system,' he noted in 1844 in his *Outlines of a Critique of Political Economy*, 'is always followed by an absolute increase in crime'. Thefts motivated by want were seen by Engels as a clear sign of this, but so too were the street crimes committed by the 'surplus population' of casual labourers, street sellers and the like.

Engels' explanation of crime also encompassed petty crimes, such as drunkenness, brawling and prostitution. In part, such actions were due to the alienation of working men and women; in part, they were due to upperclass neglect and the failure to provide the necessary moral training:

> While burdening them with numerous hardships the middle classes have left them only the pleasures of drink and sexual intercourse . . . If people are relegated to the position of animals, they are left with the alternatives of revolting and sinking into bestiality.[18]

At this point the demoralizing pressures are so great that working men and women are swept into criminal behaviour. Engels' explanation of criminal behaviour is not entirely consistent. At one point, the demoralized individual is driven to crime as if by natural laws. As water turns into steam at boiling point, so the working man turns into a criminal when the demoralizing influences of capitalist society act upon him in a more powerful and more concentrated form. But in a later passage Engels ascribes a greater degree of control and decision making to the individual. In general terms, he saw crime as a form of rebellious resistance, albeit of 'the crudest and least fruitful form', consciously entered into by the working man who could not understand why he contributed more to society than the idle rich but also suffered more. Thus driven by 'sheer necessity', he took his revenge for the injustices perpetrated upon him by the rich.[19]

The best-known mid-century ethnographer was Henry Mayhew. In the opening pages of his monumental study of *London Labour and London Poor*, he distinguished between settlers and wanderers. The latter were inherently savage. Mayhew, drawing on Prichard, described them in vivid language. They are characterized by 'a greater development of the animal than of the intellectual or moral nature of man' and by such physical features as 'their high cheek bones and protruding jaws'. In addition, they exhibit such worrying characteristics as 'lax ideas of property', 'general improvidence', 'repugnance to continuous labour', 'disregard of female honour', 'love of cruelty', 'pugnacity' and an 'utter want of religion'. Despite sharing that wider confidence in the possibility of developing self-control among the working classes, Mayhew had grave doubts about the 'wanderers', who seemed to be incapable of this and he exhorted his readers to distinguish between the respectable and worthy class of 'honest, independent working men' and the degraded and vicious class of 'vagrant beggars and pilferers', of whom only 5 per cent could be classified as deserving.[20]

The threat from the dangerous classes appeared to be at its greatest in the second quarter of the nineteenth century. Thereafter, the authorities began to win the battle against crime. The language became less extreme and attitudes more tolerant and understanding. There was a recognition that poverty could be an important causal factor and greater emphasis was placed upon the impact of environment. The criminal was presented more as a product of his circumstances and of wider defects in society at large. In 1896, Henry Thomas could write that 'as poverty increases so does crime' and that most criminals were 'slaves to their surroundings'. Therefore 'reform of those environments' was the first step towards reform, though education and character training were also important. Despite a superficial continuity with mid-century environmentalist explanations, Thomas' views were clearly influenced by less optimistic ideas of his day. The improvement in conditions, important in its own right, was an essential step in the more important task 'to define the habitual criminal'.[21]

The essentially optimistic belief in the rationality of the individual came under heavy attack from the 1860s onwards. Doubts about the free will of the individual and the perfectibility of man were not new. The discovery of patterns of human behaviour which suggest organizing principles beyond the collective decisions of individuals can be traced back to the 1830s, if not before. Scientific advances also created a more pessimistic outlook on the criminal. The writings of Henry Maudsley in the 1860s and 1870s cast serious doubt on old beliefs. Preaching self-control to the criminal was as foolish as 'to preach moderation to the east wind, or gentleness to the hurricane'.[22] Even more starkly, he argued that 'No one can escape the tyranny of his organisation; no one can elude his destiny that is innate in him, and which unconsciously and irresistibly shapes his ends, even when he believes that he is determining them with consummate foresight and skill.'[23]

The idea of the criminal as a defective individual, blighted from birth by the defects of his parents and liable to add to the process of degeneration, was but one strand in a more general concern for the continuing healthiness and efficiency of the nation. The habitual criminal, the persistent and seemingly irredeemable offender, was the starkest reminder of the corrupting effect of urban growth. Increasingly, influential Victorians, despite living in the wealthiest and most powerful nation in the world, expressed doubts about the internal stability and external standing of the country. There was a growing sense of despondency brought about by the discovery of a greater degree of poverty than had previously been imagined and the emergence of socialist groups who focused on these social problems. There was concern about the loss of economic dominance to the rapidly expanding economies of Germany and America and the growing imperial difficulties, culminating in the second Boer War, in which the world's greatest imperial power struggled to assert itself with an army in which many working-class men from the towns and cities of Britain had been found to be unfit to serve. In what was seen as a Darwinistic struggle between nations for survival, Britain seemed to be among the unfit.

A further element in the reconstruction of the criminal came from the writings of Cesare Lombroso, who challenged free will thinking and introduced the idea of the born criminal.[24] Lombrosian ideas were brought to Britain by writers such as Isobel Foard and Havelock Ellis. Unlike many Lombrosian popularizers, Ellis stressed the difficulty of distinguishing between both normal and abnormal and the different types of abnormality. Nonetheless, he still saw the criminal as analogous to a savage, 'a simple and incomplete creature' set apart by the failure to match civilized standards.[25]

The importance of such ideas in Britain has generally been played down, with emphasis being placed on traditions of empiricism as exemplified by the work of Charles Goring. However, on closer examination the picture is less clear-cut. Goring was highly critical of Lombroso's idea of the born criminal, which he saw as a superstitious dogma which distorted scientific criminology. His massive study, *The English Convict*, based on extensive research funded by the Home Office, was a three-phase investigation of Lombroso's claims. The first element was a detailed statistical analysis to establish the existence of Lombrosian characteristics in the criminal population. Based on a study of almost two and a half thousand male prisoners, classified from first offenders to habitual criminals, 37 Lombrosian characteristics were tested for and very weak correlations were found for all. The findings from this first phase were then compared with the characteristics of the non-criminal population as reflected in a motley collection of men – including Oxbridge undergraduates, a company of Royal Engineers and inmates of the Middlesex General Hospital – whose common characteristic was the absence of a criminal record. No significant differences were discovered between the two populations. Finally, Goring and his team analysed the general physical characteristics of the criminal population. Evidence of physical inferiority was found, but it was concluded that this was not the result of any inbred criminal trait.

It might be felt that this was a classic example of English empiricism confounding continental theorizing. However, the contrast can be overstated. In his conclusions, Goring explicitly rejected environmental factors as an important element in the explanation of the criminal. Drawing on a belief that intellectual, social and moral qualities were distributed normally in any large population, he argued that

> there is a physical, mental, and moral type of person who tends to be convicted of crime . . . In every class and occupation of life, it is the feeble mind and the inferior forms of physique – the less physically and mentally able persons – which tend to be selected for a criminal career.

Although the idea of a distinctive and atavistic criminal type had been rejected, Goring had still identified a criminal type characterized by physical and mental deficiencies, determined more by heredity than environment. He had little faith in education as a solution to the problem of the criminal, but rather argued for either segregation and supervision of the unfit or, and this he saw as 'attacking the evil at its very root', the regulation of 'the reproduction of those degrees of constitutional qualities – feeble mindedness, inebriety, epilepsy, deficient social instinct etc. – which conduce to the committing of crime'.[26] This was a fundamentally different explanation of criminal behaviour and one which had profound policy implications.

The Female Criminal

Throughout the nineteenth century the problem of the criminal was discussed largely in terms of deviant male behaviour. However there was a real and continuing concern about female criminality. The Victorians were aware that, according to the official crime statistics at least, there were fewer female than male criminals. This fact, which could be explained in terms of the natural religiosity and superior moral qualities of women, was a source of comfort in a difficult and threatening world, but only up to a point. The moral fibre of the nation was seen to be threatened by such diverse forces as the spread of factory employment for women – a high-profile concern in the 1830s and 1840s which saw a gross exaggeration of the extent of factory employment for women, let alone of its allegedly deleterious effects – and the growth of popular leisure which encouraged vice rather than virtue.[27] More specifically, women were more heavily involved in those moral crimes, notably prostitution and drunkenness, which so exercised the minds of contemporary commentators. Fears were intensified in the late nineteenth century when it was discovered that the habitual criminal was more likely to be female. Habitual drunkenness appeared to be a peculiar female failing. A new folk devil appeared. The demoralized and demoralizing habitual drunkard, personified by the likes of Ellen Sweeney and Jane Cakebread, both with almost 300 convictions to their name, was seen as a threat to the very survival of the race. A drunken mother was worse than a drunken father as she would bring into the world a new generation of degenerates.

Discussions of female criminality were profoundly influenced by the dominant gender ideologies of the day. Although the male criminal was a deviant figure, much of his behaviour was consistent with accepted, if not wholly acceptable, male characteristics. Men were expected to be physically strong and brave. There was a fine line dividing a manly display of strength and a criminal assault. Indeed, precisely because of prevailing codes of masculinity, many cases of assault never appeared before the courts. A female criminal was more likely to be seen as a deviant, breaching strongly held beliefs about the nature of femininity, than her male counterpart. Women were seen to have peculiar moral qualities and responsibilities that did not fall on men. While it is easy to overstate the extent of change in gender definitions in the modern period, the years spanning the late eighteenth and early nineteenth centuries and, even more so, the troublesome decades of the 1830s and 1840s, saw a marked increase in the volume of didactic literature which stressed the peculiar role and responsibilities of women and warned of the calamities that would befall society if women failed in their natural and God-given task.[28] Women in the nineteenth century were seen and judged in terms of a simple (and simplistic) madonna/whore dichotomy and the most common accusation levelled at deviant or criminal women focused on their sexuality and their alleged uncontrolled sexual behaviour. The female counterpart of the irrational male criminal was characterized by precociousness and sexual promiscuity.[29]

Horror and fear went hand in hand in many contemporary accounts. Elizabeth Fry was appalled at the women prisoners in Newgate that she saw in 1813. Physically and morally degenerate, their defeminization was summed up for Fry in their habit of dressing in men's clothing. For a woman to fall from grace was more serious both for the individual concerned and for society at large. One contributor to the *Cornhill Magazine* in 1866 saw criminal women as being like wild animals or worse: 'Criminal women, as a class, are found to be more uncivilised than the savage, more degraded than the slave, less true to all natural and womanly instincts than the untutored squaw of a North American Indian tribe'.[30] The image of the defeminized woman was also used to describe, and by implication explain, women who resorted to violence. Women fighting amongst themselves or even attacking men were seen as harridans. The woman who killed her new-born child might be treated with some sympathy as a sad or mad individual, but the female murderer, more likely to have killed a member of her immediate family, was viewed with horror as unnatural, defeminized and the very antithesis of feminine virtue.

The dominant gender ideology stressed the importance of the home as the environment in which woman could fulfil her responsibilities and also be protected from the corrupting influences of the outside world. Thus women were seen to be more susceptible than men, for whom the public sphere was their natural environment, to the degrading and demoralizing effects of urban conditions. The slums of London and the factory towns of Lancashire in particular attracted considerable attention and aroused considerable fear. The weakness of woman underpinned another popular explanation of female criminality – that of the young woman seduced and exploited by men. It was a commonplace of much mid-Victorian commentary that young women did not choose to become prostitutes and thieves but had been brought to this sorry state by the philandering aristocrats in particular, who, having used these poor defenceless young women, abandoned them to a life of crime. The idea that emancipation from the home could lead to female criminality received fresh impetus in the last quarter of the nineteenth century. The emergence of the 'new woman' was viewed with concern by many conservatively minded people, while the growth of the suffrage movement added further to fears. L. O. Pike, a noted writer on criminal matters, could argue confidently that 'every step made by woman towards her independence is a step towards the precipice at the bottom of which lies a prison'.[31]

The late nineteenth century saw more 'scientific' attention being focused specifically on the female criminal. Lombroso and Ferrero's pioneering work, *The Female Offender*, was first published in 1895. Their explanation was couched in terms of degeneration and atavism. Despite the fact that their empirical evidence was weak – few of the women prisoners they studied had the minimum number of marks of degeneracy needed by their theory – they sought to preserve their central belief by arguing that women, being less developed than men, could not degenerate as far. Women were little more than 'big children' with deficient moral sense. Therefore the female criminal type did not stand out as distinctly as the male. But what female criminals lacked in quantity they made up for in quality, according to Lombroso and Ferrero. In addition to the criminal qualities of men, women brought with them the peculiar characteristics of cunning, deceitfulness, jealousy and spite. To compound matters such women lacked a properly developed maternal instinct. Whereas, they argued, in ordinary mothers 'the sexual instinct is in abeyance' the criminal woman exhibits 'exaggerated sexuality so opposed to maternity'. Such abnormalities effectively defeminized them. The female criminal was coarse-voiced and unnaturally strong and exhibited a virility that was not natural to her sex. The 'maleness' of her attributes and actions was a reflection of her genetic deficiencies and abnormalities. Thus the criminal woman was doubly damned – for her offence in itself and for her offence against true womanliness – and she was 'as a consequence a monster'.[32]

The response to Lombrosian ideas on female criminals varied considerably. Many writers, with the notable exception of Havelock Ellis, took a critical stance and such was the extent of criticism that one writer, at least, was able to ridicule the founding father of positivist criminology with the commonsense observation that 'prostitutes are of all sizes and shapes, from the very thin to the very fat'.[33] Nonetheless, one of the leading writers on the subject, W. I. Thomas, propounded a variant on the Lombrosian theme. In *Sex and Society*, published in 1907, he argued that female criminality should be explained, not in terms of abnormal, that is, masculine tendencies amongst this group of women, but rather as the product of the misuse of feminine characteristics. Such women were cold, calculating and amoral.[34] The scepticism towards Lombroso did not mean that all biological and medical explanations were out of favour in England. To the contrary, many learned medical men believed women to be at the mercy of their biological make-up. Sexual mania was called upon to explain prostitution – as in the writings of Hargrave Adams, for example – and also murder and, especially, infanticide. There was in all this an underlying continuity in the depiction of the female criminal as not being truly feminine.

A final element in the depiction of the female criminal was that of Eve-the-temptress. Not only could an evil woman drive her husband on to ghastly deeds (the Lady Macbeth syndrome) but she could also corrupt the next generation through the way in which she brought up her children, and the delinquent child was a recurring source of worry throughout the nineteenth century.

Juvenile Delinquents

Despite a clear concern for the well-being of working-class children in the late eighteenth century, there was relatively little attention focused specifically on juvenile crime. However, attitudes began to change around the turn of the nineteenth century. Demographic changes created a society which, as well as growing at a historically unprecedented rate, had a higher percentage of young people. Furthermore, economic changes appeared to create more idle young as well as undermining the basis of the family, and the process of urbanization concentrated the young and made them more visible. Thus youth itself was seen as a major problem. Behaviour which previously had been tolerated was no longer seen as acceptable. As a consequence, the identification of juvenile delinquency as a major social problem can be seen, in broad terms, as a product of new attitudes in the early nineteenth century in general and in the 1820s in particular.

Concern with juvenile delinquency, which was heightened by the transition from war to peace, led William Crawford to become the driving force behind the establishment of a committee to investigate 'the alarming increase in juvenile delinquency in the Metropolis'. Concern continued throughout subsequent years and reached its height in the 1840s and 1850s when a flood of pamphlets and essays was produced on the subject. Such was the fear that the young criminal aroused that one mid-nineteenth century writer could blame juveniles for 'the overwhelming mass of crime, now deluging our land [and] the current of iniquity which at present sweeps our streets'.[35] To compound matters, the phasing out and imminent cessation of transportation – Australia's refusal to continue to provide 'an open cesspool for the criminal sewerage of England', in the Reverend John Clay's memorable phrase – gave rise to lurid images of a nation swamped by depraved juveniles.

Virtually every commentator based his or her judgement on middle-class assumptions about the nature of family, children and childhood. As Mary Carpenter, a sympathetic observer, wrote of them in 1853: 'in almost every respect [juvenile delinquents exhibit] qualities the very reverse of what we should desire to see in childhood; we have beheld them independent, self-reliant, advanced in the knowledge of evil'.[36] For the majority of contemporary experts the problem could be explained in terms of parental, especially maternal, neglect, violations of the Sabbath, the absence of appropriate education and guidance and a corresponding influence of pernicious, cheap literature and entertainment and, to a lesser extent, lack of employment. In addition, the fundamental problem was compounded by failures in the criminal justice system, notably inefficient policing, an over-severe penal code and a corrupt system of prison discipline.

Concern with juvenile delinquency was not constant. Periods of relative self-confidence were followed by years of fear. Thus juvenile delinquency in general and hooliganism in particular became a prominent problem in the 1890s and 1900s. A panic was engendered by large-scale street conflicts between gangs of outrageously dressed young men with caps 'set rakishly forward', trousers 'very tight at the knees and very loose at the foot' and, most sinister of all, 'the substantial leather belt heavily mounted with metal'.[37]

Incidents of football hooliganism involving rival youth gangs punctuated the 1880s and 1890s. Weekends were favourite times for disturbances. August Bank Holiday brought high-profile troubles as some 300 people were involved in large-scale fisticuffs and kicking in the Old Kent Road in 1898. Nor was this the largest disturbance. The Newton Heath 'scuttle' of 1890 involved in excess of 500 youths in a pitched battle in which they used belts, stones, catapults, knives and iron bars. There were also less spectacular cases which, while not catching the national headlines, nonetheless added to local fears about a new generation of criminals. In retrospect, the theft of seven pigeons in Marton, near Middlesbrough, in 1886 was not evidence of the collapse of local order. However, at the time, the fact that a gang of five young men, aged from 16 to 19, and all with at least two previous convictions to their name, had carried out the deed created an impact locally that was out of proportion to the scale of the crime.

Hooligan troubles appeared more worrying because of the physical characteristics of the participants. Fear of racial degeneration was neatly summed up by Cyril Burt, who described juvenile offenders as 'frail, sickly and infirm', young men 'of bodily weakness and ill-health'. Furthermore, these people were seen to be a source of supply that would perpetuate that other threatening figure, the adult habitual criminal. Explanations of late Victorian and Edwardian juvenile delinquency were not dissimilar from those put forward in the 1850s: family malfunction leading to moral failure, inadequate education and pernicious literature, such as *Comic Cuts*, which encouraged the criminal and reduced respect for the law. However, there were certain important differences. Whereas early nineteenth-century writers believed that to be good required a fight against the child's nature, late nineteenth-century writers took a more optimistic view. Greater emphasis was placed on the distinctiveness of childhood and the difficulties associated with the transition to adulthood. The discovery of 'adolescence' as a distinctive phase in the development of the individual and a time of 'storm and stress' for all, irrespective of class, led, somewhat paradoxically, to a more relaxed belief that the majority of juvenile offenders would pass through this phase and settle down.

The Reality behind the Rhetoric

The changing perceptions of the criminal tell us much about the beliefs and concerns of elite figures, but do they give us an accurate indication of the nature of the criminal and the cause of crime? There are no easy answers, largely because of the limitations of the available evidence.

Despite the widespread contemporary belief in the existence of a distinct criminal class, recent detailed studies lend little support to this notion. With the possible exception of London, where sheer geographical size made possible the existence of distinct criminal areas, it is difficult to find clear-cut criminal ghettos and a distinct criminal class. This is not to say that there were not notorious crime spots, 'dangerous districts', especially in the larger towns and cities, places such as the China district of Merthyr, the old town area of Middlesbrough or even Castlegate in Huddersfield. Moreover, within such districts there were people, like John Sutcliffe, the 'King of Castlegate', who relied heavily upon the proceeds of crime to survive and even a few professional gangs who made a living out of organized theft, but this is not the same as saying there was a distinct criminal class. Even in the late nineteenth century, when the prison population was visibly ageing, it is by no means clear that these 'hardened and perhaps experienced' criminals constituted a class of their own. On the contrary, the evidence points more to the conclusion that criminals, particularly in the early and mid-nineteenth century, were drawn from a wide section of society (predominantly, but not exclusively, the working class) but with an overrepresentation of the more insecure, the more marginalized and the more stigmatized groups. By the late nineteenth century, the criminal population was less representative of the population as a whole: 'By the 1880s and 1890s those who stole by habit or had to steal to survive were more and more conspicuously the most depressed and least literate in the population.'[38]

One fact seems beyond dispute: crime was largely and increasingly a male activity. The majority of criminals appearing before the courts were male. For serious crimes tried at assize or quarter session the national average was about 80 per cent but there were considerable local variations. Men accounted for 95 per cent of those tried at assize in Sussex in the first half of the nineteenth century and 89 per cent of those tried at quarter session; in Gloucestershire, the corresponding figures were only slightly lower, while in the North Riding of Yorkshire men accounted for just under 90 per cent of all prisoners indicted for trial at quarter session. In contrast, women accounted for approximately 20 per cent of all prisoners at the assizes in London between 1810 and 1850, while in some industrial areas the percentage of women was even higher: 25 per cent in the Black Country and 30 per cent in Middlesbrough. The latter figure obscures a dramatic short-term change. In the early 1840s, female prisoners from Middlesbrough accounted for 10 per cent of all women appearing at the Northallerton Quarter Sessions. A decade later the figure had risen to 25 per cent of the total, reaching 55 per cent in 1855.[39] By the late nineteenth century there had been a sharp reduction in the percentage of women appearing in court, most clearly seen in London.

Assessing the age of criminals is more difficult. Compulsory registration of births was not introduced until 1837 and, in addition to those who genuinely did not know, there were those who falsified their age in the belief, well-founded or otherwise, that this would bring them more lenient treatment. Given the severity of punishment meted out to men in their twenties, particularly in the late eighteenth century, there was an incentive to claim to be younger or older. The official figures are likely to overstate the scale of juvenile crime, although one can but speculate on the precise scale of this problem.[40]

Contemporaries were much exercised by the problem of juvenile delinquency and at least one historian (Tobias) has argued that the increase in criminal activity was largely associated with young offenders, but the official statistics lend only qualified support to this point of view. In the period 1834–41, 40 per cent of offenders were aged 21 or under and 30 per cent were under 20 in the period 1842–7. Yet, according to the 1841 census, 46 per cent of the population was aged under 20. The greatest overrepresentation was for people in their late teens and twenties, but there was also a disproportionate number of people in their thirties.[41]

A further point needs to be made about juvenile delinquency in the early nineteenth century. As well as being exaggerated in the popular imagination, the problem was, in a sense, a manufactured one. To claim that Sir Robert Peel was the father of juvenile delinquency is an exaggeration, but changes in legislation, such as the 1824 Vagrant Act and the 1827 Malicious Trespass Act, greatly increased the number of juvenile offenders as a wide range of relatively petty actions and activities were criminalized. Equally, the extension of summary jurisdiction probably led to an increased willingness to prosecute young offenders, though this would not be reflected in the statistics from the superior courts. Other factors added to the artificial increase in the number of juvenile offenders. The growing number of policemen and the extension of their discretionary powers led to youngsters appearing before the courts for such heinous offences as playing cricket in the street, flying kites and bowling hoops. Finally, magistrates were driven by a belief that children, particularly in towns, were so precocious and depraved that they were capable of acting criminally at any age. Certainly, there was a decline in the presumption of *incapacitas* for those under 14 years of age. Thus the fear of juvenile criminality became self-fulfilling.

During the latter part of the century the prison returns, relating to both indictable and summary offences, show an ageing criminal population in which young offenders were relatively less important. In 1861 about 30 per cent of male offenders were aged 20 or under and almost 40 per cent 30 or over. By 1891, the contrast was even greater, with 50 per cent of offenders aged 30 or over but only 20 per cent aged 20 or under. The contrast for female offenders was even greater. In 1861, 25 per cent were 20 or under and just under 40 per cent were 30 or over. By 1891, some 60 per cent were 30 or over, but only 10 per cent 20 or under.

From 1893, the annual statistics distinguished by age group those convicted of indictable offences. The figures point to a decline in serious crime among juveniles. In 1895, 40 per cent of the total number convicted for indictable offences were aged under 21. By 1905 the figure had fallen to 35 per cent. More striking was the decline in the number of juvenile offenders as a percentage of the relevant age group. Between 1895 and 1905, the number of offenders aged from 12 to 16 fell from 261 per 100 000 to 218, a decline of 17 per cent, while for those aged 16 to 21 the fall was from 321 to 275, or 14 per cent.

The official figures do confirm contemporary fears about the habitual criminal. Between 1860 and 1890, the percentage of male prisoners who had previously been committed to gaol rose from 26 to 46, while for women the rise was from 42 per cent to 63 per cent.[42] Local evidence brings out the point starkly. John Campbell, found guilty of theft in Middlesbrough, was a 28-year-old engineer who had been incarcerated for the first time at the age of nine. From reformatory school he graduated to prison and was sent down a further 15 times, as well as receiving nine fines for petty offences, before he appeared at the Northallerton Quarter Sessions in April 1884. An even greater 'failure' was the 62-year-old labourer, George Clay. Found guilty in 1887 of stealing 12 rabbits in Marton, he was sent to prison for the thirty-second time since 1860.[43] Mary Fentiman, a 24-year-old married woman, found guilty of stealing a purse and £7.15s at Middlesbrough in 1883, had been imprisoned 16 times in the previous nine years for a variety of offences ranging from indecency, drunk and riotous behaviour to theft, while 22-year-old Mary Ann Smith, in court at Northallerton in June 1886, had been imprisoned on 16 occasions for a range of offences including using obscene language, prostitution, drunk and disorderly behaviour, wilful damage and theft.

However, a note of warning needs to be sounded. The people who were prosecuted in the second half of the nineteenth century were not necessarily a random sample of the criminal population. Employers and others based their judgments of whom to prosecute on prevailing stereotypes of 'the criminal'. Thus selective prosecutions, based in part on preconceived notions, may well have helped to create the older, habitual criminal, rather than simply reflect his or her existence.

Occupational status is of central importance, but not easy to establish. The court records contain information, but it is often of too general a nature. However, the fact that as many as nine out of ten people defined themselves as labourers is not without significance. As far as one can tell, the unskilled manual worker, in his various guises, was a disproportionately frequent figure in the mid-nineteenth century court records. Some occupations were heavily over-represented – canal boatmen in the Midlands, for example – as were certain ethnic groups, most notably the Irish. Skilled workmen and craftsmen were underrepresented, as were, to a greater degree, shopkeepers, professionals and gentlemen. The criminal population clearly did not reflect accurately the wider population, but there was a much greater overlap between the two than exponents of the 'criminal class' thesis allow for. Most occupations were represented, although the less well-paid occupations and the more vulnerable workers were more likely to end up in court.

In the absence of detailed studies, it is difficult to be precise about the nature and extent of change in the socioeconomic composition of the criminal body that appeared before the courts later in the nineteenth century. An analysis of just over 1800 people from the North Riding of Yorkshire who appeared before the Northallerton Quarter Sessions in the 1870s and 1880s, and for whom occupations are given, reveals, unsurprisingly, that the undifferentiated group of labourers (excluding farm servants and farm labourers) was the largest group, accounting for almost 30 per cent of the total. Looking at the specific occupations, the range reflects, albeit in distorted fashion, the economy and society of the region. A smattering of professional people are to be found – an accountant, a schoolteacher and even a bank manager – a few more petty bourgeois figures, bakers, fishmongers, grocers and green-grocers appear, as do a yet larger number of skilled working men, drawn from the ranks of carpenters, engineers, masons, plasterers, shoemakers and tailors. Local industries make their peculiar contribution: jet workers from Whitby, puddlers, furnacemen and ironworkers from Middlesbrough, and miners from the ironstone districts of east Cleveland. There was change over time. The unskilled labourer was relatively more important in the 1880s than in the 1870s, as were hawkers, tramps and rag-pickers.

The vast majority of convicted criminals were drawn from the least educated sections of society. The percentage of female prisoners who could neither read nor write was in the low to mid-40s in the mid-nineteenth century, falling somewhat but still in the mid-to-upper 30s thereafter. The percentage of men in this category remained largely constant from 1840 to 1880, hovering in the low 30s, and dropping sharply to the low 20s by 1890. However, this has to be set in the context of steadily improving literacy rates in the population at large. This is consistent with the view that the late Victorian prison population was drawn more from the illiterate and unskilled than had been the case in the early Victorian years. The explanation may well lie in the improvement in living standards in the latter part of the nineteenth century which led to a reduction in the number of those who were driven to crime by want or who felt that crime offered a better prospect of survival.

Despite the recurring preoccupation with uncontrolled sexuality, there is little hard evidence to show that this was the predominant cause of female crime. The most common offence for women was prostitution (itself seen as a step to a further life of crime) but few women became prostitutes because of their unbridled sexual urges. Nor, contrary to another popular explanation, were the vast majority of 'fallen women' the victims of seduction and abandonment. Poverty was the most important factor. For many working-class women so few and precarious were the opportunities to earn a living that prostitution was seen as an almost inevitable phase, through which many young women would pass. Indeed, despite the obvious and well-known health hazards, prostitution offered a woman the opportunity to earn much more than would otherwise be the case and, at least until the 1860s, also offered her some independence and a degree of control over her life in a way that other jobs did not. This was to change in the late nineteenth century as prostitutes became more of an outcast group and prostitution became more male-controlled.[44] As for those other women who came before the courts, their crimes also related more to poverty. This was particularly true of seamstresses and milliners and those working in the sweated trades generally. Servant girls stealing from their mistresses and widows stealing from the people who employed them as charladies are recurring figures in the courts. Receiving was also more of a female crime, but again its explanation is not to be found in the peculiar sexuality of the women concerned.

The historian will never know the totality of crime, neither will he or she know the characteristics of the criminal population. It is easier to reconstruct what eighteenth- and nineteenth-century commentators thought about the subject. To a large extent, contemporary descriptions and explanations tell us about the wider concerns that exercised their minds. It is not possible to test fully the fears and fancies of the past against the 'objective' record of the court and prison statistics. The facts arising from the official response to crime give but a crude impression of the underlying reality and were often themselves a product of the very theories that later historians wish to test. That said, one can offer a number of conclusions. First, there is little evidence for the existence of a criminal class in eighteenth- or nineteenth-century England. Second, the number of hardened, or professional, criminals was small, though possibly increasing in relative terms in the late nineteenth century. Third, the majority of the men, women and children who appeared before the courts were, if not representative of the population at large, not wholly different. Indeed, that wider population contained an unknown and unknowable number of 'criminals' who either were never caught or never appeared before a court. However, the overlap between the criminal population and the larger population may well have diminished over time. Criminals were drawn from the more precarious and more stigmatized groups of society. Working-class men and women were more likely to be seen as criminal than middle- or upper-class people. Men and women who were deemed not to be respectable were more likely to appear in court. Women who worked in factories were likely to be labelled as prostitutes and women who walked alone at night were self-evidently so!

Youths in gangs, walking the streets or hanging around street corners, were targets for the law. Itinerant traders and gypsies were under greater suspicion of criminal behaviour than the resident population, as also were the Irish. These were the people who were kept under more general scrutiny and who were more heavily policed. As more of them were brought before the courts the initial 'judgment' was confirmed and the need to keep such 'lawless' groups under control was reinforced. But this was not a failing peculiar to the eighteenth or nineteenth century. The criminal, as much as his or her crime, is to a very large extent a social construct. Thus it is not only easier but, in some respects, more valuable to discover what a society determines to be criminal behaviour than to seek to discover what makes the criminal man or woman.

4

THE ORIGINS AND IMPACT
OF THE NEW POLICE

The new police were a central element in the evolving criminal justice system. After many debates spread over much of the previous century, there was a flurry of legislation in the second quarter of the nineteenth century which established the framework within which they would develop. Peel's Metropolitan Police Act of 1829 had been followed by the 1835 Municipal Corporations Act, which required the establishment of a police force under the control of a watch committee, the 1839 Rural Constabulary Act and, finally, the 1856 County and Borough Police Act, which required the creation of police forces in all counties and boroughs and established an inspectorate to ensure efficiency. This bald summary of legislative change, which itself simplifies a more complex process of development, obscures a fierce debate that has surrounded the advent and impact of the so-called 'new police'.[1] There are three major issues to be considered. The first centres on the novelty of the new police, the second on the arguments about policing that shaped the legislative changes, and the third on the role of the new police and their impact upon early Victorian society.

Early police historians were sure about the distinctiveness of the new police. Captain W. L. Melville Lee, writing in 1901, had no doubt that 'the police constable who made his appearance in 1829 was a very different kind of man from any of his predecessors in the same office'.[2] Continuing in eulogistic tones, he described the men of the new metropolitan force as being of 'the best procurable material . . . [of] good physique, intelligence above the average, and an irreproachable character'.[3] Thus was created an efficient force, devoted to the fight against crime for the good of society as a whole. This interpretation quickly became the received wisdom and was taken up by later historians, such as T. A. Critchley.[4] The new police were also set apart from their parish predecessors by the fact that they were a uniformed, paid force under bureaucratic control. The distinctiveness of the new police was heightened by often lurid descriptions of the physical and mental deficiencies of their incompetent and corrupt predecessors. Here was a clear and vigorous interpretation. Unfortunately, it was deficient in a number of important respects.

Problems begin with definition.[5] Paid policing did not begin in 1829. In many parts of England in the late eighteenth and early nineteenth century, paid constables and watchmen were to be found. Moreover, there was an element of coordination and organization, seen most clearly in London. Well before 1829, attempts were made to recruit men of appropriate character and physique and to impose an upper age limit for recruits. In addition, there was a degree of interparochial cooperation to offset the problem of fragmentation stemming from a parish-based system of policing.[6] The emergence of the 'new' police was more protracted and less clear-cut than once had been imagined. The carefully chosen and often overstated evidence given to the 1828 Select Committee and used by Peel in his speech to parliament in 1829 was political propaganda. The distinction between old and new is further blurred when the professionalism and efficiency of the new police is subject to closer scrutiny. The first Metropolitan Police commissioners, Charles Rowan and Richard Mayne, wished to create an efficient and highly disciplined police force, but intention did not guarantee outcome. The early history of the Metropolitan Police, and indeed of other forces, was dominated by high turnover rates as large numbers of predominantly unskilled men, many coming straight from the countryside, receiving little or no formal training, proved to be totally unsuited to the job.

However, the 'new' police were intended to be different, as the simple fact of being clearly uniformed shows, and – more importantly – they were perceived to be new at the time. The explanation for this is to be found in their role and responsibilities. They carried out a variety of functions, of which crime prevention was but one. Much of their work involved bringing order and decorum to the streets and lanes of England which, in turn, involved them in the surveillance of many aspects of working-class life. Furthermore, the new police were only responsible to the community in the most generalized and vague manner. The reality was that they were directly responsible to the Home Secretary, in the case of the Metropolitan Police, the local watch committee, in the case of borough forces, and to local magistrates, in the case of county forces. Nor should the symbolism of the 'new police' be overlooked. The constable with his 'bull's eye' lamp, casting light on darkness, was the personification of reform and progress. In other words, the novelty of the new police resided, and was seen to reside, in the fact that they were effectively agents of the ruling elite, acting on their behalf, enforcing their codes of behaviour and responsible to them.

This leads to a consideration of the arguments that have surrounded the development of policing in the late eighteenth and early nineteenth century. Broadly speaking, three schools of thought can be identified. The oldest, the Whig or orthodox interpretation, is based on a consensus model of society and is essentially conservative. The development of policing is presented in a straightforward, linear manner. There is a continuity that runs through from the earliest, if unsuccessful, proponents of reform in the mid- and late eighteenth century, through the 'founding fathers' of the nineteenth century, to the present day. Modernization is seen to be unproblematic and the police, in the form that they developed, are presented as a progressive, far-sighted and effective response to the collapse in law and order in an emerging urban/industrial society. The London model was quickly adopted in the rest of the country and almost as quickly accepted by law-abiding citizens. Such an interpretation is inadequate in a number of important ways. It fails to capture the diversity of opinion among proponents of police reform and also gives a distorted view of the arguments of its opponents. In addition, it fails to give sufficient attention to the changing socioeconomic and political context in which reforms developed and minimizes the importance of short-term and 'accidental' considerations.

In contrast, revisionist historians reject the conservative assumptions of the orthodox school and set the development of policing within a conflict-based model of society. Emphasizing the perceived threat, both physical and moral, posed by the working classes, revisionists depict the police, acting as 'domestic missionaries', as the product of bourgeois concerns to maintain or extend their control of society. While presenting a more sophisticated analysis, the revisionist interpretation is not without its shortcomings. There is a danger of oversimplifying class attitudes and relationships while the concept of social control, which figures largely in such explanations, is problematic in its assumption of a degree of agreement, on both aims and methods, among the propertied classes. Finally, there is a very real danger of conflating intention and outcome.

More recent syntheses have stressed the complex and continuing nature of the debate on policing and also the immense local variation to be found in the first half of the nineteenth century. Diversity, dissension and debate were the key features. There was nothing inevitable about the form of policing that was to develop in nineteenth-century England.[7] Police reform had been on the political agenda for many years before Peel's 1829 Act. The

Fieldings and Patrick Colquhoun are among the better known voices crying in the late eighteenth and early nineteenth-century wilderness. Despite a forceful presentation of the case for reform, successive parliaments were unconvinced of the need for change and a number of bills failed to make progress. The reasons for this are varied. Fears for civil liberties, underpinned by a powerful fear of tyranny on the supposed continental model, combined with a concern to preserve local authority and a perception that crime was not at an unacceptable level intermingled. There emerged a broad-based coalition, including right-wing country gentlemen as well as radicals of the political left, which ensured that police reform was thwarted in parliament until the late 1820s.

This was to change in 1829. Robert Peel, the chief architect of the Metropolitan Police Act, in his speech to the House of Commons in April 1829, argued for his proposal primarily in terms of the alarming rise in the crime statistics for many districts of London and the inadequacy of existing law-enforcement agencies. Peel's words need to be taken seriously, but they do not necessarily give us an accurate indication of his motives. There are a number of problems with his argument. First, as a number of contemporary observers knew, the increase in recorded crime reflected more an increase in prosecutions than an increase in criminal behaviour, a fact of which Peel himself was well aware. However, we cannot entirely reject rising recorded crime rates as a causal factor. Two possibilities offer themselves. First, influential contemporaries, including Peel's parliamentary audience, believed, however erroneously, that there was a real rise in crime. Second, there was a growing intolerance of levels of crime which had been seen as acceptable in previous decades.

The second element in Peel's argument was also suspect. Existing law-enforcement agencies were not uniformly poor, as Peel himself conceded, nor uniformly condemned. The partisan nature of the evidence given to the 1828 Select Committee must not be overlooked, though, once again, we cannot totally discount this argument. If contemporaries believed the old parochial system to be hopelessly inadequate, or if they were no longer prepared to tolerate once-acceptable levels of incompetence, these attitudes have an important part to play. Significant changes in public attitudes were taking place in the early nineteenth century. Concerns with the general problem of change, a belief that criminal behaviour was symptomatic of wider social problems, changing standards of behaviour which led to greater intolerance of violence, disorder and crime and demands for greater discipline in society, new perceptions of policing and punishment and more demanding expectations of the magistracy came together to create a new climate of opinion that was more receptive to the idea of police reform. Peel was aware of the mood of the political nation and sought to exploit it in 1829. However, one has to look beyond the parliamentary speech to discover the full range of Peel's motives.

Peel's interest in police reform was long-standing, dating back to his experience in Ireland in the late eighteenth century. Of more immediate relevance were the events of postwar England which highlighted the problems of maintaining public order by traditional means. Fears were widespread that the use of the yeomanry or the regular army was counterproductive. In June 1820, concerned with signs of incipient mutiny in the Guards, Wellington informed Lord Liverpool that he was of 'the opinion the government ought, without the loss of a moment's time, to adopt measures to form either a police in London or military corps, which should be of a different description from the regular military force, or both'.[8] Peel shared these concerns, particularly after the disturbances associated with Queen Caroline. Such was the level of support, which had risen quite dramatically since her return to England and during the time of the parliamentary divorce proceedings, that, on her death in 1821, elaborate precautions were taken to ensure the untroubled passage of her funeral cortege through London. Despite a heavy concentration of soldiers in and around London, plans to keep the cortege out of the City of London failed. It was clear to all that 'the Mob' had triumphed and, for Peel, newly in office, an effective alternative had to be found.

A Select Committee was established in 1822, but failed to support Peel's known preference for police reform. Despite this setback, he was determined to establish 'a vigorous, preventive police' and drew up proposals which were very similar to the Dublin police measures of 1786 and 1808. Peel was unable to introduce these measures as the Liverpool government fell from office but, on returning to office in January 1828, he returned to his task, established another Select Committee, which was effectively a mouthpiece for his views, and finally introduced the Metropolis Police Improvement Bill in April 1829. Skilful parliamentary tactics, combined with the strategic decision not to include the City of London in the proposal, greatly facilitated the rapid passage of the bill, though police reform was slipped through parliament at a time when more important and contentious issues, not least Catholic emancipation, were attracting the attentions of politicians. Whatever the precise reasons for success, there can be no doubt that Peel had achieved his goal. Moreover, given his knowledge of the Dublin police and the nature of their work, Peel could have had little doubt but that his new police would be used to bring both order and decorum to the streets of London as well as to fight crime.

Although London was seen as a special case, the Whigs discussed the possibility of a national force in 1832.[9] Their draft bill contained proposals for a scheme of policing that would have covered corporate as well as non-corporate towns and unions of smaller towns or large rural districts. This was a dramatic advance in thinking, but even more radical was the proposal to introduce stipendiary magistrates to replace the 'great unpaid', mainly gentry, justices of the peace. Although the scheme came to nothing, it is significant for what it reveals of thinking in parliamentary circles. As the parliamentary debates of 1832 reveal, there was an emerging consensus among leading figures of different political persuasions that there was a pressing need to overhaul the machinery for maintaining order in the country. The measure that finally came forth, embodied in the Municipal Corporations Act, was very much a second-best for the Whigs. Clause 76, which required borough councils to set up watch committees and establish police forces, was not debated or amended in parliament. Melbourne hardly referred to policing powers in a long speech and made no mention of crime as a particular threat. The discussion was couched largely in terms of efficient municipal government, with police powers in the control of local government a necessary element of this.

The policing provisions of the Municipal Corporations Act were a partial solution to the problem of disorder. Many of the chartered boroughs failed to implement clause 76 and many rapidly growing towns were outside the scope of the act. The latter problem became part of a wider debate on rural policing and the responsibilities of county police forces. Disruptive industrial communities in rural settings and the persistence of highly publicized rural protest crimes, such as arson and cattle maiming, combined to bring an urgency to the debate, but there was no consensus as to the best action to take.

Even before the Swing Riots, there had been a vigorous debate about rural policing and a variety of alternatives proposed and put into practice. One short-lived practice, popular in parts of East Anglia, was to use the New Poor Law unions, set up in 1834, as the organizational basis for policing and to meet costs from the poor law rates. This experiment was brought to an end in 1836, when the practice was declared illegal. The second, and most common, practice was the adoption of the 1833 Lighting and Watching Act which enabled vestries to appoint an inspector who, in turn, appointed paid watchmen. The precise extent to which this legislation was used is unknown but examples of its use are to be found in a variety of rural parishes, notably in East Anglia, districts such as Croydon and Blackheath, as well as a variety of small towns such as Braintree, Walthamstow and Horncastle.[10]

A third model was that of the so-called 'private subscription force', such as the well-known Barnet association set up by Thomas Dimsdale. Similarly, at Stow-on-the Wold, following a brutal robbery and murder, the local gentry created 'An Association for the Better Security of Life and Property' and employed two London policemen, under the local justices, to patrol a district six miles in diameter from the centre of Stow. The distinction between privately and publicly paid forces should not be overdrawn. In a number of cases, such as Blofield in Norfolk, the subscription force was the basis of what became a regular force under the 1833 act. Historians have not given due weight to the extent of local experimentation in rural policing and its contribution to the debate of the late 1830s.[11] However, it remains the case that the bulk of England was still policed under the unreformed parochial system. Such a situation was intolerable not simply to zealous reformers like Edwin Chadwick but also to many members of the ruling elite at Westminster. It is not surprising, therefore, to find the Whig government turning its attention to the question of rural policing, especially after the introduction of the New Poor Law.

Edwin Chadwick was the dominant individual actor in the debate that finally led to the 1839 Rural Constabulary Act. His energy and determination were critical in the establishment of the Royal Commission set up to explore the matter but Chadwick was not the sole or main architect of the 1839 act, nor was the act the embodiment of his ideas. The appointment of Rowan and Lefevre as commissioners was a blow to Chadwick, as neither had great sympathy for his centralizing ideas and the report itself reflected more the interests of country gentleman than the ideals of Benthamites. Chadwick was also outmanoeuvred in the political build up to the preparation of the police bill. In February 1839 the Home Office had sought opinions from quarter sessions regarding a resolution adopted in Shropshire proposing 'a body of constables appointed by the magistrate, paid out of the County rate' as the most efficient and desirable way forward. Although positive responses came from only half of the 36 quarter sessions to reply, this was sufficient for the Home Secretary, Russell. The bill which was presented to parliament contained some, but not all, of the recommendations of the Royal Commission. For Chadwick the bill and subsequent act was a particular disappointment, being permissive in nature and containing very little in the way of central government control.[12]

The 1839 act was an important piece of legislation, but was far from being the last word on rural policing. Local initiatives continued, most notably in Kent. The magistrates there not only refused to adopt the 1839 act but also put forward a number of proposals to improve the parochial constable system. One such proposal had an important part to play in the evolution of the oft-neglected Parish Constables Acts of 1842 and 1850. The 1842 act allowed for the payment of parish constables and laid down tighter criteria for their appointment. In addition, provision was made for the appointment of a paid superintending constable. This system was to be found in several southern counties – Kent, Buckinghamshire, Dorset, Lincolnshire and Oxfordshire – and was also used in more industrial districts such as Huddersfield in the West Riding of Yorkshire.

There was little new thinking about policing in the 1840s. Indeed, the Town Police Clauses Act of 1847, which provided a *pro forma* for local acts, reinforced traditional thinking. However, changing circumstances brought new attitudes. Riots in Stockport in 1852, in Blackburn and Wigan in 1853 and the Sunday Trading riots in Hyde Park in 1855 highlighted the problem. Vivid descriptions of lawlessness were given in a Select Committee report in 1853, but Palmerston's first attempt to tackle the problem met with such opposition that the proposed police bill had to be withdrawn. However, the problem of disorder intensified. The ending of the Crimean War aroused fears of a crime wave brought about by large numbers of unemployed ex-soldiers roaming the countryside. These fears were further heightened by concern about the consequences of ending transportation. The 1853 Penal Servitude Act created a new bogey figure: the 'ticket-of-leave man'. The thought of another army, this time comprising ex-convicts, prowling the countryside, aroused considerable fears which played a critical part in the debates of 1855 and 1856 which led to the passing of the County and Borough Police Act, 1856.

The 1856 act did not introduce a centralized police force in the way that Chadwick had envisaged, but involved the government through the establishment of an inspectorate and Home Office funding for those forces deemed to be efficient at their annual inspection. There was an important break with that traditional area of local government, the parish. Centralization took place at county rather than national level. The 1856 act was essentially a triumph for 'the provincial vision of the rural police as a kind of soldiery' and, as such, a defeat for the boroughs.[13]

Hostility to the extension of policing was still to be found. Complaints that the government was acting unconstitutionally and that its proposals for police reform were 'a base attempt upon the liberty of the subject and the privilege of local government' were heard in several parts of the country, from Portsmouth to York. The old fears of 'a standing army' and 'the darkest age of tyranny' resurfaced, but there was a dated quality to many of these predictions of woe. There was a newer mood abroad. The *Brighton Examiner* saw effective policing as being 'as necessary to the proper management of a town as gas lighting' and saw 'no danger to general freedom' in the proposed reforms. The *Norfolk Chronicle* took a similar stance and was scathing in its dismissal of old fears, seeing them as 'anachronisms, mere hypothesis and exaggeration'.[14]

The County and Borough Police Act, which was passed by 259 votes to 106 in the House of Commons, laid the foundation of modern policing in England and Wales. It was the culmination of a long and tortuous process of reform. The variety of policing practices and the persistence of the old, parochial policing are striking features that should not be overlooked. Nor was police reform a simple crusade against 'the golden age of gangsterdom'. But nor should the process of reform be interpreted simply in terms of sectional interests and social control. There was more to police reform than the protection of the propertied from the threat posed by the propertyless. The demand for a higher standard of security for person and property was not the prerogative of one class. Finally, it is also an oversimplification to see the struggle as one between central and local government. Despite the presence of Chadwick, and the antagonisms that his centralizing proposals aroused, the greater, if less spectacular, tensions were to be found between the defenders of the old, parochial policing and the advocates of a county-based system. Ultimately, the needs of an increasingly urbanized and industrialized society rendered the parish inappropriate as the unit of policing, but this was by no means a foregone conclusion as late as the 1840s.

The flurry of police legislation in the second quarter of the nineteenth century was important in creating a framework for development, but the various acts were, effectively, statements of intent. Before we can assess the impact of the new police it is necessary to consider the implementation of the major pieces of legislation. The task is not an easy one. It is by no means certain how many small towns and villages took advantage of the 1833 Lighting and Watching Act, though we know that in some parts of the country, such as Kent, this legislation was adopted to avoid the Rural Constabulary Act of 1839. Similarly, we do not know precisely how many superintending constables were appointed under the 1842 and 1850 acts. More work needs to be done to establish the extent and nature of policing under the Improvement Acts or under the Town Police Clauses Act. However, it is possible to give some indication of the take-up rate for the Municipal Corporations Act and the Rural Constabulary Act.

The response to the Municipal Corporations Act was patchy, with 93 of the 171 boroughs without a police force claiming to have taken action in the following two years. In 1839, over 40 per cent of boroughs were unable to provide figures relating to police. Of those that did, only 30 per cent had achieved the desirable police/population ratio of 1:900 or better. Almost ten years later, the number of boroughs not returning figures had dropped to 30 per cent, but only 20 per cent enjoyed a police/population ratio of 1:900 or better.[15] The permissive Rural Constabulary Act was taken up by 35 counties in England and Wales, some two-thirds of whom did so in the first two years of the act. The precise pattern of adoption is complex and not easily explained. There does not appear to be a consistent link between adoption and recent disturbances. Indeed, in some counties, such as the West Riding of Yorkshire and Staffordshire, the magistrates decided not to adopt the act, notwithstanding considerable recent disturbances. Similarly, of the ten counties most seriously affected by the Swing Riots, five adopted the act and five did not. However, such variations are not entirely surprising, given the range of policing options discussed and implemented in the 1830s and 1840s. One factor that played an important part in decision making was the practical consideration of cost. Preventive policing, 'watching and suspecting', was seen to be too expensive and also ran contrary to the tradition of using police as an *ad hoc* response to a specific problem, using, for example, the provisions of the Special Constables Act. In Buckinghamshire, Lincolnshire and the West Riding of Yorkshire, such cost considerations were clearly a major consideration, while in Derbyshire the magistrates, having decided to adopt the act, were forced to reverse their decision in the face of ratepayers' opposition.[16]

A partial snapshot of the state of policing in the mid-nineteenth century is provided by the 1844 *Police and Constabulary List*. As well as the Metropolitan Police and the City of London Police, the *List* contains details for 21 counties (of which two applied to parts of counties only) and 58 boroughs. The most striking feature that emerges from this survey is the immense variety to be found in both counties and boroughs. At one extreme, among the counties, Cumberland and Herefordshire had a total of four and five men, respectively. At the other, the force totalled almost 400 men in Lancashire, just over 250 in Gloucester and almost 200 in Wiltshire, and slightly fewer in Essex and Staffordshire. A more useful comparison can be made by looking at the police/population ratio. The 1839 act provided for a maximum of one constable per 1000 population, but only the Gloucestershire force came near to this. Only four had a ratio better than 1:1500 and seven a ratio better than 1:2000. In Leicestershire the ratio was almost 1:6000 and in Cumberland in excess of 1:7000. Within the boroughs there was also considerable variation with police/population ratios varying from 1:500, or less, in Liverpool, Bath and Hull, to 1:1500 or more in Salford, Coventry, Ipswich and Whitehaven. In Walsall the figure was in excess of 1:2000 and in Macclesfield over 1:3000.

It is important to bear in mind these variations when assessing the initial impact of the 'new police'. Before 1856, there were many areas in which there had been no significant change in the practice of policing and, even where reforms had been implemented, the limited number of new police meant their role was necessarily limited. Nonetheless, historians have differed in their interpretation of their impact. The older, orthodox school emphasizes the speed with which widespread support was won, partly because of the nature of police work, combining crime prevention and detection with a range of 'public service' activities, and partly because of the manner in which they carried out their duties, seeking to police by consent and with minimum force. Whilst there was initial popular hostility, particularly in London, this, according to orthodox historians, rapidly disappeared as law-abiding citizens quickly recognized the value of the police. Revisionist historians, in contrast, have drawn attention to the class-based nature of much police work and the scale and persistence of popular opposition that this provoked, not simply in London but also in many northern towns.[17]

The varied nature of police work is a major consideration. The emphasis upon crime prevention as their *raison d'être* was a misleading oversimplification of police work which provided a powerful and convenient fiction that both legitimized the police and obscured the nature of much of their work. From the outset, policing was seen as a multifaceted job. The guidance to the Metropolitan Police, often adopted verbatim by other forces, stressed a welfare role, looking after 'insane persons and children'. In addition, there was a public service dimension which ranged from the official, such as acting as inspector of nuisances, to the unofficial, such as acting as 'knocker-up' for market porters or factory workers. However, it was the preservation of public order that was of major importance but which lent itself to a variety of interpretations. At one extreme, it involved maintaining order in the face of riotous crowds. This in turn could lead to surveillance and, in exceptional cases, infiltration, of trade unions or radical political organizations. It could also involve establishing and maintaining order and decorum in the streets. This in turn involved an unprecedented degree of scrutiny and control over a wide range of activities, involving both work and leisure, which were seen to be legitimized by long-established custom. The new police had an important part to play in the war that was being waged upon the customs and culture of the urban and rural working classes.[18]

The nature and impact of policing was conditioned by local variables, most importantly the attitudes of the local chief constable and, in the

boroughs, of the local watch committee. The determination of Superintendent Heaton in conducting his 'Huddersfield Campaign' contrasts with the
more pragmatic policy of the Middlesbrough chief constable, Saggerson,
whose unwillingness to arrest all drunks in the town led him into conflict
with the local temperance interest and their supporters on the town's watch
committee. In a more general sense, senior officers made judgements, based
on a combination of past experience and preconceived ideas, on the best
deployment of resources and effort. Almost inevitably, this meant that working-class districts were more likely to come under the gaze of the police,
while within those districts certain groups, vagrants and especially poor
Irish, were also more likely to be targets. Finally, the individual officer
exercised considerable discretion. The realities of policing were such that
decisions had to be taken on the spot. An overzealous or injudicious intervention could provoke considerable hostility, while turning a blind eye
could defuse a potentially difficult and dangerous situation. The realities of
day-to-day policing are of fundamental importance to an understanding
of popular responses to the new police but, such is the paucity of direct
evidence, this remains a subject of speculation rather than analysis.

The initial response to the new police in London was very hostile. Middle-
class as well as working-class critics condemned the Peelers for a variety of
reasons. For some, the 'blue drones' were a waste of money, failing to
improve the security of the London streets. For others, 'the crushers' were a
poorly disciplined and, at worst, a brutal force who interfered in a range of
legitimate economic, social and political activities. The disturbances at Cold
Bath Fields in 1833, which led to the death of PC Culley, revealed widespread hostility towards the police. However, according to orthodox historians, this was but a short-lived period, after which the relationship between
police and public in London was essentially a friendly one.

Such optimism is difficult to square with certain facts of London life in the
second quarter of the nineteenth century. The middle classes soon appre-
ciated the benefits of the new police. They were the most direct beneficiaries
of police actions that curtailed political disturbances and reduced the level
of street crime. Working-class attitudes were less clear-cut. For the politically active, admittedly a small number, there were obvious grounds for
concern. Meetings of working-class radicals were kept under surveillance
and infiltrated by police spies who posed a real threat to constitutional liberties. The case of Sergeant Popay, dismissed in 1833 for infiltrating
the National Political Union, certainly gave credence to popular worries.
With the benefit of hindsight, one is struck by the incompetence of
Popay but contemporary responses were, understandably, more fearful.

The report of the Select Committee set up to investigate the incident, which came to the conclusion that Popay had acted on his own initiative, brought little reassurance.[19]

The majority of Londoners were not directly involved in political activity but it is a measure of the scale of opposition that the commissioners of police were burnt in effigy during Guy Fawkes celebrations in the 1830s. For these people contact with the police was a recurring, if less spectacular, phenomenon. The early nineteenth century saw a continuing attempt to transform the streets of London. Control of public space was a central issue. The wide-ranging Vagrancy Act of 1822 fell heavily on those who used the streets for economic or recreational purposes. The establishment of the Metropolitan Police, and the extension of their powers by the 1839 Police Act, greatly increased the disciplinary powers of the authorities. Attempts to control leisure and morals were highly unpopular. The suppression of popular leisure activities, the closing down of annual fairs, as well as the use of the immensely unpopular 'move on' tactic generated tensions that could easily turn into outright hostility. So too did the attack on the street economies. Mayhew, interviewing costermongers in the mid-nineteenth century, soon discovered the extent of hatred for the police. Having recounted their grievances, Mayhew's interviewees made it clear that assaulting the police was seen as 'the bravest act by which a costermonger can distinguish himself'. The physical injuries inflicted upon the members of the Metropolitan Police provide a measure of continuing popular hostility.

However, the police did have a positive role to play. The desire for a higher standard of security was not confined to the middle classes. In so far as the new police helped to reduce street violence and thefts, they were welcomed by the working classes, who were as much, if not more, the victims of petty crimes. Nonetheless, attitudes tended to be ambivalent, not least because of the different guises in which the policeman could appear in working-class life; tolerance was very fragile and could easily break down, as happened in the summer of 1855. A proposed bill to limit Sunday trading aroused considerable popular opposition and demonstrations were organized to take place in Hyde Park on the first of July. Initially, there had been no signs of antagonism. There was friendly banter directed at the police, but no indication of the disturbances that were to follow. A series of police rushes into the crowd, the seemingly indiscriminate use of truncheons and the spectacular use of a horsewhip by Superintendent Hughes led to serious rioting.[20]

Anti-police sentiment was not confined to the capital. Indeed, the most dramatic incidents took place in northern England. The events at Colne,

although exceptional, provide a vivid illustration of the bitterness and determination with which the new police were met. The original Colne force,
some 16 men led by Superintendent MacLeod, arrived in the town in mid-
April 1840. From the outset the police were seen to act in an aggressive and
insensitive manner. The 'move on' system was unpopular enough but sensibilities were enraged by a number of physical assaults on members of the
public. Late in April, open conflict broke out, MacLeod was knocked uncon-
scious and suffered a broken arm and the police were physically driven from
the streets. This was not some chance happening. The whole matter appears
to have been well planned, with the police drawn into a trap in a town that
had been thrown into darkness by the extinguishing of every lamp. The
following day, a new superintendent sent from Burnley with 20 policemen
reoccupied the town, but it was deemed necessary to send troops, both
mounted and on foot, into the town to help keep order.

The presence of troops undoubtedly helped to bring a semblance of order
to the town. However, this was a temporary measure. The Lancashire police
authorities decided to triple the number of policemen allocated to Colne as
an interim measure. This policy of saturation policing succeeded to the
extent that there was no rioting during the next three months. At the end of
July the Colne force was reduced to its initial 'normal' level. This brought to
an end the temporary truce. The houses of known police supporters, most
notably that of a local solicitor and clerk to the magistrates, Mr Bolton,
were attacked and windows smashed. On 4 August, the police, once again,
were driven from the streets in a concerted attack and, for the second time,
the military were ordered in to restore order. In fact they were not needed, as
the town was quiet. The troops duly left, only for a group of disgruntled
Chartists to confront the town's dignitaries. The cycle was repeated: troops
returned to restore order and left, only for there to be a further upsurge of
anti-police rioting. The events of 10 August, however, were the most serious
yet experienced. At one stage the situation was akin to civil war. On one side
were 70 special constables, sworn in from the ranks of the town's 'respectable
inhabitants', in addition to the regular police whose numbers had been
doubled by the police authorities. On the other was a large crowd of disciplined and well-armed men. In the ensuing mêlée, one special constable was
killed as the police, yet again, were driven from the streets. The disturbance
had exhausted itself before the arrival of troops from Burnley, but this time it
was decided to find a lasting solution. Sir Charles Napier was ordered to
establish a permanent military force in a newly built barracks in the town.[21]

Colne was exceptional in its scale of anti-police rioting but not unique. The
new police were driven out of Middleton in the spring of 1840 by a crowd

enraged at the arrest of a local miner. There were serious anti-police riots at Lancaster races, while in the Potteries the newly created force had to be rescued by troops and police from Liverpool. Even established forces could find themselves facing considerable opposition, as was the case at Hull, Manchester and, especially, Leeds. The Leeds force had been established in 1836, but as late as the summer of 1844 it was faced by a three-day riot that involved several sections of the town's population. The disturbances started on Sunday 9 June, when two policemen arrested a number of soldiers of the 70th Regiment of Foot at the Green Man beerhouse in York Street, following an allegation of theft and assault. Fellow-soldiers attacked the police as they attempted to convey their prisoners to the lock-up and police reinforcements were sent to the scene of the fight. Fights between police and soldiers were not that uncommon, nor was it unprecedented for soldiers to seek revenge on the police the following day. The wider communal response was unusual. Having attacked some policemen in Vicar Lane, the soldiers turned into Briggate, where there was a crowd, estimated at over a thousand, which responded with enthusiasm to the soldiers' cry of 'Down with the Police'. By the end of the evening, four groups of civilians, including one composed largely of Irish, were involved in a series of anti-police skirmishes that saw the police driven from the streets of central Leeds. Finally, regrouped and better organized, the police reasserted control over the rioters, now exclusively civilian, on the Tuesday evening. The motive of the civilian rioters was clear. As the local press noted, it was not 'out of love to the soldiers themselves, but from . . . feelings of hatred towards the police' that they acted.[22] The riots were out of proportion to the immediate cause and are better seen as the outpouring of hostility that had built up over several years.

Other examples of anti-police disturbances can be found in various parts of the country, while hostility to individual policemen was a feature of both urban and rural life. Rural constables could easily find themselves labelled as 'landowners' lackeys' as they became embroiled in the poaching wars that rumbled on for much of the nineteenth century and which could involve fatalities. But even ordinary policing could involve considerable hazards, as PC Thomas Griffiths, one of 'Paddy Mayne's Grasshoppers' in Shropshire, found to his cost. Visiting the Old Three Pigeons in Nesscliff on New Year's Eve, 1841, he was faced with a hostile crowd of locals. First having been hoisted into the air, he was then thrown onto the fire, from whence he escaped only to be further assaulted and kicked under a cupboard. The somewhat belated intervention of the landlady enabled him to reach safety in the cellar, but such was the severity of the attack that it was three months before he was fit to appear before the local magistrates.[23]

As in London, the hostility towards the police can be seen to have grown out of the day-to- day experience of policing. Both work and leisure activities came under surveillance and attack. Popular leisure was a particularly fraught field. Concerns with civilizing the crowd date from the late eighteenth century, and before, but the intensity of the official assault increased with the advent of the new police. The attempt to stamp out cruel sports was not easy in the face of popular resistance; the persistence of the Stamford bull-run bears witness to this. But even when the police achieved a greater degree of success the victory carried a price in terms of continuing resentment. The newly formed Staffordshire County Police was used to crack down on 'popular and rowdy recreations' such as wakes and fairs as well as various forms of animal baiting and fighting. Police unpopularity in the mid-1840s was such that there were a number of miniature riots as police arrested people attending such activities. Anger was exacerbated when public humiliation was involved. The unpopularity of the Birmingham police was enhanced by the public display of 40 prisoners, tied in pairs with rope and paraded through the town, for attending a cockfight.[24]

Working-class opposition to the new police was widespread, extending beyond the ranks of the 'rough' and criminal elements, and also beyond the ranks of organized labour and the politically active. The very nature of policing meant that it impinged upon aspects of the everyday life of ordinary men, women and children. Furthermore, because many of the new rules and regulations were imposed by and reflected the values of the ruling elites, many working-class people had a perception of the police as agents of an alien class, sent to spy upon them and to restrict activities which were not seen as socially reprehensible, let alone criminal.

The novelty of police surveillance caused concern and conflict but the fact that many of the early constables were deliberately recruited 'outsiders' and often drawn from the lower ranks of working-class society added to these difficulties. Tensions and conflicts were exacerbated, particularly in the early years, by clumsy, insensitive and, sometimes, corrupt policing. The 'irksomeness of their arbitrary rulings' meant that the police were oft-times viewed as 'oppressors and obnoxious outsiders'.[25] Respect was more for the power at their disposal than for their enforcement of an abstract concept of justice. Anti-police rioting and assaults on police constables (and senior officers) were a continuing feature of the early and mid-nineteenth century, but it is essential to retain a sense of proportion. The situation was significantly worse in Ireland. There, the early 1840s, for example, saw some 60 major anti-police riots and at least 16 fatalities, the overwhelming majority of whom were peasants. That said, the orthodox interpretation understates the extent of opposition to the new police and, correspondingly, overstates the ease and the extent to which they gained popular support in the early years of the 'new police'.

Conflict, however, was reduced by a pragmatism born of an awareness of the limitations of police powers and the operational constraints which flowed from this. Limitations of manpower meant that priorities had to be set. More importantly, it also meant that, if the police were to implement them, they would have to have the acquiescence of a majority of the policed. To that extent, the police were constrained by the policed. The question of popular acceptance of the police is a problematic one. There was a growing, if begrudging, acceptance of the fact that the police were an established part of life. Indeed, there was a growing instrumental acceptance of the police as they were seen to do a job which brought benefits not simply to the middle and upper classes. Thus, contrary to the revisionist argument, even in the mid-nineteenth century, more positive relationships developed between working people and the police. However, there was a fragility about these relationships which could easily break down, especially in times of industrial or political crisis.

5

THE CREATION OF A PROFESSIONAL FORCE, 1856–1914

The legislation of the second quarter of the nineteenth century created a framework for the development of policing, but it was only in the second half of the century that a network of 'professional' forces was brought into being.[1] In comparison with the advent of the 'new police', these later changes have not attracted the same degree of historical scrutiny and yet, in many respects, they are of greater importance to an understanding of the development of modern policing. Furthermore, these years also saw a significant extension of police powers which brought more people into direct contact with the agents of the disciplinary state.

Prior to 1856, the development of police forces had been patchy and piecemeal. The 20 or so borough forces of 1834 had risen to about 140 by the early 1840s, at which level it remained until 1856. By the mid-1870s, there were 165 borough forces in existence, but subsequent amalgamations of small forces with county forces reduced the number to just under 130 by 1914. County forces were slower to develop. Eight were created in 1839 and a further seven in 1840 and there were only 26 by the early 1850s. Only after the passing of the County and Borough Police Act in 1856 did every county have a force.

The number of policemen increased from about 20 500 in 1861 to 54 300 by 1911. The rate of growth in the overall population was lower. Consequently, the number of persons per policeman nationally fell from 980 to 664.[2] The Metropolitan police force was the largest in the country. Initially just over 800 strong, it had grown to 5500 by 1851. In 1871, the numbers exceeded 9000, while on the eve of the First World War there were some

22 000 policemen in London. No other force could match it in size. The next largest forces were to be found in the northern counties of Lancashire and the West Riding of Yorkshire, where numbers in each exceeded 1000 in the early twentieth century. However, many of the county forces numbered their men in a few hundred and did not match the size of the largest borough forces, such as Liverpool and Manchester.

The various police forces that came into being in the first half of the nineteenth century had one common characteristic: very high turnover rates. There was a discipline and fortitude required to become a successful policeman and many men signed up only to resign within days or weeks of joining, while even larger numbers left within the first 12 months of service. However, by the late nineteenth century there had been a fundamental change. Turnover rates were much lower and attitudes towards policing had changed. Instead of being viewed simply as a stop-gap measure, or as a short-term stepping-stone to a better job, policing was increasingly seen as a job in its own right. There was a growing body of disciplined men who had made a career of policing. Indeed, there were some who consciously decided at the outset of their working life that they would make such a career, often following a father or an elder brother into the force. At the same time there was a change in the public perception of the police. The despised 'blue locust' had become the beloved 'bobby'.[3]

There was not a force in England that did not face considerable problems of recruitment and retention in its early years. This is nowhere better illustrated than in London, where a concerted effort was made to attract good-quality men who would form the backbone of the new force. Attracting good recruits in the first place was difficult enough, retaining them for a long period more so. The statistics paint a grim picture. Some 3400 men joined the newly formed force in 1829–30, of whom only a quarter were still in post four years later. Nor were the problems confined to London. The Wolverhampton force in 1859 had been in existence for 12 years and yet over 25 per cent of its men had less than one year's experience and over 50 per cent less than three years'.[4] In Middlesbrough in the 1850s, at least a third of all recruits served for less than one year and over 50 per cent for less than five years.[5] Similar problems were found in the county forces. Between 1845 and 1860, just over 40 per cent of recruits in Lancashire served for less than one year. In Buckinghamshire and Staffordshire in 1856, 47 and 46 per cent, respectively, of the first recruits served less than a year. Twenty years later matters had improved little in Staffordshire, where 43 per cent of the 1876 intake left within 12 months, though for Buckinghamshire the figure had dropped to 33 per cent.[6]

Correspondingly, annual turnover rates (that is, the number leaving as a percentage of the total force) were high. As late as 1865, the figure for the Metropolitan Police was 13.5 per cent, though this had fallen to 5 per cent by the mid-1880s. The overall turnover rate for England and Wales stood stubbornly at 14 per cent and did not fall below 10 per cent until the mid-1880s. The national average conceals two important variations. First, the turnover rates tended to be higher in borough, as opposed to county, forces and, more starkly, the turnover rate was significantly and consistently higher in the north of England than in the south. In 1856, the figures were 30 per cent in the north compared with 15 per cent in the south; but by 1880 the figures were 15 and 8 per cent, respectively. As one dispirited chief constable observed to the 1875 Select Committee on Police Superannuation Funds, 'If the men stay two years, there is some hope of them staying longer, but the vast proportion of men change within the year, or the first few months'.[7] However, the situation was to change and by the early twentieth century turnover rates had been significantly reduced as police forces became stabilized around a hard core of long-serving 'career' policemen.

To explain this transformation we need to look at the backgrounds of police recruits, their reasons for joining and attitudes towards policing, as well as at the evolving nature of the job itself. In the opinion of many chief constables and their recruiting sergeants, the ideal police recruit was an agricultural labourer who was seen to have the necessary physical strength and the appropriate mental qualities of stoicism and deference. Despite the mythology of ploughman turned policeman, the reality was different in two ways: recruitment patterns were more diverse and the agricultural labourer did not necessarily make the longest serving, let alone most able, policeman.

Given the size of the agricultural labour force in the mid-nineteenth century and the low levels of rural wages, it is not surprising to find that a large proportion of early recruits were men with experience of agricultural work. County forces drew heavily on the local pool as did borough forces such as Bristol. Labourers accounted for about 50 per cent of the recruits to the Buckinghamshire force in the 1860s, with the figure slightly less in Staffordshire, while in Lancashire, between 1845 and 1870, just under 40 per cent of recruits were classified as labourers (though not all would have come from agriculture). On a broader time span, the percentage figure was less. Between 1840 and 1910, in a sample of over 7000 police recruits, almost 40 per cent were classified as labourers, but only 11 per cent came from agricultural work.[8] The remainder of recruits were drawn from a wide range of trades: grooms, blacksmiths, thatchers, wheelwrights and carpenters became policemen in Buckinghamshire; miners, moulders, puddlers,

brickmakers, potters and even a printer in Staffordshire; and, in Lancashire, boot and shoe makers, carpenters, joiners, cabinetmakers and a
variety of textile workers.

Whatever their occupational background, recruits tended to be younger
and unmarried men. Indeed, many forces explicitly stated that married men
need not apply and it was rare indeed for a man aged over 35 years to be
appointed. In Lancashire, the mean age of recruits was 28 in 1845–50, falling to 25 in 1866–70, while in London the figures were 26 years in 1833,
24 years in 1850 and 22.5 years by the early twentieth century.[9]

The decision to become a policeman was largely an economic one.
In early Victorian England policing was a new, low-status occupation that
did not pay exceptionally well. However, for agricultural labourers, and
other unskilled workers, policing offered higher and regular wages. The
Head Constable of Norwich, Robert Hitchman, had little doubt about the
economic realities, observing that 'a police constable would rather obtain
agricultural employment if he got a shilling a week more, than remain a constable at 22s'.[10]

The patterns of recruitment reflected the distribution of poverty in the
catchment areas of the various forces. Unskilled men, however, were not
the only ones affected. Skilled men joined up when their trade was badly
hit. In 1866, the Stafford boot and shoe trade was in severe decline and in
that year six shoemakers joined the Staffordshire force. Chairmakers and
French-polishers joined the Buckinghamshire force in the early 1870s as the
local furniture industry went into decline, while in Middlesbrough the sharply fluctuating fortunes of the iron and steel industry had a clear impact on
recruitment into the local force. The long-serving chairman of the town's
watch committee, Isaac Wilson, conceded that it was 'simply a question of
wages'. As industrial wages fell it became easier to recruit and retain men,
but as they rose men left the force to return to their old occupations.[11] For
others, joining the police was a calculated move intended to improve long-
term career prospects. Becoming a policeman was one way of effecting a
move to a town, a temporary phase, a bridge to a better job. Trained ex-
policemen with good references were employable in a range of occupations.
As the Head Constable of Sheffield ruefully observed of certain recruits,
'when they have been drilled and smartened up, there is a great demand for
them as porters, timekeepers and so on'.[12]

Temporary desperation played an important part in the decision to join
up, but not all policemen were 'failures and casualties'. Nor was policing
perceived wholly in a negative light. There was an obvious attraction
for ex-servicemen, though their numbers should not be overstated. More

generally, in a rapidly changing economy with many low-paid and insecure jobs, policing, with its prospect of secure employment, regular pay and a variety of fringe benefits, had its advantages. Certainly there was a steady flow of recruits, which provides a rough-and-ready measure of the underlying attraction of policing as a job. For some recruits material considerations were part of a wider attraction. It was not simply the pay but 'the prospect, the promotion by merit, the recognition of faithful service, the appreciation of moral character' as well as the reward of a pension for old age.[13]

High turnover rates, especially in the mid-nineteenth century, can be explained, in part, by reference to the negative reasons for joining the force. Other factors, not least the nature and demands of the job, played their part. The new recruit quickly found himself working the beat. Much of this work was tedious and conducted in isolation, especially in the countryside. For the heavily uniformed policemen, adverse weather brought short-term discomfort and longer-term ill-health. A strong constitution was essential and it is unsurprising to find that many men were physically broken by these demands, to the extent of retiring through ill-health or dying on the job. In addition, beat work required self-discipline. The temptation to snatch a brief nap or take a quick drink was obvious and, as the conduct books testify, many were unable to resist.

The amount of training that a recruit could expect to receive was minimal until late into the nineteenth century. Policing skills were acquired on the job and a recruit could expect to be pitched straight into beat work, albeit accompanied by a more experienced colleague. Metropolitan Police recruits received three weeks of 'systematic instruction in police duties' before being posted to their divisions,[14] but in 1907 Peel House was opened as a training school and this enabled more rigorous training to be given.[15] Elsewhere training was of a very rudimentary nature. Exceptionally, as in Hull, it was offered as early as the 1830s but it was not until the 1890s that it became more common to offer courses in police duties and educational classes.[16]

Although there was an improvement over time, hours of work were long, even by contemporary standards: 14 hours a day, seven days a week was not an uncommon experience. In Stratford-upon-Avon in 1865 the police worked a 15-hour day. More typical were the 10–12-hour shifts, and 20-mile patrols, worked by mid-century Bedfordshire policemen. Gradually hours were reduced. In 1872, the Bristol watch committee cut the hours of duty from ten to eight and there were similar reductions in the length of shifts worked in Norwich and York. Slowly, though not always uniformly, hours of work were being standardized across the country. By the mid-1870s, the shorter eight-hour shift was common in the north, while nine hours was more usual in the south, though local variations still persisted. The introduction of rest days and holiday entitlement also brought an improvement in conditions, but these often came with restrictions. Ipswich police could only leave the town with the express permission of the mayor, while Chief Constable Bower of the East Riding constabulary refused to grant his men holidays if they stayed at home idle![17]

The ordinary constable was made very aware of his position both within the force and within society at large. He was expected to exercise self-discipline and to follow codes of behaviour, on and off duty, which were not the norm in the working-class society in which he lived and worked. Intended, in part at least, to be an agent of social discipline, the policeman was himself subject to rigorous control by his superiors. He was required not to drink, gamble or smoke in public. Attendance at fairs or race meetings, except in an official capacity, was forbidden. When he did appear in the public house or at a race course he did so to enforce codes of behaviour that were not readily accepted by many members of working-class society. He embodied, and sought to enforce, the social discipline which his superiors wished to see imposed throughout society. It followed, therefore, that his private life was to be conducted in exemplary manner. Debt was to be avoided, wives maintained and religion publicly observed. As late as 1898, a standing order instructed all Watford policemen to attend divine service once on Sunday. Married men, accompanied by their families, were allowed to wear plain clothes, but men attending alone were to wear uniform. Nor was this unusual. From Buckinghamshire and Bedfordshire to Shropshire, county policemen were instructed to attend church in uniform at least once each Sunday. Similar instructions went to borough forces from Luton to Hull. Likewise, personal appearance was subject to close scrutiny. Non-shavers in the Watford force were given very precise instructions. Those with whiskers and a moustache were told that 'the whiskers must be cut short, and must not come lower than on a level with the mouth' while there had to be 'the space of an inch between the whiskers and the moustache'. Among Monmouth policemen, beards could not be longer than two inches. In Maidstone, until 1873, beards were compulsory, but in the East Riding constabulary they were banned until 1872.[18]

There were other restrictions. Uniforms had to be worn even when off duty in the early years. It was only in 1890 that the men of the East Riding force, for example, were allowed to wear plain clothes when off duty. Even in plain clothes there could be restrictions. Robert Bruce, chief constable of Lancashire from 1868 to 1876, felt it necessary to issue a general order, informing his men that 'a shooting jacket and wide-awake hat is not the dress in which they should appear in public, and more especially when visiting . . . such towns as Liverpool and Manchester'.[19]

There was also intervention in more personal matters. County forces, for the most part, insisted on 'approving' spouses and required them not to work. It was essential to demonstrate that a constable had the wherewithal to establish himself and his family in the appropriate manner. In certain forces, for example, constables were refused permission to marry until they were in a position to sign a declaration stating that they were free of debt and owned property to the value of £20 or possessed £20 in cash. Once married, domestic respectability was expected. As well as being expected not to work, constables' wives in many forces were not allowed to keep pigs, fowls and even dogs. Personal behaviour had also to be beyond reproach. Somewhat harshly, PC George Stewart was requested to resign from the Essex police in 1859, 'his wife being insane'. Less surprisingly, Richard Buckle was dismissed from the Middlesbrough force for attempting to poison his wife. One final aspect of police life deserves emphasis: isolation. Although drawn from the working classes, the policeman, by the very nature of his job, was set apart from them. He, and his family, might live in the community but they were never truly part of it. Furthermore, this isolation was compounded by the constant moving that took a man, and his family, from one post to another. Alfred Jewitt of the East Riding constabulary moved station nine times in a career of 28 years, while Richard Hann of the Dorset constabulary served in 13 different places. During his 27-year career his longest stay, his tenth posting, was four and a half years.[20]

In view of this demanding, closely regulated and often isolated life, it is hardly surprising to find that many men left of their own accord or fell short of the required standards and were dismissed. Resignation was a reflection of the individual's dissatisfaction with the force,[21] and became an increasingly important reason for leaving as length of service increased, while dismissal was a reflection of the force's dissatisfaction with the individual, and was the most important cause of leaving in the first year of service.

Dismissals, Discipline and the Emergence of the Career Policeman

In the early years of the new police forces, dismissals ran at extremely high levels. In the first year alone of the East Riding constabulary, 42 men, that is the equivalent of the full establishment, were dismissed. Even more startling was the case of Ipswich, the force which was adjudged to be so incompetent in 1842 that it was dismissed *en masse*. Staffordshire was more typical, with roughly a third of its early intake dismissed. Furthermore, the level dropped over the course of the nineteenth century. In the late 1840s, 37 per cent of the Lancashire force were dismissed; by the late 1860s, the figure had fallen to 18 per cent. In the Metropolitan Police, dismissals accounted for just under 30 per cent of the intake as late as the 1880s, but had fallen to a mere 6 per cent by the early twentieth century.[22] The reasons leading to dismissal are well recorded: drunkenness, neglect of duty, insubordination and the more general failure to act in a manner expected of and befitting a constable. In town and country, men succumbed in their thousands to the lure of strong drink. From the very outset this was a major problem. Although not all officers were paragons of virtue, this was a problem heavily concentrated in the lowest ranks. The first police commissioners, Rowan and Mayne, confessed that four out of every five dismissals were due to drunkenness. Nor was the problem peculiar to London. The reasons are not difficult to find. The temptation to slip into a public house, or simply take a strategically left drink, when working a beat in the cold, wet and wind-swept streets of Manchester or Middlesbrough during the winter, or while tramping the dusty lanes of Wiltshire or Norfolk during the summer, is easy to appreciate. Some men acted more foolishly. Constable Hodges of the Dorset constabulary was dismissed in July 1857, having spent 'several hours in a Public House at Iwerene and playing skittles, whilst there he had his pocket picked of his handcuffs'; while Constable Collins of the same force was dismissed after regaling his prisoner with strong drink at several hostelries, including the Green Dragon Inn at Piddletrenthide.[23]

Drunkenness was also commonly linked with neglect of duty. Constable Audus of Hull was dismissed for being drunk and incapable on his first day of duty. Others combined neglect of duty with insubordination and verbal, even physical, assaults on senior officers. Thomas Taylor and Jewitt Hardy, dismissed from the Middlesbrough force for neglect of duty and insubordination, restricted their attentions to a sergeant, but Harry Bickley verbally assaulted a superintendent before destroying property in his office. John Bottomley went to the top and was dismissed for attempting to assault the Chief Constable of Oldham.[24]

Sexual misconduct was the downfall of many policemen. Constables Caddy, Metcalf and Robinson were dismissed in 1888, having been discovered in a Middlesbrough brothel at 2 o'clock on a Sunday morning, while constables Blakeborough and Nash lost their jobs as the result of their 'highly improper conduct'; that is they were married men who were keeping the company of a widow and a single young lady, respectively. The actions of other men were even more blatant. Constable Cook of the West Suffolk police not only allowed a prostitute to stay in his room at Mildenhall police station, but left his keys with her when he went on duty. Even more foolhardy was James Brook, a policeman whose career with the Oldham police was short-lived but not without incident. In the space of one week he was disciplined for 'misbehaving' with a married lady, being found asleep on duty and, in the act that finally led to his dismissal, 'taking liberties with the daughter of Inspector Winterbottom'. Yet this was as nothing compared with the folly of one member of the Worcestershire constabulary who was dismissed after 'having intercourse...with a girl on two occasions on Sunday afternoon April 18th. 1880, in full uniform and broad daylight'. The offence was compounded by the fact that this 'conquest' had been witnessed by two men and several children.[25]

Men were also dismissed for a wide variety of other reasons but many, if not all, had some bearing on the respectability of the man concerned. 'Eating tripe at a market stall' led to the dismissal of two Oldham policemen; having been found 'covered in vermin' spelled the end of policing for Constable Davis of Essex; while being 'connected with Mormons' led to the termination of Constable Marchbank's career in the same force some three years later. In one sense the pattern of dismissals reveals a determination to remove men who failed to give value for money but, in a more profound sense, the forces' dissatisfaction, as expressed through dismissals, was more a moral judgment on the character of the individual.[26]

Discussions of discipline and dismissals focus, understandably, on the lower ranks, but one should not overlook the problems of senior officers. The Head Constable of Bury St Edmunds was dismissed in 1845 for drunkenness, while Superintendent William Baxter of the Shropshire constabulary was dismissed for embezzlement in 1850. Nor were such cases confined to the early years. In 1902, the recently appointed Chief Inspector Grey of Middlesbrough was dismissed for stealing from prisoners. Such cases were exceptional, but not as rare as earlier histories have suggested. The experience of the newly formed East Riding constabulary in the 1860s and 1870s well illustrates the point. Despite repeated exhortations from the Chief Constable, Major Layard, there were persistent problems with the superintendents in the force. Superintendent Green, fined 15s for laughing and joking with members of the Rifle Corp and 'making water with his men outside the house of Dr. Watkins', hardly set a good example, but was not the worst offender in the senior ranks. Superintendent Ward was found guilty of gross carelessness and bad bookkeeping, while Superintendent Lazenby, already in disgrace for having been improperly dressed on parade, having rusty spurs and mould on his weights and measures, was fined £2. 3s in 1871 for employing constables to dig his garden when they should have been on duty. To add to the catalogue of woe, the first Deputy Chief Constable, Superintendent Gibson, having been found guilty of a gross case of drunkenness and neglect of duty, absconded from the force. However, the most spectacular miscreant was Superintendent Joseph 'Jack the Lad' Young, who was fortunate to be retired on an annual pension of £40 in 1872. In an eventful career he was found guilty, *inter alia*, of drunkenness, withholding information, falsifying divisional accounts, forging the signature of a police officer, not once but on three separate occasions, and helping out in his son's butcher's shop, cleaning game, dressing meat and serving customers, all while in police uniform.[27]

By the late nineteenth century, the level of dismissals had dropped in most forces. The reasons for this are varied. In part it was the product of a lowering of standards of discipline. The Metropolitan Police, for example, took an appreciably more lenient stance in the 1890s and 1900s than in the 1830s and 1840s. In part it was the product of a better quality of applicant. The labour force of late Victorian England, taken as a whole, was more disciplined and self-disciplined than its early Victorian counterpart. Furthermore, the decision to become a policeman became less opportunistic with the passing of time. Police forces grew and the number of men with direct experience, or indirect knowledge, of police work increased. This resulted in less ill-informed recruitment decisions being made by would-be policemen.

The emergence of the 'career' policeman is the crucial element in the development of a disciplined and quasi-professional police force. The number of men remaining in the force and receiving a pension on retirement increased steadily in the second half of the nineteenth century. Although they may not have joined with the express purpose of spending their working life in the force, the fact remains that they chose to do so. Historians have tended to focus their attention on the years of formation and the first generation of new policing, that is up to c.1880. Consequently, there have been very few detailed studies of the development of individual forces into the second and third generation. Of the men recruited to the Metropolitan Police between 1889 and 1909, only one in five of all recruits and one in four of all men serving five years or more achieved some form of promotion. Moreover, the bulk of these did not gain promotion beyond the rank of sergeant.[28] This gloomy picture was not untypical of several forces around the turn of the twentieth century, but the situation had not always been so bleak. The history of one borough force in the north-east of England throws light on the longer-term pattern of change and the variations to be found within even a small group of men.

The Middlesbrough police force effectively started with the appointment in 1853 of William Hannan, who began a programme of expansion and improved efficiency before the 1856 County and Borough Police Act, which greatly facilitated his reforms. The long-term transformation that took place is easily demonstrated. In the 1850s, less than 10 per cent of recruits went on to a career in policing. In the 1890s, the corresponding figure was over 55 per cent.[29] As the number of long-serving policemen increased, different career patterns emerged. Only a few men who joined in the 1850s made a long-term career of policing, but the opportunities for promotion were very good; 75 per cent reached the rank of inspector and one became a superintendent. Moreover, the first two promotions in a policeman's career were rapid. Promotion opportunities for those recruited in the 1860s remained good, although double promotions, that is beyond the rank of sergeant, were less frequent and took longer to achieve. Of 15 long-term policemen, 13 became sergeants, taking an average of five years to do so, and seven of this number went on to the rank of inspector, taking just over an average of seven and a half years. For a minority of the 1860s recruits there was no promotion at all and this created tensions which were to become more pronounced among later intakes. One-third of the 1870s recruits did not get beyond promotion to the long-service class. The numbers becoming sergeants or inspectors were significantly lower. Furthermore, the rate of progress was appreciably slower. In this respect Middlesbrough was not typical: it took an average of ten years to become a sergeant when the national average was five years.

Nor did the situation improve in the 1880s. Indeed, it now took an average of 12 years to reach the rank of sergeant. This figure obscures an important difference between those who gained promotion before reaching long-service status and those who did so afterwards. It took the latter more than half as long again as the former to win their stripes. For the few who were promoted to inspector, the time taken in the 1870s (about eight years) was very similar to that of their counterparts of a decade earlier and almost exactly in line with the national average. The situation worsened in the 1890s. Recruitment levels were at their lowest since the 1850s and yet a higher percentage than ever (55 per cent) served for ten years or more. However, their promotional opportunities were limited. Little more than a quarter became sergeants and a mere 4 per cent became inspectors. The problems of frustration which had emerged in the 1860s were felt most keenly with this cohort of men. Thus, at a time when policing was being seen as a more attractive long-term proposition for working-class men, promotion opportunities were actually diminishing.

However, there could be no doubting the growing maturity of the force. The contrast between the force of 1857, dominated by men with less than two years' experience of policing, and the Edwardian force, in which almost two-thirds had served for more than five years and nearly half for ten, is striking indeed. Although Middlesbrough cannot be seen as a typical force – the peculiar development of the town alone ensured that – its over-all pattern of development has a wider applicability. The second and third generations of policing saw a consolidation and maturation in forces across the country. As in Middlesbrough, internal hierarchies became well established, with a cadre of experienced men in senior positions, having worked their way up through the ranks. There was a body of practical experience to hand which could be used as part of the training initiatives that dated from the 1880s onwards. As a consequence there was a growing sense of identity for both the individual policeman and the force of which he was a part.

The voice of the ordinary policeman is rarely heard in the historical record. Consequently, it is not easy to explain this transformation, but a large part of the answer is likely to be found in economic matters. From the outset, the policeman had enjoyed a number of advantages compared with workers in other industries. First and foremost, the work, and therefore the pay, was regular. Policemen did not suffer from the seasonal unemployment that beset building workers, or from the longer-term cyclical fluctuations that hit those in the iron and steel trades. In addition, the policeman could look forward to promotion. Recruitment from within the ranks was a deliberate policy and a man, if fortunate, could work his way to the top of a borough, though not a county, force. Clearly only a few reached such exalted heights, but there was a promotional ladder and this was augmented by the introduction of merit and long-service classes to ensure that all men had an opportunity of some form of promotion. At the end of his career the policemen could hope for a pension and, after 1890, expect one as of right.

Furthermore, there were a number of valuable perks to the job. Subsidized housing was available in several forces. Others provided cheap coal or helped with gas and water bills and even local rates. In some cases policemen were provided with a uniform and often given their old uniform for off-duty use, in others boot allowances were paid and, for more senior men, there were a variety of additional responsibilities, such as acting as assistant poor law relieving officer, which brought in a few extra pounds a year. Escorting prisoners, attending trials at quarter sessions or assizes, or even acting as a javelin man, escorting the judge at the latter, could bring a welcome supplement to the wages of a long-serving constable with little chance of moving far up the promotional ladder. There were also some unofficial perks, several of which were frowned upon by the police authorities. In many towns policemen expected to travel free on the trams and to receive complimentary tickets for the music hall or theatre. An entrepreneurial bobby could earn a shilling or two by acting as a 'knocker up' for factory workers or market traders.[30] And there was always the free food and drink slipped surreptitiously to the man on the beat. The precise scale of such activities will never be known, but anecdotal evidence suggests that most policemen took advantage of one or more of these perks at some stage in their career.

The question of police pay and pensions was not unproblematic. Tensions existed very close to the surface and broke forth on several occasions in a variety of forces. However, the point remains that there were certain financial advantages to being a policeman. The crucial question, however, remains: how did policing compare with other jobs in financial terms? There were real benefits for a man, especially if unskilled, joining the police in the 1850s and 1860s, and the police gained more than many working-class men during the so-called Great Depression. Police wage rates increased steadily during the second half of the nineteenth century, while food prices in particular were falling from the 1870s to the 1890s. The use of wage rate data only gives a crude indicator of change; by looking in detail at actual earnings in a particular police force it is possible to provide a more sensitive measure of change.

Middlesbrough was a Victorian boom town, noted for the high wages paid in the local iron and steel industry. Men and women were attracted from all parts of the country and the Middlesbrough force was recruited predominantly from local unskilled workers. Wages were of paramount importance if men were to be recruited and retained. Taking into account actual earnings, the evidence suggests that career policemen recruited in the 1870s and 1880s enjoyed a higher rate of growth of real earnings than men working in the local iron and steel and engineering industries. This was particularly true of men promoted beyond the rank of sergeant. For recruits of the 1890s, the situation was somewhat different. The material standard of living of those who remained constables throughout their careers rose at roughly the same rate as those in the town's major industries. However, for those who gained a sergeant's stripes, or more, the rate of growth of real earnings was clearly greater.[31] Not all forces would conform to this precise pattern but, given the problems in gaining promotion noted above, men in other forces may well have fared better than those in Middlesbrough.

Although economic considerations were of central importance, other factors played their part. First, the nature of the job was changing and becoming less arduous. In other ways conditions improved. The provision of canteens and rest-rooms with bagatelle and billiard tables, the opening of reading rooms with illustrated and comic papers, and the creation of police bands and sporting clubs, while serving a variety of purposes, eased some of the worst hardships of the job.[32] The hard graft and dangers remained but, in comparison with the first generation of new policemen, the late Victorian and Edwardian police enjoyed improved work conditions. The passing of time and the emergence of the career policeman brought with them, part cause and part effect, a developing police culture with a distinct self-image and an *esprit de corps* that was not to be found among the transitory constables of the 1840s and 1850s. The 1856 act, with its inspections and measures of 'efficiency', helped create a sense of pride in belonging to a team. There was also a sense of being part of a nationwide group of men. Government inspection, once again, was important, but more so were the in-house journals, such as the *Police Service Advertiser*, or *Police Review and Parade Gossip*, in which even ordinary constables could express their views as well as learning those of others.

Camaraderie was important but so too was the developing self-image of 'the loyal servant' and the ethos that went with it. It was an image cultivated in part by the middle classes in the avuncular figures to be found, for example, in the cartoons of *Punch*. More importantly, it was policemen who developed a more positive image of themselves and their work and articulated it through contributions to in-house journals or in evidence given to select committees. Central to this image was the figure of the constable, set apart from the community he policed but watching over it, through day and night. He was the faithful and trustworthy servant *par excellence*. Further, this self-image was strengthened and developed by a growing sense of the skills (as well as the worth) of the job. Policing was seen to be akin to a craft or trade with an apprenticeship to be served, a body of knowledge of the law to be learned and a series of practical skills to acquire.

There was also a sense in which policing was seen to provide an opportunity for personal improvement. There was the notion of the man made good by becoming a policeman. Almost as a latter-day Bunyan, the idealized policeman was seen as finding his salvation as he journeyed through the travails of his working life, rewarded for doing good, moving up the police hierarchy and finally receiving his pension as recognition for a working life of service for others. In a variation on this theme, Richard Jervis openly talked of his life as a crusade. Nor should this be surprising. In a broader sense, policemen were expected, and expected themselves, to set an example to others in their conduct. Theirs was a life governed by such virtues as obedience, sobriety and decency. It is no coincidence that police manuals stressed the importance of personal conduct. Clearly, not every policeman achieved these ideals, but it would be over cynical to deny the importance of this developing self-image and its accompanying sense of self-worth.

It is also significant that the public's perception of the police changed over the course of the second half of the nineteenth century. Among the middle classes, initial hostility soon abated. By the end of the century there were clear signs of growing sympathy for the police. *Punch* cartoons show the policeman increasingly as the victim rather than the perpetrator of violence. The London bobby, in particular, was a man with a weakness for a hot cup of tea and flirting with the maids – an activity which reinforced the servant image of the police. Affectionate, if somewhat patronizing, obituaries in local papers indicated the esteem in which they were held. But the question of popular attitudes towards the police is problematic. *The Times'* reference to the 'handyman of the street'[33] says more about elite perceptions and elite wishes than about popular sentiment. Nonetheless, outright hostility to the police was diminishing in the late Victorian and Edwardian years and there was a growing popular acceptance of the police, albeit begrudging and based on pragmatic considerations rather than affection.

The late nineteenth or early twentieth century was not a 'golden age' of policing. The police were still commonly viewed with suspicion and, at times, outright hostility. Flora Thompson's picture of the unliked policeman is reinforced by the bitter observation of a Norfolk labourer, Billy Dixon. Looking back to his youth in the early part of the century, he noted: 'Course the police were against the population in them days . . . the police was sort of a bit of an enemy'.[34] Communal hostility could lead to very public protest. In one notorious case, the inhabitants of Stebbing in Essex, were so incensed by the behaviour of the local constable, Enoch Raison, that they burnt him in effigy on 5 November 1888. An attempt to smuggle the unfortunate Raison from the village was bungled and he left in ignominious fashion, catcalls ringing and missiles flying round his ears.[35] More common were the assaults that continued to be part of the policeman's daily experience, particularly when he interfered in popular customs. However, the frequency of such actions must not be overstated. More often than not, police and public viewed each other with suspicion and went their separate ways. Non-cooperation rather than outright hostility was the most common response. However, this uneasy coexistence could easily be undermined and underlying hostilities laid bare.

Urban policing remained characterized by recurring outbursts of violence. In London, for example, the handling of public protests and industrial disputes revealed tensions close to the surface. The events of 'Bloody

Sunday', 1887, offer a clear example. Here, 400 arrests and over 200 casualties, including three fatalities, resulted from the clash between police and a crowd protesting at the government's failure to tackle the problem of unemployment. Furthermore, the growing responsibilities for policing morals increased the likelihood of conflict with certain groups in society, notably young working-class males. By the early twentieth century, according to Archibald's *Metropolitan Police Guide*, there were just under 650 statutes relating to police work, the majority of which referred to economic or recreational activities in the streets.[36] The situation was further compounded by the fact that the police, as well as acting as prosecutors, were also responsible for the imposition of certain punishments, such as the whipping of minor offenders.

Assaults on the police, although declining in frequency, were still very much part of a London policeman's life. One in every four constables in the Metropolitan Police had been assaulted while on duty in the early twentieth century. Certain districts, such as the notorious Campbell Bunk in Islington, popularly known as 'Kill Copper Row', remained highly dangerous for the police to enter, though the destruction of many of the old rookeries in the late nineteenth century had broken up many highly hostile neighbourhoods.[37] In certain respects, London was exceptional, but anti-police sentiment was not confined to the capital.[38]

The fact that the police were perceived to be the agents of another class, imposing alien values that resulted in working-class people being punished for actions that they did not see as reprehensible or wrong, meant 'there is hardly a man who cannot, from the working-class point of view, bring up instances of gross injustices on the part of the police towards himself or his friends or relations'.[39] Juveniles and young men were most likely to fall foul of the police and when they did so it could leave bitter memories that lasted a lifetime. Robert Roberts had no doubt as he looked back on his Salford childhood in the pre-First World War years:

> Nobody in our Northern slum, to my recollection, ever spoke in fond regard, then, or afterwards, of the policeman as 'social worker' and 'handyman of the streets'. Like their children, delinquent or not, the poor in general looked upon him with fear and dislike. When one arrived on a 'social' visit they watched his passing with suspicion and his disappearance with relief.[40]

The ordinary policeman found himself in a difficult position when dealing with strikers. In mining districts from South Wales to Lancashire, and from several parts of the country during the 1911 transport strike, come accounts of serious conflicts between police and strikers which in turn emphasized the separateness of the policeman and his family from the community he policed. There were also serious and continuing conflicts between the police and ethnic minorities, notably the Irish, in many cities.[41] The policing of the Irish, and other outcast groups, raises a number of interesting questions about popular responses. Although unpopular with the particular target group, the policing of groups who were perceived to pose threats to the well-being of society as a whole may well have increased the standing of the police with members of the indigenous working classes as well as with those of the middle and upper classes. On the other hand, the ease with which an individual, a relative or friend, could end up on the wrong side of the law was such that working-class suspicion was difficult for the police to counter.

That said, it would be misleading to suggest that it was impossible to gain acceptance or that attitudes had not changed since the mid-nineteenth century. Even in Campbell Bunk, some policemen were accepted. Arthur Harding, a small-time crook from the East End, constantly in trouble with the police before and after the First World War, nonetheless counted policemen among his friends. Even more striking was the huge crowd that lined the streets of Leicester for the funeral of PC Stephens in 1908. For many people, irrespective of class, the police were seen to do a valuable job. Middle-class complaints tended to be more vociferous, but working-class people were as much, if not more, victims of theft and violence and sought the protection of and redress from the law. The easily parodied social service role, which saw parents united with lost children at the local station and old ladies helped across roads, also played a part in establishing the image of the policeman as a public servant. The extent of the change in attitudes is impossible to measure precisely, but working-class men and women born in the 1880s and 1890s tended to have a more benign image of the police. The reputation of the police was further enhanced by the bravery they showed in a variety of circumstances. Stopping runaway horses and dealing with dangerous dogs are but two mundane examples. Prompt action in times of emergency – fire or flood – likewise brought a positive public response.

A changing and more positive perception of the police was an important element in the transformation to 'professional' policing but it is also central to an understanding of the second major theme, police legitimacy. In the mid-nineteenth century, the establishment of new police forces was accompanied by considerable violence and, in some quarters at least, a profound challenge to their very existence. By the late nineteenth century the situation had changed. In pragmatic terms there were very few, if any, who did not accept that the police were here to stay. The simple fact that there were more policemen on the streets, that they were more disciplined and had more extensive power than in the 1850s, meant that their presence was more readily accepted. More importantly, there was a broadening acceptance, extending beyond the middle classes into the working classes, that, like them or not as individuals, the police were a necessary part of modern society. In that sense, the Edwardians, though more closely policed than their early Victorian counterparts, accepted that theirs was a policed society.

The complexities of society and the multi-form nature of policing meant, either collectively or individually, that there was not a uniform working-class experience of or response to the police. The late Victorian and Edwardian policeman appeared in a variety of guises to one and the same person. In one circumstance, he was a genial figure returning a lost child; in another, a welcome defender against petty thieves. But equally he could appear at other times, to the same person, let alone to different members of society, as a heavy-handed and insensitive figure, brusquely enforcing laws and even exacting punishments for actions that did not appear to be 'criminal' while, even worse, in other circumstances he could be a positive threat to cherished rights as he escorted 'scab' labour to work during a strike or broke up a crowd of demonstrators, male and female, demanding the right to vote. The analogy between the police and peace-keeping troops is a useful, if not entirely exact, one. There was a fine balance to be struck and the friendly peace-keeper/constable could quickly become a hostile soldier in an enemy country. Notwithstanding these problems, public support for the police had broadened considerably by 1914, in no small measure because of the improvements in policing that had taken place.

6

COURTS, PROSECUTORS AND VERDICTS[1]

At the heart of the criminal justice system were the courts. Here those accused of crimes were tried and, if found guilty, sentenced to death, transportation, imprisonment or some other form of punishment. There were a wide variety of courts to be found in eighteenth-century England, but the most important were the Court of King's Bench and the assize courts, which heard the most serious cases; the county and borough courts of quarter sessions, which heard less serious cases; and, finally, the courts of summary jurisdiction, which dealt with misdemeanours. Over the course of the eighteenth and early nineteenth century, two important shifts took place in the distribution of cases. First, a number of felonies, notably grand larceny, were transferred from assize to quarter session, leading ultimately to the position whereby the former dealt with capital offences and the latter with non-capital offences. Second, there was a transfer of offences from quarter session to petty session as the scope of summary justice was expanded, most notably in the first half of the nineteenth century. In 1857, it was estimated that justices at quarter sessions dealt with four times the number of indictable offences dealt with at assizes, while justices in petty sessions dealt with 20 times the number of cases dealt with in all other courts.[2] By the late nineteenth and early twentieth centuries the predominance of summary justice was overwhelming. Of all those dealt with by the courts, 98 per cent were tried summarily (91 per cent for non-indictable offences, 7 per cent for indictable) while the remaining 2 per cent were dealt with by the superior courts. Although the precise pattern of change in the distribution of criminal cases between these courts cannot be ascertained, the most

106

common experience of the law, even at the beginning of our period and certainly at the end, was an appearance before magistrates sitting in petty session.

Summary Justice

The conflicts of the seventeenth century in particular had highlighted the importance of the rule of law in guaranteeing the liberties of the individual and offering protection against arbitrary arrest and punishment. Trial by jury, in particular, was seen to be of fundamental importance and gave a distinctiveness and superiority to English justice. As a consequence, summary justice was viewed with some suspicion and any extension was a source of concern to libertarians such as Blackstone, for whom the jury was 'the grand bulwark' of English liberties. However, despite his wish that 'this palladium remains sacred and inviolate',[3] there was a steady increase in the scope of summary justice, starting in the late eighteenth century and accelerating in the first half of the nineteenth, notably as a result of Peel's Criminal Justice Act of 1826 and the 1855 Criminal Justice Act. Eighteenth-century magistrates were untrained and their practices were informal and lacking in uniformity across the country. From the seventeenth century, in some parts of the country, magistrates had come together in petty sessions, but the practice, though well-established in some counties, was absent in others. The situation was further complicated by the difficulty of finding suitable men to take on magisterial responsibilities, particularly in the rapidly growing urban centres and those neighbouring rural districts where the volume of work was appreciably greater. To some extent this was offset by the creation of rotation offices at which two or more county magistrates would sit. This strategy was adopted by the Middlesex bench in the 1780s and similar offices were established for Manchester in 1795 and Birmingham in 1799. These were the exceptions. For other rapidly growing industrial centres (and indeed for some rural districts) much depended upon the accident of personality. Energetic and able justices were found in some parts of the country, but not in others. Nonetheless, the scope of summary justice continued to be increased.

This trend reflected a powerful and persistent desire for cheap and speedy justice, particularly when the volume of cases coming before the magistrates was increasing markedly, rather than any weakening of the commitment to individual liberty. Although the process of change was unplanned, actions were taken to improve the efficiency with which petty sessions were

conducted. Concern with the lack of clear procedure and a code of practice
for summary jurisdiction led to legislation in 1848 which clarified matters
considerably.[4] The conduct of the courts also became more professional as
trained lawyers became stipendiaries and recorders.

Nonetheless, the extension of summary justice aroused fears that the law
was being used in a partial manner to protect the interests of certain well-to-
do members of society. One of the most important extensions of summary
justice in the eighteenth century centred on the new game laws. Concerns
about injustices were expressed by both contemporaries and later historians.
Shock stories, such as that told by Brougham of the Duke of Buckingham,
hearing in his own home a charge brought by his gamekeeper against a
local farmer, are not difficult to find. However, caution should be exercised.
While there were undoubtedly a number of oft-quoted scandalous cases,
they were not typical of the administration of the game laws.

If recent research has exculpated, in part at least, the eighteenth-century
landowner from charges of imposing class-biased legislation, the same
cannot be said about mid-nineteenth-century industrialists. There is a growing body of evidence, mainly from the West Midlands, suggesting that the
newer magistrates, drawn from the ranks of ironmasters and industrialists,
were unwilling to enforce such legislation as the Truck Act and took a very
partial stance when enforcing the Master and Servant Act.[5] Moreover, this
bias was not confined to the administration of summary justice. The sharp
increase in the percentage of cases of industrial larceny tried on indictment
suggests a determination on the part of these magistrates to use the law to
protect their own interests. It is difficult to evaluate the significance of the
West Midlands evidence. Swift's claim that the experience of Wolverhampton was replicated in the industrial towns of South Lancashire, the West
Riding of Yorkshire and South Wales rests on a relatively narrow basis.
Furthermore, not all industrializing areas followed this pattern. In some
parts of the industrial north-east, for example, local industrialists made
little use of their powers as magistrates in a narrow fashion.[6] It also remains
to be seen whether such attitudes persisted into the late nineteenth century
or whether they were a product of the particularly difficult years of the mid-
century. Evidence from the London police courts in the second half of the
nineteenth century points in a somewhat different direction.[7]

The 13 police courts of the mid-nineteenth century dealt with a wide variety of offences, many under the 1839 Police Act. However, the legislation of
1855 greatly increased the volume of work dealt with by the stipendiary
magistrates. Such was the growth of the regulatory powers of the state that
a growing percentage of the population was likely to fall foul of the law. This

was particularly true for young working-class men. In such circumstances upholding the law and retaining its legitimacy in the eyes of a population who were disproportionately its victims was not an easy task. However, conscious efforts were made to overcome these difficulties. From an early date, magistrates were expected to exercise considerable discretion in dealing with the London poor. Moreover, they accepted that they had a responsibility to look after the interests of the poor as well as to deal with the problem of crime. Much of their work was concerned with defending the property rights of shopkeepers and employers, but a significant minority of prosecutors were working-class men and women, though formal and informal sanctions coexisted. In addition, the courts appear to have been important local centres for advice, informal justice and even charity. The police courts were popular with many in the local working-class community, reflecting the fact that they (the courts) fulfilled, and were seen to fulfil, a useful purpose in the everyday lives of ordinary people. The 'new' police courts were run in a way that had much in common with 'old', eighteenth-century, practice. The exercise of discretion, the willingness to make strategic concessions in the short term, were an important and necessary tactic in gaining and retaining longer-term influence over a population not universally enamoured of the law as personified by the local policeman.

Pretrial and Trial Procedures in Superior Courts

The volume of summary justice was increasing both absolutely and relatively over the course of the nineteenth century but a substantial amount of work was still conducted at quarter sessions or assizes. While eighteenth-century courts have been subjected to close scrutiny, much less work has been done on their nineteenth-century counterparts. Nonetheless, it is clear that a number of important developments took place which significantly altered the nature of the trial process.

It is necessary first to consider pretrial practices. The victim was the central actor in the process of prosecution well into the nineteenth century. He or she had a variety of options from which to choose. The decision to take formal action involved the weighing up of a variety of considerations. The appropriateness of going to court, the dangers of retaliation by the accused or hostility from the community and the cost in time and money had to be carefully weighed.

We will never know how many 'victims' decided either not to take action or to pursue informal sanctions; or why they chose to do so. However, a growing number of observers in the late eighteenth and early nineteenth centuries believed that the inconvenience and cost of bringing a prosecution was a considerable factor. Rough estimates for the late eighteenth century suggest minimum costs for bringing a prosecution at assize to be in the region of £1 to £3 and at quarter session to be less than £1.[8] More detailed figures for the mid-nineteenth century show average expenses at assizes varying from £16 to £22 and at quarter session ranging from just over £3 to over £10.[9] A number of expedients and changes in practice were introduced with the express aim of facilitating prosecutions. One such response was the creation of an association for the prosecution of felons. Depending for their resources upon membership subscriptions, such organizations – some 450 were scattered unevenly across England and Wales in the years between 1744 and 1856 – offered rewards for evidence leading to successful prosecution and expenses to cover the costs of prosecution incurred by their members.[10]

In addition, a series of acts, dating from the mid-eighteenth century, sought to ease the financial burden on prosecutors. A poor prosecutor in a felony case, if the accused was convicted, could receive expenses from the court under an act passed in 1752, while poor persons appearing as witnesses on their own recognizances in felony cases could also get expenses in the case of a successful prosecution under legislation passed two years later. This provision was broadened to all prosecutors in 1788. Although the payment of expenses was supposedly dependent upon a successful prosecution, in some parts of the country, such as Essex and Nottingham, courts were prepared to pay expenses even if a conviction was not obtained. Further legislative changes meant that the court was obliged to pay reasonable expenses incurred by constables in bringing offenders to prison (1788 and 1801) and to meet the fees of the Clerk of Assize and of the Peace on conviction and acquittal in felony cases (1815). Yet further financial assistance was granted under Benet's Act of 1818, which enabled courts to pay an allowance for loss of time and trouble to all prosecutors and witnesses in felony cases, irrespective of outcome, while Peel's Criminal Justice Act of 1826 extended the scope of recognized expenses to include attendance at the magistrate's pretrial hearing. It is difficult to determine the impact of these changes. John Beattie, after his exhaustive study of the courts in Surrey, concluded that the payment of costs was of 'marginal importance' as an incentive to prosecution, though removing a disincentive may be seen as distinct from creating a positive incentive.[11] Yet as late as 1845, the criminal law commissioners were still lamenting the fact that 'the injured party would rather forego the prosecution than incur expense of time, labour and money'.[12]

A further disincentive to prosecution may have been the severity of the law. Contemporary observers believed that would-be prosecutors were unwilling to proceed because they believed the punishment to be disproportionate to the crime. This opinion was shared by solicitors and police magistrates as well as by laymen. Alderman Harmer, commenting on a case of non-prosecution in 1836, summed up the general sentiment: 'Had the punishment been short of death, no consideration would have induced the gentleman to whom I allude to forbear prosecuting.'[13]

Opinion elsewhere was divided on the matter. Certain London magistrates rejected the whole idea that the severity of punishment was a deterrent to prosecution, while others stressed the greater importance of cost and inconvenience.[14] Whatever the precise importance of these factors, concern continued to be expressed that justice was being thwarted. However, such concerns may well reflect an elite misunderstanding of popular conceptions of justice. For many people, throughout the nineteenth century, the courts were still seen as a last resort and alternative, informal measures were not simply cheaper and less inconvenient, but actually a more desirable way of settling matters.

Having chosen to seek formal redress through the legal system, and having been able to find a magistrate, the private prosecutor was, to an increasing extent, in the hands of the magistrate.[15] Over the course of the late eighteenth and early nineteenth centuries the pretrial role of the magistrate was to change significantly. If the offence was a misdemeanour he had considerable latitude. In such cases it was deemed appropriate for the magistrate to act as a mediator to prevent further legal action being taken. Sir John Hawkins, chairman of the Middlesex Quarter Sessions, in his 1780 charge to the grand jury, expressly stated that, 'where the injury is but small, the magistrate to whom the complaint is made, cannot better exercise his humanity, and I may add, his wisdom, than by persuading the parties to peace and reconciliation'.[16]

A variety of tactics were adopted, such as the return of stolen goods, financial recompense for lost goods or an injury inflicted, or a public apology and a declaration of future good intent. In peacetime the accused might be persuaded to join the East India Company, while in wartime he might be similarly persuaded to join one of the armed forces. However, if the complaint related to a felony, there was far less scope for informal action. Indeed, to agree a financial settlement – compounding a felony – was a crime in itself. Strictly speaking, in these circumstances, the magistrate was constrained by the Marian legislation of 1554 and 1555 which required him to ensure that the accused went to trial and that the strongest case against him was assembled. In 1752, Henry Fielding spelled out the legal position as follows:

> By the law of England as it now stands, if a larceny be absolutely committed, however slight the suspicion be against the accused, the justice ... is obliged in strictness to commit the party ... Nor does the trifling value of the thing stolen, nor any circumstances of mitigation justify his discharging the prisoner.[17]

In practice things were different. By the mid-eighteenth century it seems clear that there was a discernible shift towards a more judicial hearing at the pretrial stage. The eighteenth-century legal system continued to be concerned with obtaining pretrial confessions which would then be proved in court, but magistrates were dismissing weak cases in contradiction of a strict reading of the law. As a part of this new emphasis, the position of the defendant changed. Under the old laws the defendant had few rights. He or she did not know the precise charge; nor was he or she present when depositions were given. Two points should be made about these practices. First, the role of the magistrate was conceived to be that of assistant to the prosecutor. It was his responsibility to put together as strong a case as possible and, although he could include evidence favourable to the defendant, he was under no obligation to do so. Second, the decision to keep the defendant in a state of ignorance was not a tactic to guarantee a successful prosecution, though this may have been the outcome in many instances, but was based on the belief that the truth of the case could be best determined if the defendant was confronted with the evidence *only* in the courtroom. There the jury could assess the quality of his or her immediate and unprepared response in a direct oral conflict between prosecutor and defendant. There was also a suspicion that a defence counsel could be positively harmful in preventing the accused from making the necessary impression upon the jury. William Hawkins, writing in the early eighteenth century in his *Treatise of the Pleas of the Crown*, summed up the traditional view:

> it requires no manner of Skill to make a plain and honest Defence, which in Cases of this kind is always the best; the Simplicity and Innocence, artless and ingenuous Behaviour of one whose Conscience acquits him, having in it something more moving and convincing than the highest Eloquence of Persons speaking in a Cause not their own.[18]

This attitude changed during the second half of the eighteenth century. Rules of evidence were modified. Depositions were only allowed in court if the accused had had the opportunity to cross-examine the witness when the statement was made to the magistrate in the pretrial phase and greater emphasis was placed on the necessity for pretrial confessions to be 'free and voluntary'. By the early nineteenth century the slightest doubts led to the rejection of pretrial confessions.[19]

The prisoner's position was further strengthened by the emerging practice of allowing access to a lawyer for advice. This was not universally popular, not least because attorneys employed by prisoners advised them 'to hold their tongues, not to answer any questions, and to say nothing'.[20] Frustrating as this was to traditionalists, it was but part of a wider process of change whereby the magistrate's role was more concerned with ascertaining the merits of the case, and whether it should proceed, and less with assembling a case for the prosecution. However, change was piecemeal and unplanned and it was not until 1848 that the situation was regularized. The Indictable Offences Act, the first of the three Jervis Acts, required the magistrate to act as a preliminary judge at the pretrial stage. The act also stipulated that the examination of prosecution witnesses had to take place in the presence of the accused, and/or his counsel or solicitor, who had the right to cross-examine. Finally, the act gave, for the first time, statutory recognition to the cautioning of the accused.

Important changes were not confined to the pretrial stage. There were to be a number of significant changes which transformed the nature and practice of the courtroom trial, but important elements of continuity, not least the importance of ritual, particularly at assizes, persisted into the nineteenth century. Eighteenth- and nineteenth-century justice was intended to be a theatrical experience. There was a heavy symbolism that surrounded the whole administration of justice, from the arrival of the circuit-court judge to the dispatch of the convicted criminals. The panoply of state power was on display. The greeting of the assize judge by the local dignitaries and the elaborate progression through the town were meant to be visible demonstrations of the majesty of the law and were intended to be quite literally awesome. Similarly, the assize sermon, and the rituals of the court itself, were all part of this theatrical demonstration directed at the populace as a highly visible reminder of the power of the state and its agents. As late as 1903, the President of the Huddersfield Law Society could talk of 'the spectacle of a highly trained and highly paid judge of the High Court making a stately progress through the country accompanied by all the paraphernalia of sheriffs, chaplains, marshal associates, clerks, trumpeters [and] javelin men'.[21]

Behind this largely unaltering facade a number of important changes took place. The most visible of these was the change from the direct, face-to-face confrontation of the accused and the prosecutor to the confrontation between lawyers acting on their behalf. The 'invasion of the lawyers' was a gradual process. In the late eighteenth century, it was common practice for lawyers to be used to prosecute felonies. Defence counsels were less common. At the Old Bailey one in eight people accused with a property offence was represented by a lawyer in the late 1780s, rising to almost one in three by 1800.[22] Although surprising to modern eyes, the infrequent appearance of defence counsel in the late eighteenth century was explained partly in terms of the nature of trials, in which the accused was presumed to be innocent until proved otherwise, thus putting the onus on the prosecution to make its case; and partly in terms of the role of the judge, who had a responsibility to look after the interests of the accused. The situation is less clear-cut on closer examination. First, the presumption of innocence was not an automatic feature of eighteenth-century trials. Indeed, until the latter part of the century, the defendant was expected to demonstrate his or her innocence by virtue of his performance in response to the evidence brought forward by the prosecution.[23] Even in the nineteenth century, the presumption of innocence in itself was of secondary importance to the firmly held principle that the prosecution had to prove guilt. In practice, defence counsels were available to those who could afford the fees, but the standard fee of a guinea for a 'dock brief' did not bring high-quality service. Second, the role of the judge as the defendant's friend was often less than clear-cut. While few judges were as unhelpful as Justice Marshall who, in 1847, told the jury that 'we cannot have any doubts as to the prisoner's guilt; his very countenance would hang him',[24] few were sufficiently helpful to offset entirely the disadvantages faced by a defendant.

The situation gradually changed with the balance slowly shifting in favour of the accused. As well as permitting the cross-examination of prosecution witnesses, an important late eighteenth-century development, allowing counsel to speak on behalf of a defendant, was accepted as contributing to 'the discovery of truth and the consequent advancement of justice'.[25] The growing number of defence counsels, formally recognized by the 1836 Prisoner's Counsel Act, and the more rigorous cross-examination of prosecution witnesses clearly strengthened the position of the defendant, but the extent of change should not be overstated. In the Black Country in the 1840s, 46 per cent of cases still had no counsel for the prosecution or for the defence; 52 per cent had a counsel for the prosecution and 25 per cent for the defence. In more serious cases, the figures rose to 63 per cent and 49 per cent, respectively, but there were still 30 per cent of cases in which neither side hired counsel.[26]

Nor were such gains evenly distributed. Some contemporary critics were highly critical of the 1836 act, believing that it allowed the professional criminal to gain an advantage over his poorer counterpart and to thwart justice. In the absence of state aid, the poorest were disadvantaged. As a correspondent to the *Law Times* commented in 1851, the Prisoner's Counsel Act was 'a cruel aggravation of the distinction between the man who had a guinea or friends and the man who had not'.[27] The matter was addressed, though not satisfactorily in the eyes of critics such as the *Law Times*, in the 1903 Poor Person's Defence Act, whereby limited legal aid was made available to those prisoners who had disclosed their defence. In contrast, a prisoner who paid for his own lawyer could reserve his defence until he came to court.[28]

The defendant was not permitted to give evidence on oath. This became the subject of considerable debate in the late nineteenth century. Proponents of reform argued that the defendant was disadvantaged by enforced silence in court, to the extent that innocent people were convicted. Others felt that exposure in the witness box would weaken the position of the defendant, particularly if he or she were easily confused, liable to outbursts of temper or prone to lying. Eventually, legislation was passed in 1898, though this probably owed more to a desire to secure convictions by subjecting the defendant to cross-examination than to any wish to strengthen the rights of the accused or prevent miscarriages of justice.[29] A further, though belated, safeguard came in 1907 with the establishment of the Court of Criminal Appeal, following the scandals surrounding the *Eddji* and *Beck* cases.[30]

There were also important changes in thinking about evidence and proof, which was part of a wider eighteenth-century intellectual debate. The emergence of the concept of 'beyond reasonable doubt' was of paramount importance.[31] More specifically, there were developments in the rules of evidence, particularly in the earlier part of our period, which worked in favour of the accused. Hearsay evidence was increasingly excluded from court. The testimony of accomplices turning king's evidence was no longer accepted without corroboration, while confessions were also treated with greater suspicion, especially if there was any suggestion of duress having been used.

The defendant was also favoured by the 'obsessive technicality' regarding evidence in the early and mid-nineteenth century. The commissioners on criminal law in their first report in 1834 drew attention to the confusion surrounding the precise definition of theft, which could lead to problems for prosecutors.[32] Minute and unimportant discrepancies between the charge as contained in the indictment and the evidence produced in court could provide an escape clause for the defence. In murder cases the murder

weapon and the precise nature of the allegedly fatal wound had to be specified in the indictment and if it transpired that death had not occurred in the
manner specified the prosecution case fell. Similarly, an acquittal would
result if the accused, having been accused of stealing sheep, was shown to
have stolen lambs. Ascribing stolen goods to the wrong person had a similar
consequence. When Gerald Plunket Tunney came to give evidence against
Mary Ann Boam, the case collapsed because the indictment specified that
the stolen property belonged to George Plunket Tunney. Even worse was
the case of John Harris, charged with the manslaughter of seven-year-old
Maria Griffiths, who had been knocked down and killed by a wagon.
Although the fact that the killing had taken place as alleged had been
proved, no evidence had been given 'that the name of the child who had
been so unfortunately killed was Maria Griffiths, as stated in the indictment . . . his Lordship directed a verdict of not guilty'.[33] This situation was
first addressed by the 1851 Criminal Procedure Act, which allowed the
amendment of the indictment regarding names, places, ownership and
descriptions of property, but only where these were judged not to be material
to the merits of the case. Old habits died hard: the commissioners reporting
in 1879 could see no justification for drawing up indictments on different
principles and yet this was happening in practice. In murder cases it was no
longer necessary to detail precisely the cause of death, but in cases of obtaining goods by false pretences the precise details of the alleged deceit had to be
specified and proved.[34]

In more general terms, the 'invasion of the lawyers' brought a more rigorous and formal tone to court procedures. The somewhat chaotic court scenes
of the eighteenth century were replaced by the more orderly proceedings of
the nineteenth. Interventions by juries became far less frequent and the
defendant was also relegated to a less prominent and more passive position
in proceedings. As a newer conception of the court-room trial as a contest
between two cases rather than two individuals emerged, the form of the
trial became more regular, with the sequence of prosecution case followed
by the defence becoming the norm. Unsurprisingly, the length of trials was
increased by these developments. The very rapid justice of the late eighteenth and early nineteenth century in which cases, including capital
offences, could be dispatched in 30 minutes or less, became less common.
In the 1840s, a case lasting a day was sufficiently unusual to merit comment,
but not by the turn of the century. The appearance of counsel for the defence
also brought a change in the role of the judge. Whereas in the eighteenth
century judges played an active role in examining witnesses, this gradually
diminished. The judge became a more detached figure, sitting over and

above the confrontation between prosecutor and defendant, and providing guidance to the jury at the conclusion of the hearing in a way that had been rare earlier in the century.

A key element in the trial was the petty jury, called upon, in theory at least, to decide solely upon questions of fact. Irrespective of the unpleasant conditions of many courts, jury service was certainly irksome and, for many, expensive and arduous. Despite the importance attached to trial by jury, there were several causes for concern. The demands of jury service led to a strong desire to reach a quick verdict – a desire that was further reinforced by the fact that a jury could be locked up overnight 'without meat, fire or candle' if it did not bring in a verdict on time. Although having the right to retire, it was unusual for late eighteenth-century juries to leave the court to reach a decision. More commonly, they would huddle together in the court to discuss the matter. Experienced jury men could exercise considerable influence over new men and it was alleged that on occasions dissenting voices were silenced by mental or even physical intimidation. Decisions could also be arrived at capriciously. The jury in the 1858 case of *Smith* v. *Great Northern Railway* allegedly reached its decision by playing pitch and toss.[35] Furthermore, the absence of a detailed summing-up by the judge must have added an element of chance to a decision-making process that relied heavily upon the memory of lay persons.

Finally, the changing role of the magistrate in the pretrial stage undermined the position of the grand jury which was charged with the responsibility of determining whether a true bill had been found. Its position was further weakened by the increasing role of the new police from the mid-nineteenth century onwards. Calls for abolition were heard as early as 1836 and criticism surfaced at regular intervals throughout the nineteenth century. By 1885, it was considered highly unusual for a grand jury to ignore a bill.[36] However, despite having largely lost its effective role by the third quarter of the nineteenth century, if not before, it was not until 1933 that the grand jury was finally abolished.

The cumulative effect of these changes was to transform the old trials of Georgian England, with their distinctive procedures and presumptions, into a recognizable modern form. Wider intellectual developments, a growing awareness of the changing nature of society and internally generated developments combined to transform the English court. There were visible differences in the personnel and practices of the courts but, more importantly, there were fundamental changes in thinking regarding the nature of evidence and proof and especially regarding what constituted a fair trial. The transformation of trial procedures was part of a wider process of reform in the criminal justice system. Justice was now to be administered in a more formal, impersonal and impartial manner. The old personal justice of the eighteenth century, in which 'mercy from the judge' was central, was seen to be inappropriate in a rapidly urbanizing society. Uncertainty and inefficiency threatened to bring injustice. To combat this, the absurdities of a system that relied heavily on discretion had to be removed if the legitimacy of the law was to be maintained. Thus 'humanity in the law' was to be achieved by those reformers who sought to create a new justice system with a new image.[37]

The Decisions of the Courts

In the absence of national statistics our knowledge of the decisions of eighteenth-century courts is heavily dependent on local studies which relate almost exclusively to the capital and those counties in its immediate vicinity. A prosecution could fall at the first hurdle if the grand jury was not convinced by the prosecution case. Between 1660 and 1800, approximately 22 per cent of cases brought at quarter session and 17 per cent at assizes in Surrey were ignored. There were a number of important variations between different offences: 44 per cent of rape cases were ignored by the grand jury as were 27 per cent of infanticide cases; just over a quarter of assault and wounding cases were ignored whereas for capital property offences the figure fell to about 12 per cent. There was a clear gender division, with women more likely to see cases against them dismissed than men, particularly in murder cases, where a third of all cases involving women were ignored. In contrast, by the mid-nineteenth century, reflecting the diminished importance of the grand jury, the proportion of cases ignored, at least in the Black Country, was well below 10 per cent.[38]

The figures for the eighteenth century show that a verdict of guilty was returned in just under 50 per cent of cases. A further 14 per cent were partial verdicts, that is where the defendant was found guilty of a lesser charge, and some 37 per cent of verdicts were not guilty. This pattern varied according to the nature of the crime. For example, although the total numbers are relatively small, not guilty verdicts were significantly more common in cases of rape, infanticide and forgery.[39] Looking more specifically at property crimes, which dominated the work of the courts, we see two important contrasts. The first relates to time. There was a clear increase in the percentage of guilty verdicts returned over the course of the century. Whereas in the late seventeenth and early eighteenth century the proportion of guilty verdicts stood at around 40 per cent of all cases brought to trial, by the end of the eighteenth century the figure had risen to 60 per cent. At the same time the percentage of partial verdicts dropped from around 25 per cent to less than 10 per cent. The second contrast is between old property offences and new (that is, created by recent legislation). Verdicts of guilty were significantly higher for 'old' capital property offences (47 per cent) than for the new (22 per cent). But even within these categories there were clear variations. Thus those charged with horse theft and robbery were most likely to be found guilty. Furthermore, in almost half of the 'new' capital property cases a partial verdict was returned.

Interpreting these figures is not straightforward. It is tempting, but misleading, to see the fall in the percentage of not guilty verdicts as an indication of a hardening of attitudes. It is more likely that this trend was the product of changes in the administration of justice (the weeding out of weaker cases at the magistrate's pretrial hearing) and changes in the availability of secondary punishments. Indeed, the high percentage of partial verdicts for 'new' property offences lends further support to the argument that eighteenth-century juries acted in a discriminating manner that enabled them to express disapproval of certain crimes but also of several laws. Grand juries did not accept that all capital offences merited the death penalty and took action to see that this was not the outcome. The practice of pious perjury, whereby individuals were charged with the theft of goods artificially valued at less than 40 shillings, in cases of theft from a house, or less than five shillings in cases of theft from a shop, saved many men and women from the gallows. Likewise petty juries could return verdicts that ensured the guilty individual escaped the gallows. Early nineteenth-century law reformers seized upon examples of blatant 'pious perjury' – gold rings and jewellery stolen from a ship and valued at £300 in the indictment but valued at 39 shillings by the jury, or 23 guineas stolen from a house but valued at 39 shillings – to support their case.

The process was not completed with the decision of the jury. There remained the possibility of a reprieve by the judge and a recommendation for a royal pardon. This could take place if a judge was not satisfied with a verdict, or in the case of a woman 'pleading her belly' or in the case of a petition for pardon, especially if supported by the prosecutor. Of just over 1200 people sentenced to death in Surrey in the eighteenth century, 60 per cent were pardoned. The chances of escaping the gallows were higher for those found guilty of simple larceny and of theft from a shop or a house, while murderers, unsurprisingly, were least likely to be pardoned. The practice of pardoning was central to the administration of justice in the eighteenth and early nineteenth century, but the scale of pardons reached such a level in the 1800s that the credibility of the system was greatly strained. In London and Middlesex, the percentage of pardons was around 55 per cent for much of the eighteenth century, rising to over 60 per cent exceptionally, for example in the early 1770s. However, in the 1790s the figure leapt to almost 80 per cent, rising to almost 90 per cent in the early nineteenth century. In England and Wales during the second decade of the century, 85 per cent of all people convicted of capital offences were reprieved.[40] Romilly was not alone in arguing that justice was now a lottery.

Discussion of eighteenth-century punishment is understandably dominated by a concern with the death penalty. As a consequence it is easy to overlook the very important developments that took place in secondary punishments. In the third quarter of the eighteenth century transportation was the dominant secondary punishment. Some two-thirds of those found guilty of property offences in Surrey during this period, for example, were transported, whereas a mere 6 per cent were sentenced to imprisonment. However, by the end of the century the proportion transported had fallen to 30 per cent while those imprisoned had risen to 40 per cent.[41]

Charting change in the nineteenth century is considerably easier because of the availability of national statistics. Looking at the century as a whole, it is notable that the number of convictions as a percentage of the number brought to trial rose steadily, from around 60 per cent in the early nineteenth century to around 80 per cent a hundred years later. The fate of those found guilty changed significantly over the course of the nineteenth century. As the number of capital offences was dramatically reduced, fewer people were executed. Furthermore, as transportation disappeared in the 1850s so the number of people imprisoned increased. By the late 1860s, four out of every five persons found guilty in the higher courts of England and Wales were sentenced to a period of imprisonment, with a further 13 per cent sentenced to penal servitude. Approximately 60 per cent of those imprisoned served sentences of up to six months and little more than 10 per cent were sentenced to more than a year.[42]

The overall figures obscure certain variations between the treatment of different offences. Malicious wounding was most commonly punished with imprisonment, even before the phasing out of the death penalty and transportation. Over the course of the second half of the nineteenth century, 80 per cent and more of sentences took the form of imprisonment, with rarely more than 10 per cent of those found guilty of this crime sentenced to the harsher penalty of penal servitude. In contrast, penal servitude was a more common punishment for crimes of violence against property, accounting for over a third of sentences in the late 1850s and 1860s. However, in subsequent decades there was a shift away from the use of penal servitude, towards imprisonment. By the late nineteenth century, 80 per cent or more offenders were sentenced to terms of imprisonment and only some 13 per cent to penal servitude. The use of imprisonment diminished for both these categories of crimes in the early twentieth century. The trend is apparent from 1900 onwards in the case of malicious wounding but does not become clear until almost ten years later in the case of property crimes with violence. The move away from the use of imprisonment is seen at its earliest and most clear in the case of larcenies. In the early 1880s, two-thirds of those found guilty were imprisoned. By the outbreak of the First World War, this figure had fallen to one-third, with almost all of the remainder receiving punishment other than imprisonment.[43]

Victims and Prosecutors

Although the new police came to play an important role in the process of prosecution from the mid-nineteenth century onwards, it was the individual victim of crime, or someone acting on his or her behalf, who was of central importance. There is a tendency in some quarters to adopt a simplistic model of the law, especially in the eighteenth century, which in its crudest form sees the wealthy as the victims of crimes perpetrated by the poor. The vast bulk of people tried in the courts of England and Wales came from the poorer sections of society, but victims/prosecutors were a diverse group drawn not simply from the very wealthy but also from the 'middling sorts' and the working classes. In late eighteenth-century Essex, roughly one-third of all prosecutions at quarter sessions were brought by farmers, and a similar proportion by tradesmen and artisans.[44] Of the remaining third, 7 per cent were brought by members of the gentry and professional classes, while over 20 per cent were brought by those categorized as husbandmen and labourers. When assault cases alone are considered, the number of cases brought by this latter group rises to almost 30 per cent of all prosecutions. Such evidence runs contrary to Hay's influential interpretation and lends support to the assertion made by Brewer and Styles that the law was a 'multi-use right available to most English men'.[45]

Other evidence from the first half of the nineteenth century confirms the broad picture. In Sussex, just over a quarter of all victims appearing at the quarter sessions were shopkeepers or merchants, about a fifth were farmers but some 13 per cent were labourers. In Gloucestershire, the pattern was somewhat different, with 25 per cent of all victims at assize and quarter session combined being shopkeepers, 20 per cent farmers and a further 14 per cent householders. Labourers, although accounting for about 10 per cent of all victims in the early nineteenth century, accounted for only 6 per cent over the period from 1815 to 1850 as a whole. In London, during the same period, shopkeepers accounted for an even greater proportion, almost 50 per cent of victims at the Old Bailey.[46]

Employers and tradesmen made considerable, if selective, use of the Metropolitan police courts. Industrial theft was no less a problem in London, particularly in the docks, than in the industrial heartlands of England and Wales. In the late 1850s and 1860s, employers accounted for between a fifth and a quarter of all prosecutions, with small employers accounting for the bulk of these prosecutions. Tradesmen accounted for a slightly higher proportion, in excess of one in four of the total, while members of the working classes accounted for almost as many as employers as a whole. The fact that employers accounted for a substantial proportion of prosecutions is, in one respect, to be expected, but their unwillingness to resort to the courts is somewhat surprising. It is abundantly clear that in London in the second half of the nineteenth century there was a considerable degree of discretion used by victims in a manner that is more reminiscent of eighteenth-century practices. A variety of responses were to be found, ranging from the turning of a blind eye to the use of informal sanctions, most notably dismissal. Equally striking is the relatively high percentage of prosecutions brought by members of the working classes. This does not necessarily mean that there was a greater acceptance of and therefore greater willingness to use the courts in these years. Again, it would appear to be the case that the use of formal sanctions coexisted with the use of a variety of informal sanctions. The contrast which some historians have indicated between the attitude of the working classes towards the law in the early and late nineteenth century may well be overdrawn.[47]

A slightly different picture, reflecting different economic circumstances, emerges from the evidence of the Black Country in the mid-nineteenth century. Victims of crime tried at the Black Country quarter sessions in Staffordshire and Worcestershire were drawn from all sections of society. Unsurprisingly, retailers were the most frequent victims, accounting for between a quarter and a third of the total, and also the most frequent prosecutors. A second, and equally predictable, group of victims and prosecutors were the local industrialists. However, whereas large numbers of retailers continued to prosecute on their own behalf in the mid-nineteenth century, this was not the case with industrialists. Indeed, at the 1851 Worcestershire

Quarter Sessions, only 5 per cent did so. The figures also reveal a significant minority of victims and prosecutors drawn from the ranks of the skilled and unskilled manual workers.[48] Nonetheless, if working-class prosecutors remained a not uncommon feature of the courts, the advent of the new police did affect the overall pattern of prosecution, albeit slowly.

In conclusion, the overall picture that emerges is a complex one. In a number of important ways the courts changed in the period under review. The old oral confrontation between accused and defendant was replaced by the longer confrontation of prosecution and defence lawyers. Rules of evidence changed, the rights of the defendant were strengthened and the role of the judge altered. And yet in other respects there was a striking degree of continuity. The essential features of the adversarial approach remained.

It is clear that the context in which the law operated changed significantly over the course of the long nineteenth century. However, it is difficult to accept Rudé's claim that we see 'the replacement of one class system of justice by another; an aristocratic system geared to the land by one created in the image of a commercial and manufacturing middle class'.[49] There was never an old system of justice simply devoted to the interests of the aristocracy, or a new one reflecting the needs of the bourgeoisie. The middling sorts and some members of the labouring classes used the courts in the late eighteenth century. True there were numerous cases that were dealt with unofficially, but the courts were not perceived as the sole preserve of the propertied classes. Furthermore, in the mid- and late nineteenth century the pattern of multi-usage continues but many discretionary practices persisted. However, if prosecutors were drawn from a wider socioeconomic background than was once thought, it remains the case that the vast majority of the prosecuted came from the working classes. The concern with and action on crime was largely focused on the perceived illegalities of working-class life; white-collar crime was not prosecuted with the same vigour.

7

CAPITAL PUNISHMENT IN THEORY AND PRACTICE

While there was unanimity that convicted criminals should be punished, there were marked differences about why and how this should be done. The purpose of punishment or, more accurately, of the balance of punishment, was much disputed. Three different elements need to be distinguished: the retributive, the deterrent and the reformative. The idea of retribution is perhaps the oldest, but it would be misleading to see it simply as a 'primitive' attitude, diminishing in importance over time. The idea that punishment expresses 'society's' disapproval of crime and is the means whereby the criminal repays his debt to society for the crime that he or she has committed was a powerful and continuing one. As James Fitzjames Stephen put it, 'the sentence of law is to the moral sentiment of the public in relation to any offence what a seal is to hot wax'.[1] A second consideration was the deterrent effect of punishment. The sight of a corpse dangling at the rope's end or the knowledge that a long prison sentence was the fate of the nineteenth-century criminal was intended to deter the ordinary citizen from straying into criminal behaviour. The theatre of the gallows in the eighteenth century was seen to be a means whereby ordinary men and women could be made vividly aware of the consequences of criminal behaviour and thereby deterred from committing such acts by the 'aweful' consequences displayed before their eyes. The idea that punishment should deter persisted: 'hard labour, hard fare and a hard bed' was the late nineteenth-century formula. Thirdly, and increasingly from the late eighteenth century onwards, the reformative aspect of punishment was advocated. Whether through revelation or rationality, prisoners were to be transformed by the experience of prison. Not surprisingly, there has been a continuing, and often bitter, dispute, particularly between those who saw the reform of the criminal as the prime purpose of punishment and those who emphasized retribution and/or deterrence. Any evaluation of punishment must take into account its various and not always compatible aims.

The situation is further complicated by the fact that punishment takes place within a social and political context, which itself changed markedly over time, and serves wider social and political purposes. For Durkheim punishment served to create a sense of solidarity in society; for Marx (or those working within a broadly defined Marxist tradition) it was intimately related to the class structure of society; for Foucault, punishment also served as a means of political domination; and for Elias it was part of a wider 'civilizing process'.

Finally, the form of punishment changed dramatically in the period under review. The death penalty was prescribed for a varied and increasing number of offences in the eighteenth century. In practice relatively few men and women were executed and transportation, initially to the American colonies and later to the antipodes, emerged as the major form of secondary punishment. In contrast, by the mid-nineteenth century the scope of capital punishment had become confined, to all intents and purposes, to the crime of murder, transportation had been abolished and imprisonment was the dominant form of secondary punishment. To explain such a change requires a multicausal approach. The emergence of the prison, a shorthand for the changes that took place, cannot be explained simply in terms of the advance of humanitarianism, the emergence of capitalism or any other single factor. On the contrary, it is precisely the interplay between different elements, at both macro and micro level, which helps us understand the complex processes whereby 'modern' punishment emerged and developed.

Capital Punishment

For centuries English men and women were hanged for a variety of criminal offences. Death was seen as an appropriate and just form of punishment and the gallows had a practical and symbolic significance in the overall justice system. While in hindsight eighteenth-century justice might appear 'occasionally picturesque but thoroughly irrational', there was a rationale behind the system that was accepted by the majority. Although various critics of capital punishment were always to be found, they formed a small if vociferous minority and there was nothing inevitable about the reduction in the number of capital offences or in the abolition of public executions. The confident march of progress, which an earlier generation of Whiggish historians discerned, now appears a more faltering and uncertain progression.

Justification for the execution of those guilty of murder was easy to find in the Mosaic code of the Old Testament. God's words to Noah in Genesis were clear: 'whoso sheddeth man's blood, by man will his blood be shed'. As William Cobbett was to put it in 1823, 'The Law of God is clear: the murderer is always positively excluded from any and from all mitigation of punishment . . . He shall surely be put to death'.[2] The situation was less clear-cut as regards offences against property. The Mosaic law did not define these as capital offences but in the writings of certain clerics, such as Gilbert Burnet, Joseph Butler and William Paley,[3] and philosophers, most notably John Locke, a justification was devised. Burnet's *Exposition* on the Thirty-Nine Articles, published in 1699, argued that the Mosaic code provided 'full justification' for the use of capital punishment to defend the property of individuals from 'violent aggressors', while Locke's assertion, in his *Second Treatise of Government*, that the state had 'no other end but the preservation of property' was used to justify the use of any manner of protection, including capital punishment, without infringing the rights of the individual. Thus, whether justified in religious or secular terms, the death penalty was seen as a legitimate weapon for the state to use in the defence of society from the threat posed by those who attacked either property or the person.

The use of the death penalty was intended to serve a variety of purposes. In the first instance, it was a fitting punishment for those who had threatened the social order and was necessary to preserve the greater good of society as a whole.[4] The criminal was seen as a diseased part of the body politic and execution was the necessary removal of that diseased part to ensure the continued good health of society. It is no coincidence that assize sermons, and other writings on the subject, abound with phrases like 'as in the natural body . . . so in the body politic'. Society was seen to be analogous to the human body in that the component parts were interrelated and interdependent and the health of the whole was dependent upon the well-being and proper functioning of those components. Where an individual part was seen as diseased or malfunctioning the solution lay in excision. As one writer in the 1730s succinctly expressed it: 'the corrupt members of a community must be cut off by the sword of justice, lest by delay and impunity the malignant disease spread further, and the whole be infected'.[5]

However, if society, as a whole, was protected by the 'amputation' of diseased parts, the victim, as well as contributing to the greater good in losing his life, also was given the opportunity of redemption. Chaplains and prison missionaries were key figures in the short time between the passing of the death sentence and its execution. Not to save the soul of the condemned through true confession would have been construed as a failure on their part. James Cook, a Leicestershire murderer, on finally confessing to his crime, was consoled by a Miss Payne, one of his prison missionaries, with the following words:

> Be assured you will suffer; that you must stand before an earthly tribunal, and that it is impossible that you should be found other than guilty and worthy of death. But though the justice of man absolutely requires your forfeited life, the mercy of God offers you eternal life and pardon, if you can believe.[6]

Confession, while important to the individual, was important in a wider sense. The message of the gallows depended, in theory if not always in practice, upon the condemned person making a public acknowledgment of his guilt, delivering words of warning to the assembled crowd to prevent them from making the mistakes that he or she had made, and thus dying truly repentant. The formulaic final words of the convict, exhorting the reading of the Bible and obedience to parents, played a part in the deterrent function of public execution. If punishment were to be exemplary – and eighteenth-century wisdom stressed that the ordinary man or woman learnt only by example – then it had to be public. Quite literally, justice was seen to be done as the condemned individual was executed. Here could be seen the awful majesty of the law. Terror was of the essence. There was no idea of the proportionality of punishment. Individuals were to live in fear of both divine and secular judgment and, in ideal circumstances, 'the terror should be sufficient to prevent the evil' and thus 'the punishment [of death] should extend to none'.[7] Terror was to be reinforced or enhanced by uncertainty. There was no intention of hanging all criminals who had been sentenced to death. A selective approach to execution not only emphasized the discernment and magnanimity of the ruling elite but also added to the sense of terror as no one could be certain who would be selected to fulfil the sacrificial role.

Over the course of the eighteenth century there was a marked increase in the number of capital offences so that, by the early nineteenth century, their number had risen from around 50 to somewhere in excess of 200, although the precise number eluded both contemporaries and later historians. The reasons for this increase are varied. The Black Act of 1723, passed at a time of considerable political uncertainty, created at least 50 distinct capital offences. Indeed, if the different categories of person committing each offence is taken into account, the number of capital offences created rises to over 200. Of more significance was the removal of 'benefit of clergy' from a number of old offences and the creation of new, non-clergyable, capital offences.

Benefit of clergy was of fundamental importance to the working of the criminal justice system. It was, in effect, the widespread (and widely accepted) fiction whereby the harshness of the common law rule that almost all felonies were capital offences was tempered. Originally arising out of the claims of churchmen to be tried in ecclesiastical courts, even for secular offences, it had been secularized in the late Middle Ages. The application of a literacy, or more accurately, a memory test led to a sharp increase in the number of eligible persons.[8] By the late fifteenth century all offences, with only minor exceptions, were clergyable. However, this was to change, first in the early sixteenth century and again in the late seventeenth and early eighteenth centuries. Tudor legislation removed the benefit of clergy from all forms of murder, rape, highway robbery, piracy, burglary, theft from a house and theft from the person to the value of above 1s (5p). This process of reducing the number of offences for which benefit of clergy could be claimed continued in post-Restoration years, with legislation operating in two distinct ways. The first was by stipulating aggravating circumstances. Theft committed burglariously thus became a non-clergyable capital offence. The second was by decreasing the clergyable amount. An act of 1699 removed clergy from shop-theft of goods valued at 5s (25p) or above, while further legislation in 1713 made the theft of goods valued at £2 or more from a dwelling house non-clergyable.[9]

The eighteenth century also saw the creation of new, non-clergyable offences. Many of these were associated with new forms of property, but others dealt with articles previously considered not capable of being stolen, including objects fixed to buildings and the soil as well as animals of 'base nature' such as ferrets and dogs and animals *ferae naturae* such as hares, conies and fish. The expansion of capital offences took place in a ramshackle and unsystematic fashion. The absence of careful classification led to a multiplicity of capital offences being created as legislation was passed largely as a result of argument by analogy. Thus, by way of example, there was an act making it a capital offence to damage or deface Westminster Bridge and a further act, specifying the same crime and the same penalty, for Fulham Bridge. The application of general principles would have reduced the total number of capital offences but the introduction of a single act, for example dealing with bridges, would not have had a significantly different practical effect from the variety of acts passed to protect specified bridges.

An increase in the number of capital offences did not necessarily mean an increase in the number of people hanged. Indeed, as many commentators noted in the late eighteenth century, and afterwards, there was a paradox in the fact that relatively fewer people were actually executed at a time when the Bloody Code had become considerably more sanguinary. It might be imagined that the virtues of uncertainty would lead to a random application of the death penalty. This does not seem to have been the case. To the contrary, it would appear that careful attention was paid to the nature of the crime, the overall state of order (or disorder) and, most importantly, the character of the criminal and his position in the community in deciding upon a verdict.[10]

The nature of the offence clearly played an important part in the decision-making process. Highway robbers and burglars were twice as likely to be hanged as mere horse thieves. Evidence of premeditation or aggravating circumstances, such as the use of violence, increased the likelihood of a capital conviction. Even more so did a past criminal record or other evidence of 'bad' character. Age would also seem to have played a part. In Essex at least, those under 18 years of age and those over 35 years were less severely treated than those in their twenties or early thirties. Roughly a quarter of all under-18-year-olds and one-third of all over-35-year-olds sentenced to death actually went to the gallows. In contrast, for those in their twenties sentenced to death, the figure was three in five, while for those in their early thirties it was two in three. The reasons for this pattern are not entirely clear. The belief that a young man, not yet hardened by crime, was redeemable played a part.[11] So too did more pragmatic considerations. A healthy adolescent was an attractive proposition for the recipients of transportees, while an older man could well have had a large number of dependents, the upkeep of whom would have fallen on the parish in the event of his untimely demise.

Great effort was made to take into account the particularities of each crime and of each criminal. The judge's report on Peter Ogler in 1786 noted that his offence 'appeared to have been done from the pressure of great distress'. Ann Halford was recommended for pardon because 'she had seven children who might become chargeable to the parish and it was her first offence' while the splendidly named Rose Pluckrose, who pleaded in defence that she had 'a bad husband and three children ready to starve with hunger', was found guilty of stealing money valued at 10*d*, notwithstanding the fact that she had been indicted for stealing 5*s* 6*d* and at the trial the prosecutor 'fully proved the fact'.[12] In contrast, Thomas Heathwood was refused clemency because, in the word of the judge's report, he had 'no extenuating plea of necessity'. Similarly, William Rose, a farmer leasing some 100 acres, was left to hang in 1784 because of his wealth.[13] Economic circumstances were an important consideration, but less so than the character of the accused. First-time offenders were looked upon more leniently, while the chances of a favourable response were further enhanced by character references from people of high social status who could attest to the previous sobriety, trustworthiness and industriousness of the accused.[14]

Such verdicts came be interpreted in a number of ways. Hay has emphasized the ideological importance of the use of discretionary powers to uphold the position and reputation of a small elite. He claims that 'the rulers of England [were able] to make the courts a selective instrument of class justice, yet simultaneously to proclaim the law's incorruptible impartiality, and absolute determinacy'.[15] Thus the use of discretion enabled the ruling class to both terrorize and to command the gratitude of the petty thief. The use of discretion helped to maintain an unequal and deferential society, but there is a danger of adopting an oversimplified and overcynical point of view. The courts were not the preserve of the privileged few. Moreover, juries and judges tried to deliver justice by considering the peculiarities of individual cases. The notion of a highly individualistic and discretionary system of justice may have offended early nineteenth-century reformers but it had a rationale that was appropriate to the relatively small, face-to-face, communities of the age and thus acceptable to large numbers of people in mid- and late eighteenth-century society.

It is important to set the Bloody Code and its operation in context, but there is a danger of creating a new myth of an efficient and widely respected system of justice. This was not the case. From the last decades of the eighteenth century onwards, and particularly after the ending of the Napoleonic wars, there were growing signs that the system was beginning to collapse under its own weight. The upsurge in prosecutions that underpinned the spectacular growth in the recorded crime rate meant that far greater numbers were being sentenced to death. To keep the numbers hanged at an acceptable (and practicable) level, it was necessary to increase the percentage of those reprieved. But any judicial system that reprieved 95 per cent of those it condemned to death was open to criticism. The fact that justice (from trial to pardon) was seen to be dispensed at times in an arbitrary fashion heightened concern, particularly as these strains appeared at a time when new ideas were beginning to challenge the philosophical basis of the old system.

Having seen a substantial increase in the number of capital offences over the course of the eighteenth century, there was to be a sharp and relatively rapid reversal of this trend in the early and mid-nineteenth century.

The pattern of change is well known. Pressures for change had been building up for some years. The 1819 Select Committee on Criminal Law marked an important departure. In 1820, capital punishment was abolished for shoplifting, theft, the sending of threatening letters and the destruction of silk or cloth in a loom or on a frame, and three years later the Waltham Black Act was repealed. A further stimulus to change came later in the 1830s from the Royal Commission on the Criminal Law. Various forms of animal theft, housebreaking, burglary from a dwelling-house, coining and forgery ceased to be capital offences. By the early 1840s, when rape was no longer punishable by death, there were only seven capital offences, and 20 years later there were only four, though effectively it was only for murder that people were hanged.

Robert Peel had emerged as a central figure in the reforms of the 1820s and the process of reform was given further impetus by his Whig successors, but this is not to say that there was a seamless progression from the reforms of the 1820s to the 1830s. To the contrary, Peel's reforms were a rationalization to restore credibility to the law and prevent further, more radical change. The Whig–radical reforms of the 1830s were an unpicking of this compromise and a move to more far-reaching change. Whatever the precise reasons, the chronology of change is impressive. In a matter of years the old hanging regime effectively collapsed and was replaced by an alternative centred on the prison.

Much emphasis has been put on the contribution of new beliefs in the amelioration of the penal code, but this may reflect more the importance attached to ideas by academics than the realities of practical politics. New ideas were in circulation from the late eighteenth century onwards. Beccaria's *Dei Delitti e delle Pene* was first published in 1764 and was soon translated, albeit imperfectly, into English.[16] The notion of proportionality of punishment was accompanied by a new view of the relationship between the individual and society which reversed earlier beliefs in the primacy of society over the individual. A number of Whig–radical reformers soon became acquainted with Beccaria's ideas and used them in their campaign for changes in the criminal law. Rationalists, including a growing number of barristers and attorneys,[17] highlighted the absurdities and inefficiencies of the existing order. The severity of punishment deterred prosecutions, and juries were unwilling to return guilty verdicts, while executions failed to deter and corrupted those who watched the grisly spectacle. In similar vein, radicals with a more overt anti-oligarchical political agenda joined in the debate. The dramatic increase in the volume of debate in the opening decades of the nineteenth century was fuelled by a number of executions of women. Advocates of the emerging new chivalry seized upon such wronged women as Eliza Fenning, who was executed in 1815, to publicize their cause.[18]

Although defenders and critics of the status quo had a common desire to establish (or restore) respect for the law which, in turn, would bring protection for both person and property, differences emerged when principles and practices were discussed. The stern, pro-hanging arguments from the late eighteenth century, associated most particularly with Archdeacon William Paley and the ever-zealous Martin Madan, were still to be heard in the 1820s and enjoyed support in important quarters. Arch-conservatives, notably Lords Ellenborough and Eldon, spoke unashamedly in the language of the old order. Other conservatives emphasized the wisdom and efficacy of the existing system and most notably its emphasis on a personal system of justice in which the discretion and benevolence of individuals was central. For them the new proposals advocated by self-styled reformers, the inflexible and invariable tariff of punishment, threatened to be more inhumane and less just. Reformers, such as Romilly, rejected the idea of such personal justice, seeing it, at best, as outdated and appropriate only to a small-town world that was fast disappearing and, at worst, as uncertain, unjust and inefficient, if not counterproductive, and carrying the potential for tyrannical control.[19] At the same time as wanting an impersonal and impartial system of justice, the reformers brought a new concept of the relationship between the individual and society, and new ideas about punishment based on the belief in proportionality and the deterrent effect of certain punishment and on the belief of the redeemability of the individual through an 'enlightened' prison regime.

The importance of humanitarian concerns must not be overstated. It is tempting to see the amelioration of the penal code as a triumph for 'civilization' over 'barbarism', but there is a grave danger of misrepresenting early nineteenth-century thinking on the subject. Hanging may well appear barbarous to late twentieth-century eyes (though recent events particularly but not exclusively in America raise doubts about this judgement), but that does not mean that it offended early nineteenth-century sensibilities. Few may have shared Boswell's enthusiasm for executions as practised in Rome,[20] but more probably shared the concerns of Carlyle and Dickens over the 'mawkish sentimentality' of opponents of capital punishment. Similarly, there is a danger of overstating the extent and consistency of evangelical opposition to the Bloody Code.[21]

Attitudes were gradually changing. The unembarrassed curiosity of the mid-eighteenth century had gone and attendance at an execution had to be justified in terms of its 'grand moral example' or of the benefits of literally facing 'man's inevitable fate'. In addition, in a more general sense, attitudes towards violence were changing. New notions of masculinity were developing which placed greater emphasis on caring and protecting the weak and unfortunate in society. It is no coincidence that the language of the argument against duelling – seen as another form of gratuitous violence – was to be repeated a decade or so later in the attack on the widespread use of the death penalty. Such sentiments do not immediately translate into a humane concern for the victim of a hanging, but there was a growing disquiet with the violence that was being inflicted on behalf of 'civilized' society.

Of greater importance was the growing concern with the behaviour of the crowd. The theatre of the gallows required not simply the condemned criminal but also the crowd to play its part. An unruly and disrespectful crowd would not hold the law in due awe and would not derive the appropriate lesson from the appearance of the condemned at the gallows and his or her final words of warning. Concerns with the attitudes and actions of the crowd were not new. In 1725, Mandeville had been critical of the drunken condition of criminals on the way to Tyburn and of the violent behaviour of the mob surrounding the gallows. Similar complaints surfaced throughout the century but criticisms of the crowd intensified in the early nineteenth century as executions, particularly in London, became highly commercialized affairs. Romilly seized upon this issue. In his view, spectators at an execution saw the death of an individual rather than the punishment of a prisoner. Rather than departing in awe of the law, they were more likely to be brutalized and incited to crime by the experience. This latter point was forcefully argued by Dickens, writing to the *Daily News* in July 1840 about the crowd at the execution of Courvoisier. He condemned the absence of 'one emotion suitable to the occasion'. As far as he could see, there was 'no sorrow, no salutary terror, no abhorrence, no seriousness; nothing but the ribaldry, debauchery, levity, drunkenness and flaunting vice in fifty other shapes'. But even worse was to be seen at the double hanging of the Mannings in 1849.[22] He found himself surrounded by 'thieves, low prostitutes, ruffians and vagabonds of every kind' whose behaviour was a 'tumultuous demonstration of indecent delight' who were 'so odious in their brutal mirth or callousness' that Dickens felt ashamed.[23]

It is not easy to assess the growth and impact of 'opinion' on the hanging question. Old attitudes died hard; new concerns were often limited in their focus and inconsistently advocated; other questions were more pressing than reform of the capital code. For these reasons one should avoid the tempting but simplistic belief in a march of progress, a civilizing tide sweeping all before it. However, not all remained the same. In the 50 years between the 1770s and the 1820s unthinkable beliefs were transformed into self-evident truths. 'That English criminal law was capable not only of cruelty but also of injustice had entered the realm of the thinkable, the sayable and even the *known*.'[24] The emergence of 'opinion' was facilitated by the growth of the press and the expansion of a politically minded reading public, but in itself was not sufficient to bring change. Contrary opinions were firmly held and many of the more conservatively minded members of the elite were openly hostile to and dismissive of the views of the early nineteenth-century 'chattering classes'. Others, notably Peel, were well aware of the limitations of public opinion. And yet there was no escaping the fact that, particularly in the years after 1815, the Bloody Code was beginning to lose credibility.

Despite this growth of criticism, circumstances were not that propitious for reform. The strength of conservatism in general and of judicial conservatism in particular was considerable. However, in spite of the continuing commitment to Paleyite sentiments, there was a desire to preserve, or recover, the good reputation of the law. Further, there was scope to accommodate or adjust to those changes in 'perceptions and sensibility' to such an extent that an old order that rejected the idea of proportionality in punishment could be transformed into a new order based on starkly different principles. The scope for discussion and change was increased by the presence of a conservative figure like Peel at the helm.

Pragmatic and party-political considerations were also in Peel's mind when he set about reforming the criminal code. Aware of the criticisms that were coming from Whig–radical reformers, his reforms were as much a defensive response, that is intended to prevent more far-reaching reforms, as a positive response to the perceived inadequacies of the existing law. That said, Peel was aware of the ramshackle nature of the criminal law and shared the concern with restoring the credibility and effectiveness of the law. Thus an important element of Peel's reforms was the removal of capital offences, such as defacing Westminster Bridge, that had fallen into disuse. Superficially, the changes were impressive, as Peel himself pointed out: some 278 acts were repealed and replaced by a mere eight. However, the practical effects were less dramatic. The main hanging offences remained, as Peel intended, and the number going to the gallows was not dramatically changed: 46 people were hanged in 1824, that is, before Peel's reforms came into effect, and 46 suffered the same fate in 1830.[25]

Peel's attempt at stabilizing the existing order through judicious pruning was to prove in vain. The electoral success of the Whigs paved the way for more far-reaching reforms. Russell, the new Home Secretary, asked the criminal law commissioners to report their findings on capital offences. This they did in a series of reports that have been seen as an embodiment of the new thinking and a major spur to reform. The second report, published in 1836, argued that 'the ordinary enforcement of penal laws of so indiscriminate a character [was] impracticable'. A criminal code that resulted in the 'hungry pauper' suffering the same fate as a member of a 'gang of ruffians' was open to abuse and brought the system into disrepute. The commissioners drew attention to perversions of justice where prosecutors and witnesses had connived together, suppressed facts and coloured evidence 'to secure the escape of the offender'. But, as well as highlighting the practical inefficiencies of the existing system, the report contained a lengthy refutation of Paley's arguments.[26] The old order disappeared rapidly thereafter.

With the dramatic reduction in the number of capital offences, it was only a matter of time before total abolition was considered. Quakers such as Joseph Gurney had argued the case in the early part of the century, as had Jeremy Bentham in 1831, but the Whig government, although determined to narrow the range of capital offences, was not prepared to countenance such a radical suggestion. Influential support grew. J. S. Mill and, somewhat reluctantly, Thomas Carlyle espoused the total abolition cause in the 1840s. *Punch*, founded in 1841 and under the editorship of Douglas Jerrold, publicized the case for abolition, as did *Fraser's Magazine* and the *Spectator* while, in a series of letters to the *Daily News* in 1846, Charles Dickens, for the time being at least, gave his support. In the same year the Society for the Abolition of Capital Punishment was founded by, among others, two members of parliament, Charles Gilpin and William Ewart.

Although support for abolition was growing, it never had majority support, even within self-styled enlightened circles. An anonymous writer put the retentionist case in trenchant terms, arguing

that the number of persons executed is numerically insignificant and it affects the most atrocious criminals in the community; that the corrupting effect of public executions has nothing to do with the question of capital punishment ... that the alleged fascination of the gallows is purely nonsense; that the preventive effects of executions is silent and extensive; that it is effective as a prevention, on the authority of facts and figures which defy refutation; that the contrary has been maintained by misstatements of the result of the previous abolition of capital punishments; and lastly, we have shown that the authority of Scripture, if not in favour of executions, is at least nowise against them.[27]

Ewart introduced total abolition bills into the House of Commons on three occasions, in 1847, 1848 and 1850, where the most able champion was John Bright, who spoke forcefully against 'this last vestige of barbaric punishment'. Support, however, was limited. Accusations of 'Quaker feelings', effeminacy and of a softness towards criminals were levelled by critics, including leading Whigs such as Macaulay. By the late 1840s it was clear that the tide of sentiment was beginning to run against the abolitionists with erstwhile supporters such as Dickens, Carlyle and Mill changing their minds and becoming powerful critics of the abolitionists.

For proponents of abolition, and indeed more so for their opponents, the issue was confused by the growing concern with public executions. Dickens, writing in *The Times*, condemned the gruesome spectacle of public execution, but refused to raise 'the abstract question of capital punishment'. Others could not or would not see the distinction and there was a growing fear among the defenders of hanging that the revulsion against public executions would sweep them away and capital punishment as well. Accordingly, the sanitizing of executions became of paramount importance and, when this strategy was exhausted, the privatizing of execution was seen as the way to preserve capital punishment.[28]

Gallows crowds posed considerable threats to people and property. When John Holloway was executed in 1807 there was a crowd outside Newgate estimated at 45 000 people. In the crush that ensued, 27 people were killed and over a hundred injured. Worse, for many educated critics, was the behaviour of the crowd. To make matters worse still, the entrepreneurial zeal with which executions were exploited added to the overall sense of unseemliness. The sale of last speeches (wonderfully similar in terms of both text and illustrations!) and of gingerbread effigies had a long pedigree, but in the mid-nineteenth century mass-produced figurines of celebrated murderers were to be found on sale. Worse still was the practice of certain railway companies in offering cheap excursions to view a hanging.

The initial response to this concern was to do away with some of the worst features of existing practice. The fate of William Jobling in 1832 led to the abolition of gibbeting two years later. The murder of a local justice of the peace had aroused strong feelings, but Jobling, a minor accessory, was unfortunate to be sentenced to death as the murderer was known but had escaped. His body was gibbeted at the Jarrow stake, to which large crowds were attracted. The spectacle provided a golden opportunity for local boat owners who took eager sightseers to view the corpse. The enterprise finally collapsed when Jobling's family, in desperation, stole the body for burial. However, such was the revulsion at this 'unseemly' spectacle that, from

1834 onwards, the practice of exhibiting the corpses of executed criminals was abandoned and all corpses were to be buried in prison ground.

Such peripheral and cosmetic changes had little impact. The fact remained that hanging was, for a growing number of people, a brutal act that shocked educated sensibilities and, furthermore, attracted a crowd which itself behaved in a dangerous and depraved manner. Hanging was not a precise science, despite the introduction of the 'drop'. The worst scenes of slow strangulation disappeared but a miscalculation on the part of the executioner could lead to strangulation if the drop was overshort or decapitation if overlong. The execution of women was distressing in most circumstances, but the sight of Sarah Thomas being dragged struggling and screaming to her death by six warders aroused great concern. Bungled executions further added to public unease. In one particularly horrific incident, in 1856, the unfortunate William Bousefield succeeded in raising himself back to the platform after the drop had been opened. Having failed to push the man to his death, the inebriated executioner, the notorious and much-vilified Calcraft, finally threw himself bodily upon Bousefield and the two men disappeared into the pit.

Crowd control, especially for popular executions in London, was difficult. When five pirates were executed in February 1864, for mutiny and the murder of their captain and five fellow crew members of the *Flowery Land*, the crowd, whose size owed much to the improved transport facilities of the Metropolitan Underground railway, required a massive police presence: 300 constables, 37 sergeants and seven inspectors of the City of London Force were joined by 800 Metropolitan policemen for the day. The behaviour of the crowd that had so shocked Dickens when the Mannings were brought to execution was repeated in 1864, when Franz Muller was executed. Anti-German sentiment was strongly in evidence, and rival groups in the crowd – finally estimated at about 50 000 – kept up a barrage of jeers and songs throughout the night. The growing body of feeling was summed up in the evidence of a Dorset rector, the Revd S.G. Osborne, to the Wilberforce Committee of 1856. The gallows crowd was made up of

the very scum of mankind, who go again and again to such scenes, each time to pollute the very air with their fearful language, people to whom it is a sort of gala day, men and women blaspheming, singing obscene songs, with half drunken jollity coming to riot below the gallows, departing to follow the life that leads to it, viewing the scene without one single display of one feeling that evinces sympathy with the law, screaming a kind of fiend's welcome to the hangman ... groaning at, or, in their own way, encouraging the 'victim', ordering 'hat's off' to 'death', but damning each other's souls, – as they look upon it.[29]

Public executions clearly did not have a deterrent effect. The Wilberforce Committee had amassed a large volume of evidence to this effect in 1856, including the 'expert' evidence of such figures as John Clay, the long-serving and highly respected chaplain at the Preston House of Correction.[30] In other circles influential figures, including the Home Secretary, Sir George Grey, were expressing their opposition to public executions. In 1864, a Royal Commission was established to consider the question and came to the conclusion that the practice should be terminated. The Clerkenwell bomber, Michael Barratt, was publicly executed on 26 May 1868. Three days later, the Law of Capital Punishment Amendment Act, which abolished public executions, was passed, and on 13 August 18-year-old Thomas Wells, dressed in his railway porter's uniform, became the first person to be executed behind prison walls when he was hanged in Maidstone Gaol. Contrary to the claims of historians such as David Cooper, the abolition of public hanging was not part of an onward march of humanitarianism. In so far as the 1868 act was a triumph, it was a triumph over the vulgar crowd which had been excluded from the spectacle because of their persistent bad behaviour.

The abolition of public executions clarified another matter. The debate between abolitionists, and retentionists was no longer confused by consideration of the location of the execution itself. For abolitionists, the decision to abandon public executions was a mixed blessing. They could not but welcome the removal of an outdated and barbarous practice, but they were well aware that, as hanging disappeared behind prison walls, so the debate on capital punishment was likely to slip from public attention. Difficulties had been apparent during the work of the 1864 Royal Commission. Although four of the 12 members were committed to total abolition, they were unable to advance their cause.

Retentionist arguments were forcefully expressed in a variety of quarters. J. F. Stephen had no doubt about the matter:

no other punishment deters men so effectually from committing murder ... no other punishment gratifies and justifies in so emphatic a measure the vindictive sentiment, the existence of which is one of the greatest safeguards against crime ... no other way of disposing of great criminals is equally effectual, appropriate and cheap.[31]

Stephen was caustic in his condemnation of Quakerism and argued that

> The toleration of what ought not to be tolerated is nearly as great an evil
> as the persecution of what ought to be tolerated. There is as much moral
> cowardice in shrinking from the execution of a murderer, as in hesitating
> to blow out the brains of a foreign invader.[32]

Abolitionists had been thrown into disarray by the death of William Ewart
in 1867, but the weakness of their position was starkly revealed in 1868
during debate on the report and recommendations of the Royal Commission.
Murder was viewed as a peculiarly heinous crime which, by its very nature,
required the ultimate punishment. J. S. Mill, once an abolitionist, spoke
against the abolitionist amendment. Openly scornful of humanitarian arguments, Mill claimed that capital punishment for murder demonstrated
respect for human life: 'we show most emphatically our regard for it
[human life] by the adoption of a rule that he who violates that right in
another forfeits it for himself'. Furthermore, he argued, the death penalty
was the only true deterrent, even though, as he somewhat inconsistently continued, life imprisonment was worse than execution. Mill was confident that
there would be no miscarriages of justice. Indeed, if there were a problem it
was that 'our rules of evidence are too favourable to the offenders' – a sentiment that was echoed by other speakers. More generally, in language reminiscent of Macaulay in the 1840s, he concluded that abolition would have a
serious and detrimental effect on the spirit of the nation. It would, he told
parliament, bring 'an enervation, an effeminacy in the general mind of the
country. For what else but effeminacy is it to be much more shocked by
taking a man's life than by depriving him of all that makes life desirable
or valuable?'[33]

Hopes of total abolition effectively died in 1868. Attempts were made in
1872, 1877 and again in 1878, but on each occasion abolitionist bills were
heavily defeated. *The Times*, which had been delighted by Mill's robust
speech in 1868, editorialized, a decade later, that capital punishment was
no longer one of the 'real questions of the day'.[34]

There were still a number of scandals relating to 'unseemly' executions.
The failure to execute John Lee, despite three attempts to hang him, created
much concern as did the various stories of slow strangulation and near-
beheadings that resulted from miscalculations of the drop. However, there
was never the public outcry to compare with that of the mid-nineteenth century. The combination of private execution – the press were rarely admitted
to executions by the late 1890s – and a further sanitizing of the process of

killing meant that attention was largely focused on the appropriateness of executing specific 'problem' groups rather than on the use of the death penalty itself. Unsurprisingly, the changes that did take place before 1914 were restricted to the insane and the young.

Although capital punishment was not to be abolished until 1965, the reduction in the number of capital offences and of those executed is still striking.[35] The shift from punishing the body to punishing the mind is a crucial, if problematic, one. While not simply the product of the march of humanitarianism, there is a sense in which changing sensibilities, part of Elias' 'civilizing process', played an important part in the privatizing and sanitizing of execution. At the same time, the diminution in the use of capital punishment and the increasing use of the prison has to be set in a socioeconomic context in which a ruling elite, comprising both landowners and industrialists, sought to discipline a working class that was increasingly seen to be a threat to both property and order. Finally, a dose of realism is called for in any explanation. The pragmatic observations of a growing number of men who felt that the old Bloody Code was ineffective, if not counterproductive, were also a necessary part of the process of change.

8

SECONDARY PUNISHMENTS

Although the Bloody Code prescribed the death penalty for a wide variety of offences, there was never any intention of executing all those who were found guilty. However, some form of secondary punishment was required. The great novelty of eighteenth-century punishment was transportation; of the nineteenth-century, incarceration. These changes, and the emergence of the prison in particular, have given rise to considerable debate in two important areas which relate to the motives behind the introduction of change and to the impact of the reforms themselves.

Explanations of reform in terms of humanitarian progress have given way to more pessimistic interpretations. Marxist historians, notably Ruschke and Kirckheimer, have linked the development of the prison with the onset of the industrial revolution and the perceived need for greater controls over the poor. In an even more direct attack, Foucault challenges the 'myths of the Enlightenment' and emphasizes the shift from inflicting pain on the body to disciplining the mind of the criminal. Ignatieff, working within this framework, offers a stark reading of late eighteenth and early nineteenth-century penal reform. Revisionist interpretations have not gone without their critics, who have pointed out the difficulties of reconciling broad interpretative themes with the known chronology of change, the risk of confusing intention with outcome and the dangers of descending into conspiratorial views of society which overstate the unity and power of elite groups. Similarly, earlier optimistic interpretations of the positive effects of prison reform have been challenged by revisionists who, in turn, have been criticized for overlooking certain positive features of the new prison regimes.

Transportation

One of the peculiarities of the old penal system was the gulf that existed between capital punishment on the one hand and release upon benefit of clergy on the other. In the late seventeenth and early eighteenth centuries there was a tentative search for alternatives, driven largely by those directly concerned with passing sentence. From this background transportation emerged as the dominant secondary punishment though, even at its peak in the middle decades of the eighteenth century, there were a significant number of critics to be found. The 1718 Transportation Act was critical because it created a penal system which 'could never again operate without a centrally dominant secondary punishment'.[1] This act provided an intermediate form of punishment and although transportation, and other forms of intermediate punishment, came in for heavy criticisms there was never the suggestion that the courts should revert to past practice in which the choice was between sentence of death or release upon benefit of clergy.

Transportation, which had its origins in the earlier punishment of banishment, had been used on a limited scale in post-Restoration England. Acting on their own initiative, certain judges refused to accept claims of clergy and ordered transportation instead. However, transportation was unpopular, not least with the people in the American colonies who were the recipients, and was but one of a number of alternatives experimented with at the time. A growing body of opinion began to see distinct advantages in this form of punishment. In the language of the body politic that was common at the time, it offered an opportunity of societal cleansing. As Charles de Brosses put it, 'the political body, like the human body, has vicious humours which should be often evacuated'.[2] It was relatively cheap and it removed from society those deemed to be most dangerous. There was an element of deterrence, but it also held out the hope of a fresh start for the criminal. All in all, it was seen as an effective and acceptable means of punishing those whose crimes, while serious, did not merit the death penalty. Royal mercy could be shown without unnecessarily endangering society.

The 1718 act marked the acceptance of overall government responsibility, although the work itself was contracted out by the Treasury. It also led to a transformation in the pattern of punishment. Judges had a wider range of options and welcomed the opportunity to exercise more discretion and care in sentencing. In Surrey, in the quarter-century after the introduction of this legislation, there was a marked increase in the numbers transported. Roughly 60 per cent of non-capital punishments for men took this form, while for women the figure was 46 per cent. Despite the enthusiasm with which transportation had been used in the courts, critical voices made themselves heard, especially during and after the 1750s. It was alleged that transportation no longer held the dread that once it had. Stories of ex-criminals made good undermined the deterrent effect of punishment. Further, the advent of larger and faster boats had made America more accessible, reducing the fear of the unknown but also increasing the opportunities for criminals to return home to resume their life of crime. At least one judge in the 1760s was of the opinion that transportation had 'almost ceased to be a punishment' and there were clear signs of a diminution in its use. The ending of the transportation subsidy in 1772 was a further blow, but the initial phase of transportation was brought to an end by the outbreak of hostilities with the American colonies in 1776.

The complete loss of the dumping grounds in America was not anticipated and, accordingly, there was no government plan to deal with the emergency that developed. Transportation was no longer a practical option, in the short run at least. Consequently, a variety of short-term expedients were adopted, including the enlistment of men into the armed services. Another, the use of ex-warships known as the Hulks, was to last for a considerable time, but it was clear that an alternative longer-term policy had to be devised. The overcrowded and insanitary conditions of the highly-visible Hulks were unsatisfactory, if not downright scandalous, there were similar problems in the existing local prisons and the expense of a large-scale new prison building programme was daunting. In these circumstances, the attractions of transportation increased in the eyes of the government and its advisers. By the early 1780s, it was no longer a question of when transportation would be resumed but where. Numerous locations were suggested but found wanting. Finally, in 1786, it was decided to establish a penal colony at Botany Bay in New South Wales and the first fleet sailed in the following year.[3] Australia was to be the low-cost alternative to prison building at home. Later a link with the prison system was established with the building of Pentonville. Prisoners, selected because of their potential for reform, were to serve 18 months in separate confinement before being transported to Australia, where they immediately received a ticket-of-leave, which allowed them conditional liberty.

In excess of 160,000 people were transported on the 821 voyages that took place between 1787 and 1867. The scale of transportation increased markedly in the post-Napoleonic war years, reaching a peak in the 1830s. Initially, the development of the penal colonies was determined by the governors in Australia rather than the government in London. Consequently, conditions could vary considerably and, as contemporaries noted, the system was open to appalling abuse. Such variations explain the seemingly contradictory criticisms that surrounded transportation. The first recurring theme was the lack of deterrence, summed up in Sydney Smith's dismissive comments:

> Because you have committed this offence, the sentence of the Court is that you shall no longer be burdened with the support of your wife and family. You shall be immediately removed from a very bad climate and a country over-burdened with people to one of the finest regions of the earth, where the demand for human labour is every hour increasing, and where it is highly probable that you may ultimately regain your character and improve your future. The Court has been induced to pass this sentence upon you in consequence of the many aggravating circumstances of your case, and they hope your fate will be a warning to others.[4]

Yet other critics were appalled by what they heard of the degrading and demoralizing conditions in certain penal colonies. References to harsh conditions, barbarous regimes and 'shocking immoralities' were at the heart of this critique. In addition, the government was constantly concerned with the costs of the policy. The most far-reaching, though not impartial, critique appeared in the report of the Molesworth Committee in 1837. Amendments were introduced. The practice of assignment of convicts to free settlers was abolished and a progressive stage system, leading to the acquisition of a ticket-of-leave, was introduced. While critics were never satisfied, there were a number of influential supporters who argued for the continuation – and later the reintroduction – of transportation as the most effective and acceptable form of secondary punishment. Ultimately, the defenders of transportation were defeated. Growing opposition in the Australian states, organized by the Anti-Transportation League, emphasizing not least the demoralizing effect of transportation, began to assert itself. In Britain, influential figures, most notably Sir George Grey, shared the growing concern with transportation and were confident in the alternative of a domestic convict prison system. With the tide of opinion swinging against transportation, the shipping of convicts to Australia was first reduced and then halted. In the peak year of 1833, a total of just under 7000 men and women were transported from Britain and Ireland; a decade later the total had fallen by almost 50 per cent to just over 3700 while in 1853 the number stood at a mere 1569.[5] By 1867, despite a rearguard action by the fourth earl of Carnarvon, transportation to Australia came to an end. Attention was now focused on prisons in general and penal servitude in particular.

Prisons

The most striking development between the late eighteenth and the early twentieth centuries was in the use of prison as a means of punishment. There were two important periods of change. The first, spanning the decades of the late eighteenth and early nineteenth centuries, saw the emergence of the idea of the prison as an institution of first resort within which the criminal would be reformed; the second, spanning the decades of the late nineteenth and early twentieth centuries, saw the development of a range of alternative institutions and sentencing practices, with prison more as a last resort.[6] However, the purpose of imprisonment was to become a major and recurring source of debate between those advocating its punitive aspects and those its reformatory potential.

The prison system was never uniform. First, there were different types of institutions. The new national penitentiaries of Millbank and Pentonville coexisted with a variety of local prisons. Even after nationalization in 1877, there was a fundamental difference between the experiences in local and convict prisons. The situation was further complicated by the development in the late nineteenth and early twentieth centuries of auxiliary institutions for those who were deemed to inhabit the borderland between criminality and illness. Second, while prisons dealt mainly with adult men, there were significant minorities, notably juveniles and women, who received different treatment.

Late eighteenth-century prisons were used mainly for holding prisoners awaiting trial or execution, but the courts were already looking to prison sentences as an appropriate means of punishment in the late eighteenth century.[7] Indeed, the idea that a disciplined regime of work could be used to effect against criminally inclined vagrants and idle poor dates back to the sixteenth century. Although bridewells, or houses of correction, were theoretically distinct from gaols, the division between the two became blurred and by the early or mid-eighteenth century there were suggestions that not only petty criminals but also those responsible for serious crimes could be reclaimed, though the number of advocates remained relatively small.[8] The 'rediscovery of the prison' effectively dates from the last quarter of the eighteenth century. Traditionally, much has been made of the work of evangelical reformists who drew attention to the appalling state of England's prisons at this time. Undoubtedly, Howard's *The State of the Prisons* shocked many of its readers when it appeared in 1777, but it would be naïve to explain developments simply in terms of a humanitarian response to such findings. Howard himself was concerned with more than cleaning up prisons and more pragmatic considerations played an important part in the process of reform. Dissatisfaction with the shortcomings of the Bloody Code fuelled a debate about alternative forms of punishment, as did similar concerns with transportation, compounded by the practical difficulties following the loss of the American colonies. The use of ex-warships, the notorious 'Hulks', provided an immediate solution but, notwithstanding the length of time they remained in use, they were seen as a temporary expedient.

A new conception of the purpose of the prison began to emerge which provided 'justification and explanation' for what was already being done.[9] Hanway's advocacy of 'solitude in imprisonment, with proper profitable labour and a spare diet' exemplifies the new thinking.[10] Reformers argued for a positive role for Christianity within prisons, thereby countering the long-held belief that prisons corrupted more than they cured. Thus it was argued that prison had a positive part to play in the transformation of the errant individual. Prison, as a total institution, provided the appropriate, reformative environment in which bad was turned to good. The prison would act as a hospital for society, containing the contagion and curing the disease of criminality, and as such would play its part in that wider campaign to improve the working class. There was an optimism about mankind in these arguments. Here were purposeful individuals with a commitment to the improvement of society, who, through the institution of the prison, would exploit the perfectibility of others and 'grind men good'.[11] Such ideas were first to be found among reforming county magistrates and groups of dissenters in the late eighteenth century. This simple chronological fact is not easy to reconcile with the emphasis that both Foucault and Ignatieff have placed on the post-1815 social crisis. Further, there is little evidence to suggest that prison reformers after the Napoleonic wars sought to justify their proposals in terms of the specific problems of labour discipline facing employers. Rather, there seems to have been a fear that the old social order was breaking down as urban and industrial developments created hostile classes rather than harmonious orders. The spread of individual depravity, in this view, threatened to corrupt the industrious working classes, who needed protection. Prisons, like the reformed workhouses, were a form of social quarantine. Once again, the balance between the liberty of the individual and the security of society as a whole was the central issue. Not for the last time, a consensus emerged among an 'in' crowd of the respectable, irrespective of class, that coercive measures were necessary to meet the challenge of threatening 'outcast' groups.

There were two distinct sets of argument which, in turn, gave rise to proposals for distinct prison regimes. The first was associated with the evangelical movement. Its concern with crime and the criminal was part of a wider concern with the moral decay that threatened the world. Man's sinfulness, given greater opportunities than ever in the rapidly changing world of the late eighteenth century, threatened to destroy society. However, the forgiveness of God and the potential for redemption within man meant that disaster could be averted if only the soul of the individual could be won over to the true cause. The practical consequences of such thinking when applied to prison regimes were threefold. First, as an essential prerequisite, Christianity had to be a living presence, actively fostered by those charged with the responsibility of running prisons and influencing all aspects of prison life. Second, there was also to be the opportunity to reform the miscreant by identifying and making good his or her moral deficiencies. In practice this meant the use of solitary confinement in what was to be known as the separate system, in which criminals were isolated from their fellow convicts, thereby preventing contagion. Contact was allowed with appropriate, reforming figures, particularly the prison chaplain and, in addition, time was to be devoted to solitary contemplation and prayer. Only by giving the criminal this time alone to ponder on his or her shortcomings and to consider the mercy of God could there be a successful transformation of the individual through the rejection of old values and the internalizing of new. Third, the spiritual and moral reformation of the individual was to be buttressed by training in useful skills. Thus the criminal, having been duly punished by a term of imprisonment, would emerge as a worthy, dutiful and industrious individual fully prepared to play a positive and worthwhile part in society.

The second set of arguments was based on secular beliefs, deriving from intellectual and scientific developments of the eighteenth century which saw the universe as 'a perfect machine' inhabited by rational and perfectible individuals. The human mind was seen as a *tabla rasa* upon which values and codes of behaviour could be inscribed. Drawing on the works of philosophers such as Locke and Hume, rationalists argued that the association between experiences and sensations was fundamental in determining the attitudes and actions of the individual. The criminal was, in effect, a defectively socialized individual who had learned to associate crime with pleasure rather than pain. The application of associationism to prison meant, first and foremost, the creation of a regime in which the link between crime and pleasure would be broken and a new association, between crime and pain, established. Further, the prison regime would be devised in a way that combined both punishments and rewards so as to create new, positive and socially acceptable characteristics such as diligence and obedience. Unlike the separate system, prisoners would be allowed to associate with one another in communal work, but strict silence was to be enforced. In this, the silent system, individual reformation would be brought about as new values and new patterns of behaviour were internalized.

Advocates of reform became increasingly vocal around the turn of the nineteenth century, but there was no irresistible tide of informed opinion sweeping all before it. Enthusiasm for prison reform was strong in the 1770s and 1780s but noticeably weakened in the 1790s and 1800s, only to revive again in the post-Napoleonic war years. Nor did the new ideas go unchallenged. Late eighteenth-century critics, such as Godwin, attacked the brutalizing effects of the new regimes while others, notably Sydney Smith, advocated harsher regimes from which people would leave 'heartily wearied of their residence; and taught by sad experience to consider it the greatest misfortune of their lives to return to it'.[12] Nonetheless, as Smith recognized, by the 1820s advocates of the new prison system were winning the argument.

A Penitentiary Act, the work of William Blackstone and William Eden, passed in 1779, embodied the new thinking. Unfortunately, the act was never put into practice. However, local initiatives did take place, most notably in Sussex and Gloucestershire.[13] The two new prisons in Sussex, at Horsham and Petworth, developed distinctive regimes which foreshadowed the early nineteenth-century debate between advocates of the separate and silent systems. Local initiatives were restricted by practical considerations, notably the high costs of building new prisons. Furthermore, the practical results were not as impressive as had been hoped and thus the drive for reform lost impetus in the 1790s. However, a number of influential figures, notably Jeremy Bentham, retained their faith in the idea of the reformatory prison. They were given an opportunity as the result of Romilly's campaign against the death penalty which required an acceptable alternative to be provided. In 1810, the Holford Committee was established to look into the question of prisons and its report, accepted by the government in 1811, proposed the creation of a national penitentiary. After considerable expense, Millbank Penitentiary, capable of holding 1000 prisoners, 200 more than originally planned, was completed in 1816 and opened the following year.

Despite the high hopes of reformers, Millbank proved to be an unmitigated disaster. Poorly built on marshy ground on the banks of the Thames, it had a persistently bad health record. In 1823, the prison was temporarily closed after outbreaks of scurvy and contagious diarrhoea. To compound the problems, it proved impossible to find suitable staff and the prison had a record of continual scandals and chronic indiscipline. In 1818 there was a major prison riot, precipitated by the poor quality of food, that led to the smashing of cells and an assault on the prison governor. In the end, Bow

Street Runners restored order at gunpoint. In subsequent years, rations were reduced. In 1826–7, there were further large-scale riots. Cells were again smashed, there were disturbances in the chapel, fights between inmates and warders and even the hanging of a cat, belonging to one of the less popular warders, as prisoners sought to force the authorities to transfer them to the prison Hulks. The regime was tightened up thereafter but the prison was never a success. Official disillusionment grew until, in 1843, parliament decided that Millbank should no longer be a penitentiary, but merely serve as a convict assembly depot.

The failure of Millbank contributed greatly to the discrediting of the communal approach and the rise in favour of the separate system. Other factors also played a part. The creation of a Prison Inspectorate in 1835 saw the appointment of William Crawford and Whitworth Russell, who were fervent advocates of the separate system. Crawford, who had been greatly influenced by the prison system in Philadelphia, had no doubt that a harsh regime was essential to achieve the prime purpose of religious reformation. The embodiment of these ideas was Pentonville, opened in 1842 to take 450 men, serving a preliminary period in the penitentiary before transportation or transfer to public works prisons at Portland, Dartmoor and Chatham.

The regime was calculatingly severe. From the moment of entry, when the prisoner was washed and his head shaved, as well as being given a prison uniform (including mask) and prison number, it was made abundantly clear that the past was being rejected. There followed a period of regimented solitude, initially of 18 months' duration but later reduced to nine months, during which the prisoner was given the opportunity for that inward contemplation during which 'the still small voice will be heard and the man brought to himself'.[14] For some men it led instead to 'partial aberration of mind not amounting to insanity' and for others to more permanent madness.[15]

Change was not confined to the national penitentiaries. Local prisons were the subject of parliamentary legislation in 1823, 1835 and again in 1839. The 1823 act sought to prevent 'contamination' in gaols by means of classification, whereby the unconvicted would be kept separate from the convicted, the young offenders from the older offenders, as well as male prisoners from female. In practice its impact was limited but it was important as a statement of government intent to shape policy locally. The desire for uniformity in prison regimes led to the passing of the 1835 Gaol Act which required prison rules and diets to be approved by the Secretary of State and established a system of inspection. All five inspectors set about eradicating unacceptable local practices and the two most energetic, Crawford and

Russell, put their considerable energies towards extending the separate system. Success was by no means guaranteed. Indifference, as well as hostility to outside interference, restricted the advance of reformist ideas but, as the years passed, local autonomy was undermined. A further act in 1839, clearly influenced by Crawford and Russell, sought to move local prisons closer to the separate system.

The reformers could take some encouragement from the adoption of new prison regimes in Wakefield and Preston and later, as local prisons were rebuilt, in Birmingham, Hull, Leeds, Leicester and Manchester. But progress was limited. In 1865, of 121 prisons, 40 claimed to be running a separate system and a further 43 operated partial separation. It would be misleading to suggest, as Ignatieff does, that the reformers triumphed in the mid-nineteenth century. Local studies highlight the problems of transplanting the Pentonville model to the provinces.[16] In Lancashire, for example, although there were similarities between Pentonville and Preston, that was the extent of success for the reformers for many years. The aristocratic rulers of Lancashire did not take kindly to the suggestions of change from representatives of central government from London. Change gradually took place, none-the-less, and by the late 1850s there was a clear commitment to the separate system in Manchester and Liverpool, as well as at Preston. This pattern was repeated in other parts of the north and east of England.[17] In addition to political difficulties, there was the very real question of cost. In Exeter, for example, the creation of a new separate prison was simply too expensive to contemplate and there was no 'total institution' until the building of a county prison for Devon. Furthermore, the recruitment of appropriate staff was a continuing problem. The scandalously harsh regimes at Birmingham (Winson Green) and Leicester were exceptional and aroused public condemnation but there is little evidence to suggest that staff elsewhere were committed to the ideals of reform that motivated Crawford and Russell. Prison work lacked status and was dangerous, but was not well remunerated. As with the police, it took many years to create an efficient body of prison staff.[18]

While the intentions of prison reformers are clear, the impact of their actions is less easy to discern. Evidence of failure is not difficult to find. The incidence of insanity at Millbank and Pentonville and the scandals in provincial prisons cannot be overlooked. Furthermore, the problem of recidivism – apparent to contemporary observers – cast serious doubt on the reformatory capabilities of the new prison. Evidence of success is less easily come by. The fall in numbers in prison might be seen as such, but Frederic Hill's comments on the city prison in Norwich are a salutary caution. There had been a steady decrease in numbers in the prison for ten years, which had halved the total prison population, but this was a prison 'conducted neither on the separate system nor silent system, where there is little work, little instruction and little supervision, where many of the prisoners congregate, to their general corruption in idleness and unrestrained conversation'.[19]

However, there is a danger of being overpessimistic. Letters written by ex-prisoners to members of prison staff suggest that not all prison regimes were repressive and cruel. Instead, there was unsolicited praise for good treatment. Furthermore, there is also evidence of moral reformation which would have gladdened the heart of a Crawford or a Clay.[20] In addition, mid-nineteenth-century prisons were less unhealthy institutions than their late eighteenth-century counterparts. The dietary surveys of Dr Edwin Smith in the early 1860s suggest that prisoners enjoyed a greater quantity, but less variety, of food than the poor outside. Despite numerous press complaints about the scandal of well-fed prisoners, one should exercise caution. Equally persistent were the complaints of prisoners about the inadequacies of their diet and the unpleasant consequences that ensued. Attempts to relate prison diets (which varied considerably from prison to prison for much of the nineteenth century despite attempts to impose uniformity) to the nutritional needs of prisoners suggest that the 1878 diets were clearly deficient for adult males at hard labour and also for adolescent boys.[21]

The phasing out of transportation in the third quarter of the nineteenth century and the substitution of penal servitude brought new problems but also significant developments in the prison system. A home convict service had to be developed. Concerned that dangerous criminals were no longer removed from the country, influential figures such as Carnarvon argued for a strict regime for adult prisoners combined with greater police surveillance.[22] Using elements that were already in place, the Penal Servitude Act of 1853 effectively laid down a three-stage system involving separate confinement, followed by productive labour on public works, such as dockyards, quarries and construction sites, and, finally, parole on a ticket-of-leave. The act also laid down equivalents for transportation and penal servitude.[23] An amending act of 1857, which also marked the end of transportation, introduced a system of marks and remission of sentence for good behaviour, varying from one-sixth to one-third of the sentence, with conduct badges as the visible sign of progress towards ticket-of-leave status.[24]

From the outset the new system was under criticism for its alleged leniency and it was tightened up in the 1860s, following the garrotting panic of 1862–3, for which ticket-of-leave men were blamed. The minimum sentence was increased to five years and the mark system was made more stringent.

The garrotting panic was but one part of a wider disenchantment with the idea of the prison as reformatory. Prisons were seen to be 'soft', acting more as 'universities of crime'. Carnarvon, the driving force behind the establishment of a House of Lords inquiry into prison discipline, made clear that deterrence could only be achieved by inflicting 'pain and inconvenience' on the offender. The Carnarvon Committee, set up in 1863, rejected the idea that 'the moral reformation of the offender holds the primary place in the prison system' and expressed the view that penal servitude was 'not ... sufficiently dreaded'.[25] The emphasis on deterrence was enhanced in new legislation which introduced hard labour, including a minimum period of three months on the treadmill, or at crank labour, which involved turning, up to 10 000 times, a handle which operated a series of cups scooping up and emptying sand within a large iron drum, or a shot drill, which involved lifting and passing cannon balls down a line of prisoners under the command of a warder for an hour or more. Such 'work' was monotonous and unproductive and chosen for its deterrence value. This rejection of the primacy of 'moral reformation' and the move to greater severity was the end of the reformist experiment and an official rejection of the approach adopted not just by doctrinaire reformists, such as Crawford and Russell, but also by pragmatists, such as Joshua Jebb, who had become head of the newly created Directorate of Convict Prisons in 1850.

Hard labour was at the centre of the new convict prison regimes. The arduous and repetitive toil on construction sites or in dockyards was to act as both punishment and deterrent. Moreover, this could be reinforced by a wide range of punishments, varying from bread and water diets, confinement in dark cells and the use of restraints, to corporal punishment, though the harshness of the regime was tempered by the use of remission. The changing attitudes in penal thinking coincided with two other important considerations. First, there was a growing feeling that a uniform and centrally organized prison system was required. Second, there was a desire to reduce the burden on local rates. The upshot was the 1877 Prisons Act which nationalized the prison system. A new Prison Commission was established under the chairmanship of Edmund Du Cane. Du Cane rejected ideas of religion-based reformatory regimes. With a pessimistic view of human nature, encapsulated in his belief that 'crime is the natural tendency of mankind', and dubious as to the impact that prisons had on the level of crime, he was highly sceptical of the potential for reform of adult prisoners. He saw habitual criminals as 'a class of fools' who, by their very nature, were too weak-willed to reflect upon and learn from past crimes and to modify significantly their way of life. Thus, while the idea of reformation and the teaching of useful skills was never totally abandoned, deterrence became the prime purpose of prison.[26] All prisons were to be run in strict accordance with the rules and the regime was to be characterized, in words first used by Jebb, by 'hard fare, hard labour and hard bed'. 'Hard fare' meant that diets were set at a minimum level, determined by the particular type of work a prisoner was set to do and unnecessary extras, such as cups of tea, were cut out. 'Hard labour' involved silent work on such useful tasks as the building or extension of dockyards, as at Chatham and Portsmouth, respectively. It could also involve the construction of prisons, such as Wormwood Scrubs. To complete the harshness of the day, 'hard bed' meant the introduction of wooden beds and coir mattresses in place of hammocks and flock beds!

The influence of Edmund Du Cane was considerable. In 1863, he became a director of convict prisons (as well as being Inspector General of Military Prisons) and six years later he assumed the post of Chairman of Directors. In 1877, he also became Chairman of the Prison Commissioners, thus gaining unprecedented influence over both local and convict prisons. Indeed, for Du Cane the distinction between the two branches of the prison service was of limited meaning. Writing in 1885, he commented:

> The distinction made by the use of the term 'imprisonment' to denote sentences of two years and under, and 'penal servitude' to denote sentences of five and upwards, no longer has any significance . . . it is misleading, for both classes of prisoners are undergoing 'imprisonment' and are equally in a condition of 'penal servitude'. The only point to be kept in view is that the treatment should be adapted to the length of sentence.[27]

The 1877 Act was a measure to ensure an efficient, uniform and cost-effective prison regime. The number of local prisons was reduced dramatically. By the mid-1890s there were 56, compared with 113 on the eve of nationalization. However, the scheme was not well thought out and a variety of shortcomings became evident. The savings were far less than had been anticipated, while the new regime did not produce the expected results.[28] The system envisaged by Du Cane was based on a progressive four-stage regime. In the first stage, which lasted nine months, a prisoner would be held in strict separation and set to hard labour for six to ten hours a day. He would not be allowed a mattress during the first two weeks and only religious and educational books were permitted. In the second stage, the labour was less arduous, carried on in association and enabled a release gratuity to be earned. Further, the prisoner was allowed one library book per week. Conditions became less harsh in the third stage, where the maximum on release gratuity was raised to 1s 6d and the library book allowance doubled. Finally, in the fourth stage, the prisoner was eligible for special employment and a further increase in the release gratuity he could earn. In theory the stage system was both an incentive to the prisoner and a form of discipline for the prison authorities.[29]

The practice was somewhat different. The failure to give a precise definition of hard labour did not help the quest for uniformity. By 1880 a uniform six-hour treadwheel task was introduced, but not all local prisons had, or could afford, treadwheels. Consequently, the use of the capstan and the crank continued. Despite the attention given to prison diet, there were concerns about its adequacy, while scandals, such as the deaths of prisoners in Cold Bath Fields in the late 1870s and 1880s, raised doubts about the use of bread and water diets as part of prison punishment and, more importantly, led to concern about the secretive and autocratic way in which the prison system was run by Du Cane.[30] Opinion was steadily shifting.

The Kimberley Commission in its report of 1879 had expressed general satisfaction with the new approach, but gradually a reaction set in against the Du Cane system, which was seen to be repressive, at times cruel, but, more importantly, ineffective and inappropriate. Despite the fact that recorded crime rates were declining, there was a growing concern with the failure of the prison system to deal with the problem of recidivism. The habitual criminal was a cause for great concern but, rather than solving this problem, prisons were seen as an important contributory factor. Furthermore, as more was known about the characteristics of prisoners it became increasingly clear that strict penal discipline was both inappropriate and ineffective in dealing with those suffering from a variety of mental as well as physical disabilities. To compound matters, the harsh prison regime looked increasingly out of date at a time when new approaches to a wide variety of social problems were being advocated and adopted elsewhere. By the late 1890s, severe doubts had been raised about the mainstays of mid-Victorian penal policy: uniformity, long sentences and severe discipline. Flexibility, within and without prison, was seen to be the way forward. Criticisms mounted in the late nineteenth century. The *Daily Chronicle*, a respectable and liberal paper, produced a series of articles entitled 'Our Dark Places' in January 1894. They painted a dismal picture of prison life in which staff were overworked, prisons overcrowded and prisoners demoralized and driven to unnatural practices, insanity and suicide. In the aftermath of these criticisms the Gladstone Committee was established in 1895.

On the surface, the reasons for the establishment of this committee appear straightforward. The 1890s saw a questioning of a whole range of ideas and institutions. This climate of opinion, coupled with specific concerns about prison regimes, provides an obvious explanation. However, on closer examination the picture is less clear-cut. That there was popular concern with prisons is not in dispute. Much centred on Du Cane, who was seen by many, including influential men in the Home Office, as autocratic, secretive and overpaid. Du Cane's relationships with successive Home Secretaries had never been easy, and deteriorated markedly over time; but of greater importance were the growing conflicts between him and the civil servants at the Home Office from the late 1880s. Du Cane, for whom any questioning of his judgement was tantamount to treason, was temperamentally incapable of working with the senior Home Office civil servants and they in turn resented his high-handed manner.[31] By the early 1890s, relations had fallen to a very poor level. The Gladstone Committee was, in part, the product of a 'palace revolution' carried out by the new breed of civil servants, notably Evelyn Ruggles Brise, who had achieved high office by the late nineteenth century.

The Gladstone Committee, effectively intended to scrutinize the life work of Du Cane, has been seen as one of the major contributions to the development of 'modern' penal policy. In certain respects its report looked back to the optimism of an earlier era. Reformation was to be reinstated alongside deterrence. Prisoners were not to be seen as 'a hopeless or worthless element in the community' but as 'reclaimable men and women'. Moreover, they were to be treated as individuals in a way designed 'to develop their moral instincts, to train them in orderly and industrial habits' so that they left prison 'better men and women, both physically and morally, than when they came in'. There was also an emphasis on classification that would have been recognized and welcomed by earlier reformers. The idea of classification was taken a stage further with the proposal to create separate institutions for the different types of offenders. There was also a clear rejection of prevailing practices. The rigid application of the separate system was criticized. Hard labour was condemned and its abolition recommended. However, it is easy to overstate the importance of the committee and its report. The terms of reference were less than clear-cut, there were signs of unpreparedness in the working of the committee and a failure to use effectively the voluminous evidence that had been collected. In a dismissive phrase, McConville sums up the final report as an accurate reflection of 'the Committee's self-indulgent, meandering and lackadaisical proceedings'.[32]

The extent of practical change resulting from the work of the committee is also easily overstated. The 1898 Prison Act did not embody all of its proposals and there was no wholesale dismantling of the Du Cane system.

The separate system continued until 1922 and hard labour was not abolished until 1948. There is an irony in the fact that the 1898 Act, as well as being a triumph for Ruggles Brise and the start of a successful career, was also a triumph for the newly departed Du Cane, completing his lifelong ambition of centralizing the English prison system. Du Cane would be proud to have been able to make Ruggles Brise's claim, in 1922, that 'It is now 4.30 in the afternoon, and I know that just now, at every Local and Convict prison in England, the same things in general are being done, and that in general they are being done in the same way'.[33] Nonetheless change did take place. In the 1890s and 1900s, the basis of the twentieth-century system, with its combination of prisons and specialist institutions, catering for groups who once would have been imprisoned, was laid.

Juveniles

Concern about juvenile offenders surfaced on several occasions during the nineteenth century and it was recognized that special treatment, involving separate institutions, was required. The early advocates of classification within prisons were concerned to prevent the contamination of the young, perhaps first-time, offender by older, more hardened criminals. The idea of separate institutions developed slowly. One of the prison hulks, The *Euryalus*, was designated for the separate incarceration of juveniles. In 1838, Parkhurst was opened as a juvenile prison where young offenders would serve a preparatory period before transportation. Numbers reached their peak at around 800 a year in the late 1840s, falling to just over 600 a decade later and less than 350 in the early 1860s. Effectively undermined by the development of reformatory schools, Parkhurst closed as a juvenile prison in 1864. Deterrence and moral reformation were the twin aims, though complaints from the recipients of Parkhurst graduates do not suggest any long-term success was achieved.[34]

More significant developments took place in the 1850s with the passing of the legislation establishing reformatory schools in 1854 and industrial schools in 1857. Convicted children under the age of 16 could be sentenced to a period of from two to five years in a reformatory school, following a prison sentence. Industrial schools were intended to have a more educational purpose and were initially linked to the education rather than the prison system, catering for children between the ages of seven and 14 who had been convicted of vagrancy. These institutions owed much to reformers, notably Mary Carpenter, who had advocated the need for special treatment for children of the 'perishing and dangerous classes'.[35] However, Carpenter was not without her critics and the select committee which heard evidence during 1852 and 1853 received contradictory evidence on a number of key points. Unsurprisingly, the legislation that was passed was a compromise. Nonetheless, the fact that children were seen in the eyes of the law not to be wholly to blame for their actions and requiring treatment in distinct institutions, perceived as 'moral hospitals', was an important development.

In these institutions the paramount aim was to inculcate new and 'appropriate' patterns of behaviour, such as orderliness, punctuality and industriousness. Furthermore, the act establishing industrial schools gave the state the power, under certain circumstances, to take children (predominantly, if not exclusively, working-class) from their parents in the interests of the former. An act of 1866 which extended the legislation defined children in need of state care in broad terms to include not only those who had appeared before a court but also those deemed to be in danger of slipping into criminality, such as a child under the age of 14 found 'begging or receiving alms ... wandering, and not having a home or settled place of abode, or any visible means of subsistence, or [who] frequents the company of reputed thieves'.[36]

Despite the satisfaction expressed by many contemporaries, reformatory and industrial schools have received a critical coverage from many historians who have seen them as often brutal regimes of social control.[37] John Hurt's critique is scathing. The idealism of reformers such as Carpenter was not mirrored in the actions of local managers, who were more concerned with questions of economics, or in the attitudes of local staff, who were often indifferent, if not downright hostile, to their charges. The regimes, he alleges, were strict and regimented at best, brutal at worst. Harsh physical conditions, including poor diets, were commonplace and useful training for later life was low on the list of priorities. The inspectors' reports undoubtedly provide examples of authoritarian regimes using excessive corporal punishment, particularly on some of the Industrial Training Ships, but there is a danger of losing sight entirely of some of the positive aspects of some reform schools. The staff of the Linthorpe school, on the edge of Middlesbrough, 'treated [the boys] with obvious kindness', according to the inspectors. Physical punishment does not appear to have been a central element in the running of the school. Indeed, there was a wide range of leisure activities, from brass bands and choirs to gymnastics. The boys themselves were not isolated but took part in a variety of activities within the town. Furthermore, the school had a good record in finding employment for its boys, albeit mostly in the armed services. The official records do not record the voices of the inmates directly. Nonetheless, the low levels of absconding and the well-attended reunions of 'old boys' in the early twentieth century suggest that this was not a tyrannous regime.[38]

Contemporary concern with juvenile offenders diminished in the third quarter of the nineteenth century. In the annual report for 1875, the Inspector of Reformatory Schools noted not simply the reduction in numbers of juvenile offenders but the relative absence of that 'old thorough viciousness and premature depravity' that had been initially encountered.[39] Such optimism was eroded in the last decades of the century as different strands of concern came together. The periodically recurring fear of rebellious youth came to the fore following the hooligan outbreaks of the 1890s. Concern was given a new slant by the emerging belief, later given authority by the Gladstone Committee, that the making of the habitual criminal took place between the ages of 16 and 21, during the turbulent years of newly discovered adolescence.

Fears for the future of the nation's youth led to a variety of initiatives. Youth movements, dating from the 1880s, such as the Boys' Brigade, aimed to prevent young working-class men from offending, and some leaders, notably Baden-Powell, specifically looked to the hooligan element, believing that here was material with considerable potential for good.[40] However, there were also developments within the legal system. The apparent success of the reformatory schools, buttressed by reports of the experience of the Elmira Reformatory in New York state, led to active consideration of an alternative form of incarceration and treatment for young offenders over the age of 16. Despite the shadow of the Parkhurst failure, Ruggles Brise initiated an experiment with eight selected young prisoners at Bedford in 1900. Declared a success, the scheme was extended to Borstal convict prison in Kent in 1901 and to Dartmoor in 1903. Despite working with 'the most difficult material imaginable', as Alexander Paterson described them, the results were sufficiently positive to justify a full-scale scheme.[41]

The Prevention of Crime Act of 1908 did precisely that with its provision, in part one of the act, for the sentencing of persons between the ages of 16 and 21 to 'detention under penal discipline in a Borstal Institution'. Although a part of the prison system, borstal institutions were devised along lines that owed much to the practices of the public schools and organizations such as the boy scouts. Alexander Paterson, the leading figure, had an optimistic view of young offenders and sought to create a regime that would provide the necessary moral (and also physical) training to bring out and develop the innate goodness which he believed was to be found in every boy. The impact of the new system is difficult to assess, not least because of the outbreak of war in 1914, but contemporaries, both before and after the First World War, viewed the borstal system as highly successful. Paterson, citing the fall in the number of adult prisoners as evidence, claimed that three out of every four boys were saved, while official figures produced in 1925 showed that two-thirds of ex-borstal boys had not reoffended.

Women

The need for special treatment for women had long been recognized. In part this stemmed from a concern with the inappropriateness of certain aspects of prison regimes for men but also from a deeply held belief that criminal women were more depraved in nature, more difficult to deal with and more threatening to the wider moral order of society. Female criminals were doubly damned. Like their male counterparts they had broken the law, but, whereas male criminals were seen to be acting in a manner that was consistent with (or at least paralleling in an exaggerated form) masculine norms, female criminals, by their very criminality, were seen to have deviated from the norms of femininity. This had a profound effect on the nature of the regimes in women's institutions which were concerned with the recreation of appropriate patterns of female behaviour.[42]

The criticisms of the moral and physical squalor levelled at eighteenth-century prisons need to be understood, in part at least, in terms of the fears engendered by the destruction of gender roles that followed from the indiscriminate mixing of the sexes. It is no coincidence that Elizabeth Fry commented upon the appalling vista at Newgate of women 'dressing up in men's clothing' as well as their cursing and swearing, gambling and absence of religious knowledge. Not only for Quakers, woman's natural and rightful position was seen to be at the moral centre of society.[43] Thus a blurring of the essential differences between the sexes was both visible proof and cause of moral collapse. It followed that the separation of men and women was essential for the moral redemption of both. Thus set apart it would be possible 'to form in them [female prisoners]...those habits of order, sobriety and industry, which render them docile and peaceable while in prison, and respectable when they leave it'.[44]

Fry favoured a silent association system in which the women worked together, in silence, but slept in individual cells. A combination of religious instruction and suitable work was to effect the transformation of prisoners. The prisoners would be encouraged in developing new attitudes and habits by the example of lady visitors, to whom proper deference would be shown, and female wardens, who would provide a 'consistent example of feminine propriety and virtue', as well as by the exhortations of the prison chaplain. The 1823 Gaol Act, with its insistence on the separate confinement of men and women and the supervision of women by women, gave official expression to these ideas. The act was deficient in a number of ways. Its provisions did not cover borough and franchise prisons. Further, the large number of very small prisons, combined with an inability and/or unwillingness to spend money on prison building or modification, meant that the separation of male and female prisoners did not always take place and the regimes were more concerned with containment and deterrence than reform.

Over 95 per cent of women prisoners were held in local prisons but little is known of the conditions in them. Before 1877, there was immense diversity and one cannot talk of a typical experience. In Tothill Fields, for example, despite increases in accommodation, there was never sufficient provision for separate cells for all. In the mid-nineteenth century, there were single cells for 56 per cent of the female prison population, although this had risen to 93 per cent by 1870. There were other problems that hampered the intended reform of prisoners. It is difficult to see how any transformation could be effected when 75 per cent of sentences were for less than one month and 50 per cent for less than two weeks. Other circumstances were less than ideal: educational facilities were limited, the impact of the chaplain was marginal, the usefulness of labour questionable and the turnover of often low-quality staff high. Not surprisingly, 'the realities of prison management clearly confounded the avowed aim of penal reformers to return women to the ideal state of femininity'.[45]

Two further factors highlight the gulf that existed between theory and practice. First, the clear-cut distinction in theory between controllers and controlled (that is, warders and prisoners) was not replicated in practice. Prison management was often a matter of negotiation; compromise rather than unquestioned control was the reality. A variety of relationships between warders and prisoners developed. Some were quite mercenary – the bringing in of food, and so forth – but there is evidence of more intimate relationships, certainly emotional and possibly sexual, developing.[46] Second, the assumption that prisoners wished to be reformed so as to avoid a return to prison was flawed. For some women prison was more of a refuge, a place to return to in times of trouble. It is a measure of the harshness of life for many working-class women that prison was seen as preferable to life outside. In prison there was a respite from the threat and worry associated with a profligate or violent partner. Facilities for pregnant women were often superior and, in a more general sense, prison was for some an attractive winter alternative in terms of accommodation and food. Nor was this confined to the mid-nineteenth century. The prolific writer, Mrs Sarah Amos, told the Gladstone Committee in 1896 that it was not possible to 'make prison anything but a haven to very many'.[47]

After 1877, the situation changed as the result of the nationalization of the prison system. The number of prisons holding female prisoners fell from 61 to 32 and the determination to impose uniform regimes reduced the variations that had been found earlier. Nonetheless, certain problems remained. A large percentage of women served very short sentences. In 1895, 45 per cent of women committed to local prisons served seven days or less and almost three-quarters served no more than two weeks.[48] The quality of staff remained a problem and little interest was shown in the vexed question of appropriate labour for women. It also became apparent that prison did not appear to be effective or appropriate for the large number of women repeatedly sentenced to terms of imprisonment for drink-related offences.

The shortcomings of local prisons could be explained in part by the brief span of most sentences. The same could not be said of the convict prisons. Millbank was the main prison for women sentenced to penal servitude but, in 1853, Brixton was opened as the first purpose-built women's prison.[49] The number involved was small – some 2 per cent of all women sentenced to terms of imprisonment – but the opportunity, in theory, was great since the average sentence was some seven to eight years.[50] However, the experience of women in convict prisons was bedevilled by doubts about the appropriateness of penal servitude, problems in devising an appropriate regime and even greater problems in implementation.

The appropriateness of penal servitude was questioned largely on the grounds of the peculiar nature of women. It was felt that long-term imprisonment might be too much for weaker vessels and, even if they did survive the rigours of the regime, it would have less effect upon them, because of their sedentary natures, than upon men. Further, it was feared that they were insufficiently rational and too emotional to benefit from penal servitude. In addition, it was felt that the public works stage, an essential component of the regime for men, was simply not appropriate for women. The question of appropriate work was never satisfactorily solved, but a compromise stage system was devised. The first two stages, probation and third class, were served at Millbank. The probation period lasted two months, spent in almost total isolation, with arduous work, such as picking coir matting or heckling old ropes. After this period, and assuming good behaviour, came promotion to the third class where the work was lighter and visitors allowed. In theory, satisfactory progress was followed by transfer to Brixton for the remainder of the sentence. In practice, availability of accommodation as much as an individual's behaviour determined the move to the second class. As well as working in silent association, a prisoner in the second class received a small wage. Many women did not progress beyond this stage, but those deemed to be reformable were promoted to the first class and, generally speaking, served the last year of their sentence in the less repressive atmosphere of Fulham Refuge, which was intended to prepare women for release by training them in useful, and appropriately feminine, skills such as cleaning and cooking. A mark system was also operated, although, unlike men, women could gain marks for good behaviour alone. In addition, educational and religious support was provided, though in practice both were marginal activities and were often viewed with scepticism by the authorities.

Despite the centrality of work, attitudes to it were ambiguous. Finding appropriate work was a problem. Not all work was deemed to be acceptable for women and much that was so viewed brought its own problems. Knitting and clothes making could lead to unfair competition for law-abiding women outside prison, while laundry work was of such low repute that female convicts were in danger, as it was put, of being returned to a contaminating environment. It was also the case that many prison authorities were less interested in providing work to reform convicts and more concerned with covering costs. Laundry work and cooking had obvious advantages in this respect.[51]

The convict prisons suffered from similar problems to those facing local prisons. Much depended upon the quality and commitment of the prison staff, more so than in convict prisons for men. Staffing levels were not generous in view of the expectations made of the warders. Ratios of 1 : 15 were the average. In addition, prison work, as well as being potentially dangerous, involved long hours for relatively poor pay and there was a clear stigma attached to it. Turnover rates were high. Practical considerations dictated a regime based on compromise rather than coercion. Indeed, the belief that women needed to be treated on a more individual basis than men added to the less regimented approach in the female convict prisons. Finally, they experienced the fundamental problem of the unwillingness and/or inability of the prisoners to be reformed.

The history of the female convict prisons in the late nineteenth century is one of failure. Incidents of resistance, collective as well as individual, and the resultant use of a variety of forms of punishment were an obvious sign of this. Even the 'normal' conformity was probably little more than superficial. Less spectacular, but ultimately more telling, was the continuing problem of recidivism. By the late nineteenth century, a growing body of opinion felt that both local and convict prisons were being asked to undertake a task for which they were not fitted. A large number of recidivists were socially inadequate, or even sick, rather than threatening and sinful.

The late nineteenth century saw a growing concern with the habitual criminal in general and the habitual drunkard in particular.[52] The existence of a hard core of incorrigible 'criminals' was bad enough for a society increasingly worried by its relative decline in the world and concerned with the threat of racial degeneration. The situation was compounded by the fact that a very high percentage were women. Individuals such as Jane Cakebread and Tottie Fay became the folk devils of late Victorian England. The medical press spawned a specialist literature dealing with the problem and it was out of this concern that the first attempts to find a legislative solution emerged. The Habitual Drunkards Acts of 1872 and 1879 and the Inebriates Act of 1888 were ineffective, not least because inebriates had to volunteer to give up their freedom and then pay for their treatment. By the 1890s, informed opinion was increasingly pessimistic of finding an effective solution to the problem. The Departmental Committee on the Treatment of Inebriates saw compulsory long-term sentences as the only hope for the country, if not for the individual. Another Inebriates Act, in 1898, attempted to tackle the problem of habitual drunkards – to be dealt with by philanthropic organizations and local authorities – and those committing serious crime when drunk, to be dealt with by the state. In practice, the private response was limited and the government took over responsibility for provision in the early twentieth century.

Reformatories, predicated on the assumption that rural conditions were more conducive to rehabilitation, were established and sought to provide model conditions for the unfortunate women who were sent their way. The reformatories were an unmitigated disaster. The regimes were *ad hoc* and there was a strong and overt moral tone to the training, even though alcoholism was deemed to be a disease. The practical training was limited and inappropriate. It is difficult to see how the inmates, drawn almost exclusively from urban centres, could put to use their training in butter making, bee keeping and even hay making! Once again, the most important reason for failure was the assumption that the supposed beneficiaries wished to be reformed. The majority had little willingness or ability to change their ways and this they made abundantly clear. Disillusionment set in and the emphasis shifted from hopes of reform to a preoccupation with containment and deterrence.

However, thinking about the habitual drunkard was not unchanging. A growing body of opinion asserted that an explanation was to be found in 'feeble-mindedness' and 'moral insanity'. These ill-defined concepts blurred the distinctions between mental illness, crime and immorality but provided an alternative solution to be developed. The feeble-minded person was inadequate, irresponsible and incurable. It would, therefore, be inappropriate to subject her to a prison regime. Instead, long-term incarceration in a special institution was the appropriate treatment both for the individual, who because of her weakness was open to exploitation, and for the nation whose stock was threatened by the innate promiscuity and high fertility of the feeble-minded. Negative eugenics and late nineteenth and early twentieth-century criminology came together at a time when fears of national decline made many informed observers, across the political spectrum, sympathetic. Old morality was but thinly disguised by new science. It was 'well known' that women were peculiarly prone to mental illness, therefore it was not difficult to adjust to these new ideas.[53] The feeble-minded or morally insane woman, by definition, could not make responsible decisions to exercise sexual restraint. Pregnancy should only take place within marriage; therefore pregnancy outside of marriage was 'proof' of feeble-mindedness! The upshot of such thinking was the 1913 Mental Deficiency Act with its fourfold classification of idiots, imbeciles, feeble-minded and moral imbeciles. Thus asylums replaced prisons as the repository for these 'deviants'.

Conclusion

The emergence of the prison is the central development in the history of punishment in the 'long' nineteenth century. The history of the modern prison is one of adaptation and optimism continuing in the face of recurring failure. The initial developments from the late eighteenth century were part of a wider response by political and intellectual elites to a society that was being transformed by demographic and economic change. It drew on intellectual developments which produced new ideas of the individual and his or her workings and relationship to society and of the nature and purpose of punishment. Similarly, both secular and religious ideas, relating to the natural roles of men and women and appropriate codes of behaviour, contributed to the new penal system. Likewise, the developments of the late nineteenth century were the product of the interaction of a variety of factors. A number of external factors can be identified. Britain's relative economic decline, concerns about the long-term security of the Empire and the discovery of greater-than-imagined poverty came together with scientific ideas derived from Darwin and others to create an atmosphere of pessimism about physical degeneration and the decline of the race. Internal forces played their part too. There was a bureaucratic imperative that drove the prison system towards a more uniform, centrally controlled system. Further, the practical experiences of the prison system, the failure to reform and the emergence of the habitual criminal added to the pressure to devise alternative approaches. Non-custodial alternatives, special institutions catering for specific sub-groups of the criminal population and the medicalization of specific problems were all part of the rationalization of the prison system in late Victorian and Edwardian England.

Although imprisonment became the dominant form of punishment in the nineteenth and twentieth centuries, it was subject to continuing accusations of failure. And, for the most part, the critics had a powerful case. Prisons did not have an appreciable impact on crime rates (even Du Cane conceded this point), they did not appear to be an effective deterrent, nor did they reform the criminal, and yet their 'leniency' undermined the sense of punishment. In part, the sense of failure stemmed from the grandiose but naive claims of reformers. The idea that prison could provide an environment in which a criminal could be transformed was always optimistic: prison resources were too limited, prison sentences too short and the wider environment to which the criminal, sooner or later, returned too unhelpful. Similarly, the noble view of the perfectibility of the individual paid too little attention to the grim realities of the character and lives of the majority of criminals. In part, the explanation lies in the mismatch between policy and the perception of the problem of criminality and in the time lag between the two. Policy might better be seen as too little, too late. Well-intentioned reformers and administrators found that, once they thought they had found the solution to the question, the question had changed. The strong, rational criminal of early nineteenth-century thinking proved to be both physically and mentally weaker in reality. The early solutions were not simply inappropriate but created problems of their own. The late nineteenth-century responses drew upon practical experience, the latest scientific and medical thought and also upon a developing criminology. Some of the initiatives were quickly seen to be inadequate but others – notably borstal – seemed to offer real hopes of an effective solution.

An assessment of punishment cannot be made simply in narrow penological terms. In a wider sense, the prison was the acceptable and symbolic way in which unacceptable behaviour was punished and, in conjunction with other institutions, it played an important part in maintaining the stability of Victorian and Edwardian England. Prisons also played an important part in the identification of outcasts. They were the physical sites in which criminals were punished. The fact of having been imprisoned set certain men and women apart from their fellows in society. This contributed to the belief in the existence of a clearly defined and, allegedly, threatening criminal class which was distinct from law-abiding society. Further, this belief enabled 'respectable' society to unite across class, though not necessarily ethnic, lines in its condemnation of the antisocial criminal. In turn, this brought a broader-based legitimacy to the criminal justice system as a whole. This is not to suggest a crude conspiracy theory whereby the working classes were divided and ruled but rather to argue that the imprisonment of the habitual thief, as much as the murderer, was welcomed by a majority of the population. Not just members of the propertied classes, but also working-class victims of petty theft welcomed the protection of the law. Theft was not eradicated by the new police and the new prison but the fact that a convicted thief did receive a prison sentence had a symbolic importance that is easily overlooked.

This argument can be taken a step further. By distinguishing between different types of criminals and, accordingly, proposing distinct treatment for each group, humanity could be seen to be grafted onto justice. The more scientific approach to the problem of the criminal, particularly from the late nineteenth century onwards, was seen to have led to a more sophisticated and sensitive approach to the causes of crime, the needs of the criminal and the needs of society. Nonetheless, legal processes, if not the law itself, often appeared to be biased against the working classes and there was a widely held and well-founded belief that an element of luck was required, particularly for a young working-class male, not to fall foul of the authorities and end up in prison. Real resentments undoubtedly existed but, notwithstanding these problems, only a small minority of the population questioned the legitimacy of the criminal justice system as a whole in late Victorian and Edwardian England. To the extent that they played a part in this legitimizing of authority, prisons cannot be dismissed as unqualified failures.

CONCLUSION

This book has examined the emergence of the modern criminal justice system in England. There is something incongruous and unconvincing in writing about modernization when one lives in a country in which much of the *ancien régime* survives. Nonetheless, a clear contrast exists between the theory and practice of the criminal justice systems of the late eighteenth and early twentieth centuries. Over these years there was an underlying process of evolutionary change but also an acceleration, a coming together of change in a number of interrelated spheres, that created two transitional periods, the first in the early nineteenth century and the second in the decades around the turn of the twentieth century. As a result of the first, the criminal law was reformed, the use of capital punishment was greatly reduced and that of the prison increased, trial procedures were modified and the basis of policing was transformed. As a result of the second, there were further modifications in trial procedures, a re-evaluation of the role of the prison and the development of specialist asylums, and a significant extension of the efficiency and powers of the police.

The process of change was driven in part by internally generated forces. There was a logic to the modification of trial procedures in the late eighteenth and early nineteenth centuries and in the bureaucratic developments of the late Victorian police force. However, external factors also played a critical role. Religious and intellectual changes created the essential ideological framework; economic and social developments helped to identify areas of greatest need, while political decisions were of crucial importance in the evolution of specific pieces of legislation. But no one factor can be singled out as the dominant force for change. Humanitarian and civilizing concerns and

167

scientific enquiries played their part in the evolution of the new criminal justice system, as too did the desire to preserve the class and gender basis of society.

It is also important to consider briefly how the criminal justice system contributed to the evolution of nineteenth-century society. As well as reflecting the class and gender values of the day, the criminal justice system played a central role in defining and protecting these values and the social structures that went with them. The concern with order and decorum in public spaces, the criminalization of a wide number of working-class activities and practices and the increasingly active role of the police in the regulation of working-class work and leisure were fundamental means of preserving an essentially hierarchical society in which economic and political power remained unevenly distributed. Similarly, the passing of gender-biased legislation, such as the factory acts, was a clear indication of the willingness of the state to legislate to reinforce gender roles. The nineteenth-century state was both capitalist and patriarchal. It was paternalistic and welfare-oriented but also coercive and punitive. The criminal justice system was central to the character and actions of the state.

The long nineteenth century saw the intermixing of a variety of fundamental long-term changes. Industrialization, urbanization and the slow growth of democracy posed major challenges for the state and its elites. Historians have long stressed the growth of welfare reforms and the gradual incorporation of the working classes as sources of stability, but this focus is too narrow. Alongside a 'welfare state' there emerged a 'disciplinary state' and, as that welfare state sought to include and reward, so that disciplinary state excluded and punished. And the two processes went together. The incorporation of 'respectable' working-class men and women was often achieved by rallying their support against 'rough' outside elements who threatened (or were deemed to threaten) order, be it economic, social, political or moral.

Underlying continuities run through the period under review. On the one hand, there was the growing sophistication of the power of the state, as defined in terms of its legal and policing powers; on the other, a growing refinement in the definition and identification of the criminal enemy that threatened society. In this sense, the eighteenth-century thinking of the body politic was never totally rejected. The convenient fiction was maintained that there was a 'decent' majority threatened by a criminal minority. The body of society, as a whole, would be sound so long as the diseased elements were identified and treated. Hanging them up ceased to be the preferred option; banging them up, in prison or asylum, took its place.

Following from this, the extension of the powers of the state in general and of the courts and the police in particular was justified in terms of the need to protect society from this threat from below or without. In reality, the threat of the ordinary criminal was never that great. The number of lives lost and bones broken was relatively small. The amount of property stolen by the common thief was as nothing compared to the sums taken through fraud by middle-class criminals and scarcely justified the growing expenditure of the state on crime control.

There is a further irony in the fact that, despite the increase in the number of constables and the building of more prisons and other specialist institutions, the histories of the police and prison service were often dominated by failure. The balance of power between police and the criminal swung in favour of the former in late Victorian and Edwardian England, but the problem of crime, juvenile delinquency in particular, remained a worrying one. Even more starkly, the great hopes that had surrounded the new prison regimes had not materialized. It became increasingly apparent that prisons did not work. In many instances the prison was a wholly inappropriate institution; in others it did little or nothing to discourage, let alone reform, repeat offenders. Paradoxically, these very failures became arguments in the demands for more resources and further increases in the coercive power of the state.

J.F. Stephen was undoubtedly correct when he observed that 'The administration of criminal justice [was] the commonest . . . shape in which the state [manifested] itself to the great bulk of its subjects', but Reynolds and the Woolleys were equally correct in observing that the law imposed the values of one class upon the lives of another. In this book emphasis has been placed on the changes that took place in the criminal justice system between c. 1780 and 1914 but perhaps, in the final analysis, the underlying continuity of cooperation between the capitalist and patriarchal state and the criminal justice system is of greater significance.

NOTES AND REFERENCES

Introduction

1. V. A. C. Gatrell, 'Crime, authority and the policeman-state', in F. M. L. Thompson (ed.), *The Cambridge Social History*, vol. 3, Cambridge University Press, 1990.
2. In fact, the changes that have taken place in policing in the 1980s and the prison system in the 1990s arguably constitute a break with the pattern of twentieth-century developments.
3. D. Garland, *Punishment and Modern Society: a study in social theory*, Oxford University Press, 1994.

1   Crime and Crime Statistics

1. E. Durkheim, *The Division of Labour in Society* cited in P. Harris, *An Introduction to Law*, London, Weidenfeld & Nicolson, 1989, p. 242. D. Garland, *Punishment and Modern Society: a study in social theory*, Oxford University Press, 1994, chaps 2 & 3.
2. The pronouncements and writings of Lord Devlin show that such ideas remain an important part of the thinking of the legal establishment.
3. Harris, *Introduction*, p. 244.
4. *The Times*, 23 January 1948, cited in A. H. Manchester, *Sources of English Legal History: law, history and society in England and Wales, 1750–1950*, London, Butterworths, 1984, p. 215.
5. The ownership of property was seen to signify, indeed guarantee, such qualities as responsibility, independence and education in the owner and thereby legitimize his possession of political power. The opposition to Henry Bank's bill to protect mine owners from theft shows that legal principles were an important part of eighteenth-century parliamentary debate: C. Emsley, *Crime and Society in England, 1750–1900*, London, Longman, 1987.

170

6. A. H. Manchester, *A Modern Legal History of England and Wales, 1750–1950*, London, Butterworths, 1980, p. 191.

7. D. Hay, 'Property, authority and the criminal law', in D. Hay, P. Lindeburgh, J. G. Rule, J. G. Thompson and C. Winslow, *Albion's Fatal Tree: crime and society in eighteenth-century England*, Allen Lane, London, 1975.

8. S. Petrow, *Policing Morals: the Metropolitan Police and the Home Office, 1870–1914*, Oxford University Press, 1994.

9. See Manchester, *Legal History*, p. 194.

10. Only 'reasonable means' could be used in the case of a suspected misdemeanour, whereas force could be used to arrest a suspected felon.

11. K. S. Williams, *Textbook of Criminology*, London, Blackstone Press, 1991, p. 19.

12. There were a number of statutory offences which did away with the *mens rea* requirement. For example, possession of adulterated tobacco, contrary to an act of 1842, was sufficient, notwithstanding the fact that the accused believed the tobacco to be genuine: Manchester, *Legal History*, p. 202. Strict liability, as it is termed, generally applies to regulatory offences concerned with maintaining health or safety standards.

13. Quoted in Manchester, *Legal History*, p. 199. The following discussion owes much to Manchester's exposition.

14. First Report from the Royal Commission on Criminal Law, *Parl. Papers*, 1834(537), vol. xxvi, pp. 4ff.

15. Fourth Report of the Commissioners on Criminal Law, p. xxii.

16. Ibid., p. xxv.

17. Special Report from the Select Committee on Homicide Law Amendment Bill, *Parl. Papers*, 1847(315), vol. ix, p. iv.

18. The list included the major 'serious offences' such as murder, manslaughter, robbery, housebreaking, and various forms of larceny as well as riot.

19. J. J. Tobias, *Crime and Industrial Society in the Nineteenth Century*, London, Penguin, 1972, p. 25.

20. Ibid., pp. 272–3.

21. Rob Sindall, *Street Violence in the Nineteenth Century*, Leicester University Press, 1990, chap. 2.

22. Ibid., pp. 24 & 26.

23. To say the crime rate is artificially made is not the same as saying it is arbitrarily made. To the contrary, the distinction made between serious crimes and others is a deliberate one which gives important insights into the values of society. See K. Bottomly and K. Pease, *Crime and Punishment: Interpreting the Data*, Milton Keynes, Open University Press, 1986, p. 3.

24. The best introduction to nineteenth-century criminal statistics is V. A. C. Gatrell and T. B. Hadden, 'Criminal statistics and their interpretation', in E. A. Wrigley (ed.), *Nineteenth-Century Society: essays in the use of quantitative methods for the study of social data*, Cambridge University Press, 1972. See also V. A. C. Gatrell, 'The Decline of Theft and Violence in Victorian and Edwardian England', in V. A. C. Gatrell, B. Lenman and G. Parker (eds), *Crime and the Law: A social history of crime in Western Europe since 1500*, London, Europa, 1980; D. Philips, *Crime and Authority in Victorian England*, London, Croom Helm, 1977, chap. 2.

25. L. Radzinowicz and Roger Hood, *The Emergence of Penal Policy in Victorian and Edwardian England*, Oxford University Press, 1990, pp. 818–24.

26. S. Box, *Deviance, Reality and Society*, 2nd edn, London, Holt, Rinehart & Winston, 1981, p. 158.
27. Ibid., p. 159.
28. The figures in this section are drawn largely from Gatrell and Hadden, 'Criminal statistics'.
29. J. Beattie, *Crime and the Courts in England, 1660–1800*, Oxford University Press, 1986; D. Hay, 'War, dearth and theft in the Eighteenth Century: the record of the English Courts', *Past & Present*, vol. 95, 1982, pp. 117–60.
30. Hay has also stressed the importance of war, arguing that in times of conflict there was a fall in the levels of prosecution which in turn reflected a reduction in criminal behaviour. As Styles has pointed out, this may not be the case, as the practice of offering apprehended criminals, before indictment, the option of enlistment may be sufficient to explain the different levels of indictment in times of peace and war: J. Styles, 'Crime in Eighteenth Century England', *History Today*, March 1988, p. 39.
31. H. Perkin, *The Origins of Modern British Society, 1780–1880*, London, Routledge & Kegan Paul, 1969, pp. 162, 167–8.
32. Hay, 'War, dearth and theft'.
33. The figures in this section are drawn largely from Gatrell, 'Theft and Violence'.
34. *Criminal Registrar's Report*, 1896, p. 13, cited in Gatrell, 'Theft and Violence', p. 251.
35. J. Davis, 'Prosecutions and their context: the use of the criminal law in later nineteenth-century London', in D. Hay and F. Snyder (eds), *Policing and Prosecution in Britain, 1750–1850*, Oxford, Clarendon Press, 1989, p. 399.
36. Smaller employers were still faced with considerable disincentives in using the law, which reduced their willingness to use formal sanctions ibid., p. 412.
37. There were more panics in the period from 1840 to 1860, which would have resulted in a higher level of prosecution in these years, which in turn would lead to an exaggerated impression of decline in the last third of the century.
38. E. Dunning, P. Murphy and J. Williams, *The Roots of Football Hooliganism: an historical and sociological study*, London, Routledge & Kegan Paul, 1988.
39. J. Weeks, *Sex, Politics and Society: the regulation of sexuality since 1800*, London, Longman, 1989.

2   The Pattern of Crime

1. J. Styles, 'Crime in Eighteenth Century England', *History Today*, March 1988, p. 39.
2. K. Chesney, *The Victorian Underworld*, London, Penguin, 1974; J. J. Tobias, *Crime and Industrial Society in the Nineteenth Century*, London, Penguin, 1972.
3. G. Rudé, *Criminal and Victim: crime and society in early nineteenth century England*, Oxford University Press, 1985, p. 29.
4. D. Philips, *Crime and Authority in Victorian England*, London, Croom Helm, pp. 237–8, 256.
5. D. Taylor, unpublished analysis of York Assize records, 1855–1914.
6. J. S. Cockburn, 'Patterns of violence in english society: homicide in Kent, 1560–1985', *Past & Present*, vol. 130, 1991. Similar figures emerge from

eighteenth-century Surrey. See J. M. Beattie, *Crime and the Courts in England, 1660–1800*, Oxford University Press, 1986, chap. 3.

7. Infanticide presented a number of definitional problems which had the effect of reducing the number of successful prosecutions. However, it also seems to be the case that the courts took a lenient view of infanticide and looked to find extenuating circumstances.

8. Philips, *Crime and Authority*, p. 258. See also notes 57 & 58 below.

9. Frances Power Cobbe, 'Wife Torture in England', *Contemporary Review*, 1878. The often very trivial incidents that precipitated many savage assaults are discussed in N. Tomes, '"A Torrent of Abuse": crimes of violence between working-class men and women in London', *Journal of Social History*, vol. 11, 1978. See also E. Ross, '"Fierce Questions and Taunts": married life in working-class London, 1840–1914', *Feminist Studies*, vol. 8, 1983; and her *Love and Toil*, Oxford University Press, 1993.

10. M. E. Doggett, *Marriage, Wife-beating and the Law in Victorian England*, London, Weidenfeld & Nicolson, 1992.

11. Anna Clark, *Women's Silence, Men's Violence: sexual assault in England, 1770–1845*, London, Pandora Press, 1987.

12. *Middlesbrough Weekly News*, 2 June 1860.

13. C. Conley, *The Unwritten Law: criminal justice in Victorian Kent*, Oxford University Press, 1991, p. 19

14. B. J. Davey, *Rural Crime in the Eighteenth Century: North Lincolnshire 1740–1780*, University of Hull Press, 1994, p. 150; D. Taylor, 'Crime and Policing in Early-Victorian Middlesbrough, 1835–55', *Journal of Regional and Local Studies*, vol. 11, 1991, p. 58; Philips, *Crime and Authority*, p. 237.

15. For full details see the tables in Gatrell and Hadden, 'Criminal statistics', pp. 387–96 and Gatrell, 'Theft and Violence', pp. 339–70.

16. Beattie, *Crime and the Courts*, pp. 148–61.

17. F. McLynn, *Crime and Punishment in Eighteenth-Century England*, Oxford University Press, 1991, chap. 4.

18. Rudé, *Criminal and Victim*, pp. 29–30.

19. Ibid., Table 2.3, p. 29.

20. D. Philips, *Crime and Authority*, pp. 246–7.

21. *Police Gazette*, 22 January 1866.

22. Rob Sindall, *Street Violence in the Nineteenth Century: media panic or real danger?*, Leicester University Press, 1990; J. Davis, 'The London Garotting Panic of 1862: A moral panic and the creation of a criminal class in mid-Victorian England', in V. A. C. Gatrell, B. Lenman and G. Parker (eds), *Crime and the Law: A social history of crime in Western Europe since 1500*, London, Europa, 1980.

23. Although, strictly speaking, garrotting referred to strangulation by use of a rope, the term quickly lost its specific meaning and was applied indiscriminately to street assaults and robberies.

24. *Spectator*, 19 July 1862, cited in Davis, 'London Garotting Panic', p. 199.

25. McLynn, *Crime and Punishment*, p. 89

26. These examples were taken from the *Police Gazette* for December 1866. A perusal of other editions reveals a similar pattern.

27. Philips, *Crime and Authority*, p. 239.

28. There is a danger of understating the seriousness of these thefts. At a time when an agricultural labourer could be paid 10s (50p) a week, or less, £1 was a not inconsiderable sum of money.

29. The destruction of one's own dwelling house was classified as a misdemeanour in the eighteenth century. Insurance companies, worried by this loop-hole in the law, agitated for change, which came in 1803. This ended one of the most popular forms of defrauding insurance companies.

30. McLynn, *Crime and Punishment*, p. 86.

31. J. E. Archer, '*By A Flash And A Scare': arson, animal-maiming and poaching in East Anglia 1815–1870*, Oxford University Press, 1990, pp. 70–71.

32. Archer stresses the importance of the invention of the lucifer match in 1829–30 which greatly facilitated the work of the arsonist. At the same time, worsening socioeconomic conditions, and in particular the 1834 Poor Law Amendment Act, led to an intensification of hostility in the countryside. Not all the evidence points in this direction. Thomas Overman, a farmer of Maulden, Bedfordshire, giving evidence to the 1838 Select Committee on the Poor Law Amendment Act, commented on 'night-poaching, setting fire, cutting and maiming of animals and such like depredations' *before* 1834: N. E. Agar, *The Bedfordshire Farm Worker in the Nineteenth Century*, Bedfordshire Historical Record Society, vol. 60, 1981, p. 92.

33. E. Hobsbawm and G. Rudé, *Captain Swing*, London, Penguin, 1973, p. 170.

34. Cited in A. J. Peacock, 'Village Radicalism in East Anglia, 1800–1850', in J. P. D. Dunbabin (ed.), *Rural Discontent in Nineteenth-Century Britain*, London, Faber & Faber, 1974, p. 35.

35. Some incidents of animal maiming had more to do with ritual magic and others, involving the poisoning of horses, appear to have been the result of overzealous actions by grooms.

36. *The Times*, 29 July 1844.

37. Hobsbawm and Rudé, *Captain Swing*, p. 167.

38. Ibid., p. 318.

39. Ibid., p. 175.

40. E. P. Thompson, 'Crime of Anonymity', in Hay *et al.* (eds), *Albion's Fatal Tree: crime and society in eighteenth-century England*, pp. 311–12.

41. A. Charlesworth, *An Atlas of Rural Protest in Britain, 1548–1900*, London, Croom Helm, 1985; T. L. Richardson, 'The Agricultural Labourers' Standard of Living in Lincolnshire, 1790–1840: social protest and public order', *Agricultural History Review*, vol. 41, 1993, pp. 1–18.

42. J. M. Neeson, 'The opponents of enclosure in eighteenth-century Northamptonshire', *Past & Present*, vol. 105, 1984, pp. 114–39.

43. The death penalty for these offences was replaced by a mandatory sentence of life transportation under the 1832 Punishment of Death Act.

44. Rudé, *Criminal and Victim*, chap. 2.

45. Ibid. The Northallerton Quarter Session records reveal a very similar picture for the North Riding of Yorkshire.

46. See Philips, *Crime and Authority*, p. 201.

47. J. Rule, *The Experience of Labour in Eighteenth-Century Industry*, London, Croom Helm, 1981; C. R. Dobson, *Masters and Journeymen: a prehistory of industrial relations, 1717–1800*, London, Croom Helm, 1980.

48. The practice of taking coal was not easily stamped out. Some colliery owners, recognizing this fact, either allowed traditional perks to be retained or offered their employees cheap, concessionary coal.
49. P. King, 'Gleaners, farmers and the failure of legal sanctions in England, 1750–1850', *Past & Present*, vol. 125, 1989, pp. 116–25.
50. J. E. Archer, 'Poachers Abroad', in G. E. Mingay (ed.), *The Unquiet Countryside*, London, Routledge, 1989; H. Hopkins, *The Long Affray: the poaching wars in Britain*, London, Macmillan, 1986; P. B. Munsche, *Gentlemen and Poachers*, Cambridge University Press, 1981; R. Wells, 'Sheep rustling in Yorkshire in the age of the industrial and agrarian revolutions', *Northern History*, vol. xx, 1981.
51. The notable exception is G. Robb, *White-Collar Crime in Modern England, 1845–1929*, Cambridge University Press, 1992.
52. P. W. J. Bartrip, 'British Government Inspection, 1832–1875: some observations', *Historical Journal*, vol. 25, 1982, pp. 605–26.
53. A. E. Peacock, 'The Successful Prosecution of the Factory Acts, 1833–55', *Economic History Review*, 2nd ser., vol. 37, 1984, pp. 197–210 and P. W. S. Bartrip, 'Success or Failure? the prosecution of the early factory acts', *Economic History Review*, 2nd ser., vol. 38, pp. 423–7.
54. This paragraph owes much to Robb, *White-Collar Crime*.
55. Robb, *White-Collar Crime*, pp. 147 & 150.
56. D. Taylor, 'The Antipodean arrest: or how to be a successful policeman in nineteenth-century Middlesbrough', *Bulletin of the Cleveland and Teesside Local History Society*, vol. 58, 1990, pp. 26–30.
57. C. Dickens' *Dombey and Son* and *Martin Chuzzlewit* are but two of the more obvious examples.
58. T. Plint, *Crime in England*, London, Charles Gilpin, 1851, pp. 14–25
59. G. Sturt, *Change in the Village*, London, 1912, reprinted London, Caliban Books, 1984.
60. M. Feeley and D. Little, 'The Vanishing Female: the decline of women in the criminal process, 1687–1912', *Law & Society Review*, vol. 25, 1991, pp. 719–57.

3   The Criminal: Myth and Reality

1. See R. Swift, 'Another Stafford Street Row', *Immigrants and Minorities*, vol. 3, 1984, pp. 5–29.
2. S. J. Stevenson, 'The "habitual criminal" in nineteenth-century England: some observations on the figures', *Urban History Yearbook*, vol. 14, 1986, pp. 37–60.
3. T. Plint, *Crime in England*, London, Charles Gilpin, 1851, pp. 148–9.
4. Thomas Mayo, in a 1829 review, cited in M. J. Weiner, *Reconstructing the Criminal: culture, law and policy in England, 1830–1914*, Cambridge University Press, 1990, p. 44.
5. J. Symons, *Tactics for the Times as Regards the Condition and Treatment of the Dangerous Classes*, London, John Olliver, 1849, p. 49, cited in Weiner, *Reconstructing*, p. 19.
6. Taken from John Clay's twenty-third report as chaplain of Preston Gaol quoted in Mary Carpenter, *Our Convicts*, reprint, New Jersey, Patterson Smith, 1969, p. 73.
7. Ibid., p. 76. see also H. Mayhew, '*Of the Penny Gaff*'.
8. Carpenter, *Our Convicts*, quoting from Clay's twenty-seventh report, pp. 76–7.

9. J. Clay, 'On the Relation between Crime, Popular Instruction, Attendance on Religious Worship, and Beer-houses', *Journal of the Statistical Society*, 1857, pp. 22–32.

10. Cited in W. Hoyle, *Crime in England and Wales in the Nineteenth Century*, London, Effingham, Wilson & Co., 1876, p. 107.

11. Ibid., p. 87

12. Royal Commission on Constabulary, *Parl. Papers*, 1836, vol. xix. Tobias identifies this as a turning point in attitudes: *Crime and Industrial Society in the Nineteenth Century*, London, Penguin, 1967, p. 153.

13. Chadwick emphatically told the 1839 Royal Commission on Constabulary that, 'in the great mass of cases [theft] arises from the temptation of obtaining property with a less degree of labour than by regular industry', while Clay argued that prosperity rather than want was a cause of crime.

14. See also E. Hobsbawm and G. Rudé, *Captain Swing*. A sympathetic cartoon, 'The Home of the Rick-Burner', from *Punch* is the frontispiece to the book.

15. Hoyle, *Crime*, p. 21.

16. J. Fletcher, 'Moral and educational statistics of England and Wales', *Journal of the Statistical Society*, 1849, p. 233. He also noted that there was not 'any commensurate recoil when the prices are lowered'. See also P. S. Maxim, 'An Ecological Analysis of Crime in Early Victorian England', *The Howard Journal*, vol. 28, 1989.

17. *The Economist*, 1856, p. 281.

18. F. Engels, *The Condition of the Working Class in England in 1844*, 1845, translated by W. O. Henderson and W. H. Chaloner, London, Macmillan, 1973, pp. 144–5.

19. Ibid., p. 242.

20. Mayhew takes a far more sympathetic view in his contributions to the *Morning Chronicle*: B. Taithe (ed.), *The Essential Mayhew*, London, Rivers Oram Press, 1996.

21. H. Thomas, 'Poverty and Crime', *Westminster Review*, vol. 145, 1896, pp. 75–7.

22. H. Maudsley, *The Physiology and Pathology of the Mind*, London, Macmillan, 1867, pp. 83–4, cited in Weiner, *Reconstructing*, p. 168.

23. H. Maudsley, *Body and Mind*, London, Macmillan, 1873, p. 76.

24. Lombroso's ideas were more complex than this and were modified a number of times as his central text, *On Criminal Man*, ran through five different editions. The born criminal with atavistic characteristics was one of four criminal types that he identified. The others were insane criminals, including idiots, imbeciles, epileptics and alcoholics; occasional criminals, more opportunistic in the commission of crime but still having innate personality traits that predisposed them to criminality; and criminals of passion, driven by an 'irrestible force' such as anger or love. See D. Pick, *Faces of degeneration, a European disorder, c.1848–1918*, Cambridge University Press, 1989.

25. Havelock Ellis, *The Criminal*, London, Walter Scott, 1890, p. 205.

26. C. Goring, *The English Convict: a statistical study*, London, HMSO, 1913, pp. 370, 371, 373.

27. Mayhew's account of a penny gaff, noted above, is illuminating. Shocked by the entertainment on offer, he was more appalled by the number of women and young girls in attendance who clearly understood and enjoyed every innuendo and obscenity.

28. A. Vickery, 'Golden Age to Separate Spheres?', *Historical Journal*, vol. 36, 1993, pp. 383–414.

29. For many male Victorian commentators there was no distinction between the prostitute and the criminal. The term 'prostitute' was used in a variety of ways to cover practices deemed unacceptable by members of 'respectable' society. Mayhew, for example, used the term to describe coster-women who were not formally married but, in all other respects, lived with their partners as man and wife.

30. Cited in L. Zedner, *Women, Crime and Custody in Victorian England*, Oxford University Press, 1994, p. 43.

31. L. O. Pike, *A History of Crime in England*, London, Smith, Elder, 1876, vol. ii, p. 529, cited in Zedner, *Women, Crime and Custody*, p. 70.

32. C. Lombroso and W. Ferrero, *The Female Offender*, 1895, reprinted New York, 1955, p. 152.

33. Hargrave Adams, *Women and Crime*, London, T. Werner Laurie, 1914, p. 107, cited in Zedner, *Women, Crime and Custody*, p. 83.

34. Thomas' ideas changed and in his later works, such as *The Unadjusted Girl*, first published in 1923, he moved away from his initial Lombrosian position.

35. Rev. Worsley, *Juvenile Delinquency*, London, Gilpin, 1849, cited in G. Pearson, *Hooligan: a history of respectable fears*, London, Macmillan, 1985, p. 157. A similar sentiment was expressed by the reformer and Recorder of Birmingham, Matthew Davenport Hill.

36. Mary Carpenter, *Juvenile Delinquents: their condition and treatment*, London, W. & F. G. Cash, 1853, p. 17

37. *Daily Graphic*, 18 August 1898, cited in Pearson, *Hooligan*, pp. 93–4.

38. V. A. C. Gatrell and T. B. Hadden, 'Criminal statistics and their interpretation', in E. A. Wrigley (ed.), *Nineteenth-Century Society: essays in the use of quantitative methods for the study of social data*, Cambridge University Press, 1972, p. 379.

39. G. Rudé, *Criminal and Victim: crime and society in early nineteenth century England*, Oxford University Press, 1986, pp. 41, 45, 51; D. Philips, *Crime and Authority in Victorian England*, London, Croom Helm, 1977, p. 147; D. Taylor, 'Crime and Policing in Early Victorian Middlesbrough, 1835–55', *Journal of Regional and Local Studies*, vol. 11, 1991, p. 59.

40. Philips found that repeat offenders in his sample gave ages that were consistent with the age they claimed to be on their first appearance before the courts. This may simply show that Black Country criminals were consistent liars!

41. Gatrell and Hadden, 'Criminal statistics', Table 7, p. 384.

42. Ibid., p. 382.

43. D. Taylor, unpublished analysis of Northallerton Quarter Session, 1835–1893. Copies of the original records are held on microfilm at the North Yorkshire Record Office, Northallerton.

44. See especially J. Walkowitz, *Prostitution and Victorian Society: Women, Class and the State*, Cambridge University Press, 1980.

4   The Origins and Impact of the New Police

1. D. Taylor, *The new police in the nineteenth century: crime, conflict and control*, Manchester University Press, 1997.

2. Captain W. L. Melville Lee, *A History of Police in England*, London, Methuen, 1901, p. 241.
3. Ibid.
4. T. A. Critchley, *A History of Police in England and Wales*, London, Constable, 1967. See also the earlier and highly influential writings of C. Reith: *The Police Idea*, Oxford University Press, 1938; *The British Police and the Democratic Ideal*, Oxford University Press, 1943; *A Short History of the Police*, Oxford University Press, 1948; *A New Study of Police History*, London, Oliver & Boyd, 1956.
5. J. Styles, 'The Emergence of the Police – Explaining Police Reform in Eighteenth and Nineteenth Century England', *British Journal of Criminology*, vol. 27, 1987.
6. R. Paley, '"An Imperfect, Inadequate and Wretched System?"': Policing London before Peel', *Criminal Justice History*, vol. 10, 1989.
7. For recent syntheses, see R. Reiner, *The Politics of the Police*, 2nd edn, Hemel Hempstead, Harvester Wheatsheaf, 1992; C. Emsley, *The English Police: a political and social history*, Hemel Hempstead, Harvester Wheatsheaf, 1991; D. Taylor, *The New Police*. On the diversity of local experience, see especially C. Steedman, *Policing the Victorian Community: the Formation of the English Provincial Police from 1856 to 1880*, London, Routledge, 1984; R. Swift, *Police Reform in Early Victorian York, 1838–1856*, University of York, Borthwick Papers, vol. 73, 1988; R. Swift, 'Urban Policing in Early Victorian England, 1835–1856: a reappraisal', *History*, vol. 73, 1988; Taylor, *New Police*.
8. Cited in D. Philips, 'A new engine of power and authority: the institutionalization of law enforcement in England, 1780–1830', in V. A. C. Gatrell, B. Lenman and G. Parker (eds), *Crime and the Law: A Social History of Crime in Western Europe since 1500*, London, Europa, 1980, p. 183.
9. D. Philips and R. D. Storch, 'Whigs and Coppers: the Grey Ministry's National Police Scheme, 1832', *Historical Research*, vol. 67, 1994.
10. R. D. Storch, 'Policing Rural Southern England before the Police: opinions and practice, 1830–1856', in D. Hay and F. Snyder (eds), *Policing and Prosecution in Britain, 1750–1850*, Oxford University Press, 1989; M. Scollan, *Sworn to Serve: Police in Essex*, Chichester, Phillimore, 1993; B. J. Davey, *Lawless and Immoral: policing a county town, 1838–1857*, Leicester University Press, 1983.
11. See the discussion in D. Eastwood, *Government and Community in the English Provinces, 1700–1870*, Basingstoke, Macmillan, 1997, pp. 139–47
12. A. Brundage, 'Ministers, Magistrates and Reform: the Genesis of the Rural Constabulary Act of 1839', *Parliamentary History*, vol. 5, 1986; D. Foster, *The Rural Constabulary Act, 1839*, London, Bedford Square Press, 1982; Storch, 'Policing'.
13. C. Steedman, *Policing*, p. 27.
14. S. H. Palmer, *Police and Protest in England and Ireland, 1780–1850*, Cambridge University Press, 1988, pp. 510 & 514; R. Swift, *Police Reform*.
15. J. Hart, 'Reform of the borough police, 1835–56', *English Historical Review*, vol. 70, 1955.
16. Storch, 'Policing', p. 252.
17. The most powerful expression of the revisionist argument is to be found in two articles written by Robert Storch: 'The policeman as domestic missionary', *Journal of Social History*, vol. 9, 1976, and 'The Plague of Blue Locusts: Police

Reform and Popular Resistance in Northern England, 1840–57', *International Review of Social History*, vol. 20, 1975.

18. The situation was further compounded by the proliferation of local by-laws which sought to restrict such activities as singing obscene songs, flying kites, bowling hoops, shaking rugs and carpets in the streets before 8 am and throwing orange peel on the flagstones! See Taylor, *The New Police*, esp. chap. 4.

19. Report of the Select Committee on the Petition of Frederick Young and William Popay, *Parl. Papers*, 1833(627), vol. xiii.

20. P. T. Smith, *Policing Victorian London*, Connecticut, Greenwood Press, 1985, chap. 6; *Parliamentary Debates*, 3rd series, 139, 1855, cols 368–463.

21. Storch, 'Plague' pp. 76–83; Bob Dobson, *Policing in Lancashire, 1839–1989*, Staining, Blackpool, Landy, 1989, p. 24.

22. Storch, 'Plague', pp. 74–5.

23. H. Hopkins, *The Long Affray: the poaching wars in Britain*, London, Macmillan, 1986; D. J. Elliot, *Policing Shropshire, 1836–1967*, Studley, Brewin Books, 1984, pp. 26–7.

24. D. Philips, 'Riots and Public Order in the Black Country, 1835–60', in J. Stevenson and R. Quinault (eds), *Popular Protest and Public Order*, London, Allen & Unwin, 1974; J. K. Walton and R. Poole, 'The Lancashire Wakes in the Nineteenth Century', in R. D. Storch (ed.), *Popular Culture and Custom in Nineteenth Century England*, London, Croom Helm, 1980; R. Malcolmson, *Popular Recreation in English Society, 1750–1850*, Cambridge University Press, 1981; B. Weinberger, 'The police and the public in mid-nineteenth century Warwickshire', in V. Bailey (ed.), *Policing and Punishment in the Nineteenth Century*, London, Croom Helm, 1981.

25. C. T. Clarkson and J. H. Richardson, *Police!*, London, Leadenhall Press, 1888, p. 149.

5   The Creation of a Professional Force, 1856–1914

1. In a strict sense, policing cannot be viewed as a profession. However, the term is used more loosely here to indicate a force characterized by a core of long-term men who have made a career of policing and in so doing have developed skills and practices which in turn are handed on to others.

2. J. P. Martin and G. Wilson, *The Police: a study in manpower. The evolution of the service in England and Wales, 1829–1965*, London, Heinemann, 1969, p. 32.

3. For a more detailed discussion of these issues see D. Taylor, *The new police in the nineteenth century: crime, conflict and control*, Manchester University Press, 1997.

4. D. Philips, *Crime and Authority in Victorian England*, London, Croom Helm, 1977, pp. 66–8.

5. D. Taylor, 'The standard of living of career policemen in Victorian England: the evidence of a provincial borough force', *Criminal Justice History*, vol. 12, 1991, Table 1, p. 108.

6. W. J. Lowe, 'The Lancashire Constabulary, 1845–70: the social and occupational function of a Victorian police force', *Criminal Justice History*, vol. 4, 1983,

Table 3, p. 55; C. Steedman, *Policing the Victorian Community: the Formation of English Provincial Police Forces, 1856–80*, London, Routledge & Kegan Paul, 1984, p. 94.

7. Martin and Wilson, *The Police*, p. 13; Steedman, *Policing*.

8. Steedman, *Policing*, pp. 86–7. Lowe, 'Lancashire Constabulary', pp. 47–8; C. Emsley, *The English Police: a political and social history*, Hemel Hempstead, Harvester Wheatsheaf, 1991.

9. Lowe, 'Lancashire Constabulary', p. 45; H. Shpayer-Makov, 'A portrait of a novice constable in the London Metropolitan Police, c.1900', *Criminal Justice History*, vol. 12, 1991, p. 139.

10. Select Committee on Police Superannuation Funds, *Parl. Papers*, 1875, vol. xiii, Q. 1309.

11. Ibid., Q. 3234.

12. Ibid., Q. 1803.

13. A. Jessop, *Arcady: for Better, for Worse*, London, Fisher Unwin, 1887, p. 117.

14. C. T. Clarkson and J. H. Richardson, *Police!*, London, Leadenhall Press, 1888, p. 83.

15. *The Times*, 25 December 1908, p. 10.

16. A. A. Clarke, *The Policemen of Hull*, Beverley, Hutton Press, 1992, p. 62; B. D. Butcher, *A Movable Rambling Force: an official history of policing in Norfolk*, Norwich, Norfolk Constabulary, 1989, p. 66; Emsley, *The English Police*, p. 191.

17. A. F. Richter, *Bedfordshire Police, 1840–1990*, Kempston, Hooley, 1990, p. 19; B. Howell, *The Police in Late Victorian Bristol*, Bristol Historical Association Pamphlet, 1986, p. 5. Butcher, *Movable Rambling Force*, p. 11; R. Swift, *Police Reform in Early Victorian York*, University of York, Borthwick Papers, No. 73, 1988, pp. 15 and 56; L. C. Jacobs, *Constables of Suffolk*, Ipswich, Suffolk Constabulary, 1992, p. 22; A. A. Clarke, *Country Coppers: the story of the East Riding Police*, Bridlington, Arton Books, 1993, p. 38.

18. N. Pringle and J. Treversh, *150 Years Policing in Watford District and Hertfordshire County*, Luton, Radley Shaw, 1991, pp. 7 & 47; Clarke, *Country Coppers* and *Hull*, D. J. Elliot, *Policing Shropshire 1836–1967*, Studley, Brewin Books, 1934; Richter, *Bedfordshire Police*; T. J. Madigan, *The Men Who Wore Straw Hats: policing Luton, 1870–1974*, Dunstable, Book Castle, 1993.

19. Bob Dobson, *Policing Lancashire, 1839–1989*, Staining, Landy, 1989, p. 87.

20. M. Hann, *Policing Victorian Dorset*, Wincanton, Dorset Publishing, 1987, p. 4. The isolation of the policeman and his family is noted by a variety of writers, including Flora Thompson, *Lark Rise to Candleford*, London, Penguin, 1973, p. 484; R. Jervis, *Chronicles of a Victorian Detective*, first published 1907, reprinted Runcorn, P. & D. Riley, 1995, p. 84; D. Taylor, 'Policing and the Community: late twentieth-century myths and late nineteenth-century realities', in K. Laybourn (ed.), *Social Conditions, Status and Community*, Stroud, Sutton, 1997.

21. There is less evidence relating to why men left. The scattered evidence suggests that better pay and less arduous work conditions were the key factors. The judgement was couched largely in financial terms: too much was asked for too little reward.

22. Clarke, *Hull*, p. 24; Lowe, 'Lancashire Constabulary', p. 24; H. Shpayer-Makov, 'The making of a police labour force', *Criminal Justice History*, vol. 24, 1990, p. 109.

23. *S. C. Police of the Metropolis*, QQ. 107–8; Hann, *Dorset*, pp. 14, 37–8.
24. Clarke, *Hull*, p. 51; D. Taylor, *999 And All That*, Oldham Corporation, 1968, p. 63. The Middlesbrough examples are taken from the Constables' Conduct Register in Cleveland County Archive, CB/M/P, 29–31.
25. Jacobs, *Suffolk*, pp. 20 & 42; Taylor, *999*, p. 54; Emsley, *English Police*, pp. 201–2; Middlesbrough Constables' Conduct Register.
26. Taylor, *999*, p. 63; anon, *150 Years of Service*.
27. Clarke, *Country Coppers*, pp. 22–4.
28. H. Shpayer-Makov, 'Career prospects in the London Metropolitan Police in the early twentieth century', *Journal of Historical Sociology*, vol. 4, 1991, pp. 380–408.
29. Taylor, 'Standard of Living', includes details of individual experiences.
30. For people who had to start work in the early hours of the morning, it was well worth their while to pay for an early morning call from the bobby on night duty therby guaranteeing no lost time because of oversleeping.
31. For full details, see Taylor, 'Standard of Living', esp. Tables 6–8, pp. 127–8.
32. Rest-rooms and the like were intended to keep the constable from temptation, while sporting clubs and bands were useful in building up links with the local community.
33. *The Times*, 24 December 1908, pp. 6–7.
34. Alun Howkins, *Poor Labouring Men: Rural Radicalism in Norfolk, 1870–1923*, London, Routledge & Kegan Paul, 1985, p. 34.
35. *Essex Weekly News* 9 November 1888, cited in M. Scollan, *Sworn to Serve: Police in Essex*, Chichester, Phillimore, 1993, p. 43. See the photograph in J. Woodgate, *The Essex Police*, Lavenham, Dalton, 1983, p. 69.
36. S. Petrow, *Policing Morals: the Metropolitan Police and the Home Office, 1870–1914*, Oxford University Press, 1994, p. 294, fn. 2.
37. Behind many of the most opulent streets in London were slum areas that comprised a maze of alley-ways and lanes with houses that had been thrown up indiscriminately. The sub-dividing of larger houses and the infilling of courtyards and other spaces led to considerable overcrowding (with the attendant threats to health) in the the so-called 'rookeries'. For a fictionalized account, see A. Morrison, *A Child of the Jago*, which was based on the Old Nichol district.
38. S. Reynold, B. Woolley and T. Woolley, *Seems so! A Working-class View of Politics*, London, Macmillan, 1911, p. 86.
39. Ibid., p. 87.
40. Robert Roberts, *The Classic Slum*, Harmondsworth, Penguin, 1971, p. 100.
41. For a more detailed discussion, see Taylor, 'Policing and the Community', esp. pp. 17–25.

6   Courts, Prosecutors and Verdicts

1. The reader may find it useful to refer back to Chapter 2, and particularly Table 2.1.
2. *Report of the Commissioners appointed to inquire into the operation of the Acts relating to Transportation and Penal servitude*, vol. 1, 1863, 6457, Appendix H, p. 127, cited

in B. Abel-Smith and R. Stevens, *Lawyers and the Courts*, London, Heinemann, 1967, p. 31.

3. W. Blackstone, *Commentaries*, 15th edn 1809, vol.4, pp. 342–2.

4. Jervis's Acts of 1848 sought to establish codes of practice and procedure for justices of the peace acting 'out of Sessions', that is other than at quarter sessions. It was the second, Summary Jurisdiction, Act that clarified matters for magistrates in petty sessions.

5. D. Philips, 'The Black Country Magistracy 1835–60: a changing elite and the exercise of its power', *Midland History*, vol. 3, 1976, pp. 161–90; D. C. Woods, 'The Operation of the Master and Servant Act in the Black Country 1858–75', *Midland History*, vol. 7, 1982, pp. 93–115; R. Swift, 'The English Urban Magistracy and the Administration of Justice during the early nineteenth century: Wolverhampton 1815–60', *Midland History*, vol. 17, 1992, pp. 75–92.

6. This seems to be particularly the case in Middlesbrough where, despite the presence of the town's major entrepreneurs on the bench of magistrates, there were remarkably few cases of industrial larceny.

7. J. Davis, 'A Poor Man's System of Justice: the London Police Courts in the second half of the nineteenth century', *Historical Journal*, vol. 27, 1984, pp. 309–35. The following paragraph owes much to this article.

8. J. M. Beattie, *Crime and the Courts in England 1660–1880*, Oxford University Press, 1986, p. 46.

9. D. Philips, *Crime and Authority in Victorian England*, London, Croom Helm, 1977, p. 117.

10. R. P. Hastings, 'Private law-enforcement associations', *Local Historian*, 1981, pp. 226–32; A. Schubert, 'Private Initiative in Law Enforcement: Associations for the Prosecution of Felons, 1744–1856', in V. Bailey (ed.), *Policing and Punishment in Nineteenth-Century Britain*, London, Croom Helm, 1981; D. Philips, 'Good men to Associate and Bad Men to Conspire: Associations for the Prosecution of Felons in England 1760–1860'; J. King, 'Prosecution Associations and Their Impact in Eighteenth Century Essex' both in D. Hay and F. Snyder, *Policing and Prosecution in Britain 1750–1850*, Oxford University Press, 1989.

11. Beattie, *Crime and the Courts*, p. 48. It is also very difficult to evaluate the impact of improvements in transport. One would expect that the reduction in the travel time to increase the likelihood of prosecution.

12. Eighth Report of Her Majesty's Commissioners on Criminal Law, *Parl. Papers*, 1845(656), vol. xiv, p. 24.

13. Second Report of Her Majesty's Commissioners on Criminal Law, *Parl. Papers*, 1836(343), vol. xxxvi, p. 20.

14. C. Emsley, *Crime and Society in England 1750–1900*, London, Longman, 1987, pp. 146–7.

15. On the importance of the role of the magistrate at this stage in proceedings, see D. Oberwittker, 'Crime and Authority in Eighteenth Century England: law enforcement on the local level', *Historical Social Research*, vol. 15, 1990, pp. 3–34.

16. Sir John Hawkins, *Charge to the Grand Jury of Middlesex*, 1780, pp. 26–7, cited in Beattie, *Crime and the Courts*, pp. 268–9.

17. *Covent-Garden Journal*, 25 February 1752, cited in Beattie, *Crime and the Courts*, p. 274.

18. Cited in J. H. Langbein, 'Shaping the Eighteenth Century Criminal Trial: a view from the Ryder sources', *University of Chicago Law Review*, vol. 50, 1983, p. 123.

19. Ibid., pp. 103ff.

20. Cited in Beattie, *Crime and the Courts*, p. 276.

21. *Law Journal*, vol. 38, 7 November 1903, cited in Abel-Smith and Stevens, *Lawyers*, p. 88.

22. Elsewhere, Beattie strikes a cautious note, observing that seven out of ten defendants at the Old Bailey in 1800, including many on capital charges, did not have a defence counsel, *Crime and the Courts*, p. 375.

23. Beattie quotes an example from 1739 of a defendant stating 'I am no thief' only to be told by the judge, 'You must prove that', *Crime and the Courts*, p. 349.

24. J. R. Lewis, *The Victorian Bar*, London, Robert Hale, 1982, p. 29.

25. Second Report of Her Majesty's Commissioners on Criminal Law, *Parl. Papers*, 1836(343), vol. xxxvi, p. 2.

26. Philips, *Crime and Authority*, pp. 104–5. Not surprisingly, in the more common but less serious larceny cases 52 per cent of cases involved no counsel, 48 per cent involved a prosecution lawyer, but in only 16 per cent of these cases was there a counsel for the defence.

27. Cited in A. H. Manchester, *Modern Legal History*, Butterworths, London, 1980, p. 100. Barristers were obliged to accept dock briefs, for which service a defendant paid a fee of one guinea, plus the clerk's fee, to obtain the services of counsel.

28. Abel-Smith and Stevens, *Lawyers*, p. 151.

29. W. R. Cornish, 'Criminal Justice and Punishment', in W. R. Cornish *et al.* (eds), *Crime and Law in Nineteenth Century Britain*, Shannon, Irish University Press, 1978, p. 58; G. Parker, 'The Prisoner in the Box – The Making of the Criminal Evidence Act, 1898', in J. A. Guy and H. G. Beale (eds), *Law and Social Change in British History*, London, Royal Historical Society, 1984.

30. Concern with wrongful convictions was not new but despite a series of notorious cases, leading to Home Office pardons, in the third quarter of the nineteenth century, faith in the working of the justice system remained strong enough to thwart proposed reform until the early twentieth century. See R. Pattenden, *English Criminal Appeals, 1844–1994*, Oxford University Press, 1996, chap. 1.

31. J. M. Beattie, 'Scales of Justice: defence counsel and the english criminal law trial in the eighteenth and nineteenth centuries', *Law and History Review*, vol. 9, 1991, pp. 221–67; D. Hay, 'Controlling the English Prosecutor', *Osgoode Law Journal*, vol. 21, 1983, pp. 165–86; S. Landsman, 'From Gilbert to Bentham: the reconceptualization of evidence theory', *The Wayne Law Review*, vol. 36, 1990, pp. 1149–86; J. Langbein, 'The Criminal Trial before the Lawyers', *University of Chicago Law Review*, vol. 45, 1978, pp. 263–316; B. Schapiro, ' "To A. Moral Certainty": theories of knowledge and Anglo-American juries, 1600–1850', *The Hastings Law Review*, vol. 38, 1986, pp. 153–93.

32. Among other things, they drew attention to the need to prove that stolen goods had been taken into the possession of the accused. Cutting a purse and allowing it to fall to the floor did not constitute a theft unless and until the purse was picked up: First Report of Her Majesty's Commissioners on Criminal Law, *Parl. Papers*, 1834 (537), vol. xxvi, p. 13.

33. The last two examples are taken from Philips' *Crime and Authority*, pp. 107–8.

184

Notes and References

34. Report of the Royal Commission on the Law Relating to Indictable Offences, *Parl. Papers*, 1878–9 (2345), vol.xx, p. 36.
35. Lewis, *Victorian Bar*, p. 29.
36. F. W. Maitland, *Justice and the Police*, London, 1885, p. 139.
37. Beattie, 'Scales of Justice'; R. McGowen, 'The Image of Justice and Reform of the Criminal Law in Early Nineteenth Century England', *Buffalo Law Review*, 1983.
38. Beattie, *Crime and the Courts*, pp. 402 and 404, Philips, *Crime and Authority*, p. 103.
39. Beattie, *Crime and the Courts*, pp. 411, 419, 425, 428.
40. V. A. C. Gatrell, *The Hanging Tree: Execution and the English People, 1770–1868*, Oxford University Press, 1994, Appendix 2, pp. 616–17.
41. Beattie, *Crime and the Courts*, pp. 546 & 597
42. S. McConville, *A History of English Prison Administration, vol.1, 1750–1877*, London, Routledge & Kegan Paul, 1981 Table 11.2, p. 334. Little is known of regional variations, but my analysis of the Northallerton Quarter Sessions shows a similar trend in the North Riding of Yorkshire.
43. Gatrell, 'Decline of Violence', Tables B1–3, pp. 368–70.
44. P. King, 'Decision-Makers and Decision-Making in the English Criminal Law, 1750–1800', *Historical Journal*, vol. 27, 1984, pp. 25–58.
45. J. Brewer and J. Styles, *An Ungovernable People*, London, Hutchinson, 1980, p. 48.
46. G. Rudé, *Criminal and Victim: Crime and Society in Early Nineteenth Century England*, Oxford University Press, 1985, pp. 65, 68, 72.
47. J. Davis, 'Prosecutions and their context', in D. Hay and F. Synder (eds), *Policing and Prosecution in Britain, 1750–1850*, Oxford University Press, 1989.
48. Philips, *Crime and Authority*, p. 124.
49. Rudé, *Criminal and Victim*, p. 116.

7   Capital Punishment in Theory and Practice

1. Cited in D. Garland, *Punishment and Modern Society: A Study in Social Theory*, Oxford University Press, 1991, p. 58.
2. W. Cobbett, *Twelve Sermons*, 1823, p. 154, cited in H. Potter, *Hanging in Judgment: Religion and the Death Penalty in England*, London, SCM Press, 1993, p. 54.
3. Ibid., pp. 10–14.
4. Considerable importance was attached to property as the basis of the social, political and moral order.
5. Samuel Moody, *The Impartial Justice of Divine Administration*, London, 1736, p. 7 cited in R. McGowen, 'The Body and Punishment in Eighteenth-Century England', *Journal of Modern History*, vol. 59, 1987, pp. 651–79, at p. 662. In an age when gangrene and septicaemia were incurable and amputations more common, such imagery had considerable resonance.
6. *Mrs. Lachlan's Narrative of a Conversion of a Murderer in Letters addressed to a Clergyman*, 1832, p. 151, cited in Potter, *Hanging in Judgment*, p. 28. The body of James Cook was exhibited on a 33-foot pole in an iron cage, with specially made shoes to prevent his legs falling off.
7. *Parliamentary Debates (Commons)*, vol. xix, 29 March 1811, col. 625, cited in Potter, *Hanging in Judgment*, p. 9.

8. T. A. Green, *Verdicts According to Conscience: Perspectives on the English Criminal Trial Jury, 1200–1800*, University of Chicago Press, 1985; J. H. Langbein, 'Shaping the Criminal Trial: a view from the Ryder', *University of Chicago Law Review*, vol. 50, 1983, pp. 1–136. Those pleading benefit of clergy had to read the opening verse of psalm 51: 'Have mercy upon me, O God, according to thy loving kindness: according unto the multitude of thy tender mercies blot out my transgressions.' The reading test was abandoned as the result of legislation in 1706 and offences were deemed to be clergyable or not.

9. Ibid. See also J. M. Beattie, *Crime and the Courts in England 1660–1800*, Oxford University Press, 1986, esp. pp. 141–6.

10. P. King, 'Decision-makers and Decision-making in the English Criminal Law, 1750–1800', *Historical Journal*, vol. 27, 1984, pp. 25–58. See also J. H. Langbein, 'Albion's Fatal Flaws', *Past & Present*, vol. 98, 1983, pp. 96–120; Beattie, *Crime and the Courts*.

11. William Ludlow: 'sent to transportation solely with a view to his reformation ... if the Foundling Hospital will find him another master in some remote part of the kingdom, some hope may be entertained of his reformation' and John Brown, given three years' hard labour: 'the prisoner being a young man may under such superintendence be reformed': King, 'Decision-makers' p. 45.

12. Ibid., pp. 41–2, 46, 47.

13. Ibid., p. 47.

14. Other factors could also be taken into account, such as the suspicion of a malicious prosecution or an unfair verdict.

15. D. Hay, 'Property, authority and the criminal law', in Hay *et al.*, *Albion's Fatal Tree*.

16. Editor's introduction, C. Beccaria, *On Crimes and Punishment and other writings*, edited by Richard Bellamy, Cambridge University Press, 1995.

17. The role of such distinguished figures as Bentham, Blackstone, Eden and Romilly has been recognized consistently by historians, but that of the 'workaday barristers and attorneys' has not despite the fact that their work almost certainly had a far greater cumulative effect. See Gatrell, *Hanging Tree*, pp. 329ff.

18. There is a full discussion of the Fenning case and the publicity it engendered in Gatrell, *Hanging Tree*, pp. 353ff.

19. R. McGowen, 'The Image of Justice and Reform of the Criminal Law in early nineteenth-century England', *Buffalo Law Review*, vol. 32, 1983, pp. 89–125.

20. 'The criminal is placed upon a scaffold, and the executioner knocks him on the head with a great iron hammer, then cuts his throat with a large knife, and lastly hews him into pieces like an ox in the shambles. The spectators are struck with prodigious terrour; yet the poor wretch who is stunned into insensibility by the blow does not actually suffer much' J. Boswell, *The Hypochondriak*, ed. M. Bailey (2 vols), Stanford, California, 1928, ii, p. 284, cited in Gatrell, *Hanging Tree*, pp. 286.

21. The Quakers' contribution to the reform campaign was more selective than commonly suggested and was often focused on specific issues, such as the forgery laws, which particularly affected them.

22. The Mannings case was a *cause célèbre*. It was the first double hanging of a husband and wife for 150 years and, to make matters worse, Mrs Manning was a foreigner, born in Belgium.

23   *The Times*, 13 November 1849.

24.   Gatrell, *Hanging Tree*, p. 441.

25.   Ibid., p. 581.

26.   Second Report of the Commissioners on Criminal Law, *Parl. Papers*, 1836(343), vol. xxxvi, pp. 19, 20, 29–32.

27.   Anon, 'Capital and Prison Punishments', *Law Magazine*, vol. 4, 1846, pp. 223–250, at p. 235. For good measure, the author condemned the corrupting influence of prisons.

28.   It was also argued, echoing a point made by Fielding in the mid-eighteenth century, that concealed hangings would hold greater terror and thus be a greater deterrent.

29.   *Parl Papers*, 1856 (366), vol. vii, p. 24, cited in R. McGowen, 'Civilizing Punishment: the end of the public execution in England', *Journal of British Studies*, vol. 33, 1994, pp. 257–82, at p. 267.

30.   Such expert opinion was not unanimous. The chaplain of Pentonville, Joseph Kingsmill, argued that public executions still acted as a deterrent. One of the arguments he put forward to support this claim was that great efforts were required to prevent condemned prisoners from committing suicide.

31.   J. F. Stephen, 'Capital Punishments', *Fraser's Magazine*, vol. 69, 1864, pp. 753–72, at p. 753.

32.   Ibid, p. 762.

33.   *Parliamentary Debates (Commons)*, 3rd series, 141 (21 April 1868) cols 1047–55.

34.   *The Times*, 14 March 1878.

35.   The five-year trial period laid down in the 1965 act was made indefinite in December 1969.

8   Secondary Punishments

1.   J. M. Beattie, *Crime and the Courts in England, 1660–1800*, Oxford University Press, 1986, p. 513.

2.   Cited in A. G. L. Shaw, *Convicts and the Colonies*, London, Faber & Faber, 1966, reprinted Melbourne University Press, 1981, p. 49.

3.   Shaw, *Convicts and the Colonies*; R. Hughes, *The Fatal Shore*, London, Pan, 1988.

4.   Cited in L. Radzinowicz and R. Hood, *The Emergence of Penal Policy in Victorian and Edwardian England*, Oxford, Clarendon Press, 1990, p. 475.

5.   Shaw, *Convicts and the Colonies*, pp. 147–8.

6.   See D. Garland, *Punishment and Welfare: a history of penal strategies*, Aldershot, Gower, 1985.

7.   In the late eighteenth century by far the most numerous of long-term prisoners were debtors. The King's Bench, the Fleet and the Marshalsea, later to be described so vividly by Dickens, operated under distinctive 'rules' and 'liberties'.

8.   See for example Bishop Butler, *Sermon Preached before the Lord Mayor*, 1740, cited in S. McConville, *A History of English Prison Administration, vol.1: 1750–1877*, London, Routledge & Kegan Paul, 1981, p. 97. See also Beattie, *Crime and the Courts*, chap. 10.

9.   Beattie, *Crime and the Courts*, p. 568.

10. J. Hanway, *Solitude in Imprisonment, with Proper Profitable Labour, and a Spare Diet, the Most Humane and Effectual Means of Bringing Malefactors . . . to a Right Sense of the Conditions*, p. 4, ibid.

11. Despite the author modifying his ideas later, M. Ignatieff, *A Just Measure of Pain: the Penitentiary in the Industrial Revolution, 1750–1850*, Columbia University Press, 1978, remains a stimulating read. McConville, *Prison Administration* is a very thorough account that is more wide-ranging than the title might suggest. W. J. Forsythe, *The Reform of Prisoners 1830–1900*, London, Croom Helm, 1987, and C. Harding, B. Hines, R. Freland and P. Rawlings, *Imprisonment in England and Wales*, London, Croom Helm, 1985, are two very useful survey histories. D. Philips' article on 'Crime and Punishment', in S. Cohen and A. Scull (eds), *Social Control and the State*, Oxford, Martin Robertson, 1983, provides an incisive critique.

12. In addition Smith condemned 'the present lenity of jails, the education carried on there – the cheerful assemblage of workmen – the indulgence in diet – the shares of earnings enjoyed by prisoners' as a 'great cause of the astonishingly rapid increase of commitments': cited in Harding *et al.*, *Imprisonment*, p. 137.

13. Sir George Onesiphorous Paul was the driving force behind the Gloucester Penitentiary, which was envisaged as a harsh but reformatory regime for those awaiting transportation.

14. Earl of Chichester to the Home Secretary, 23 September 1856, cited in Ignatieff, *Just Measure of Pain*, p. 199.

15. Ibid., esp. chap. 1.

16. M. de Lacey, *Prison Reform in Lancashire, 1700–1850: a study in local administration*, Manchester University Press for the Chetham Society, 1986; E. Stockdale, *A Study of Bedford Prison, 1660–1877*, London, Phillimore, 1977; W. J. Forsythe, *A System of Discipline: Exeter Borough Prison, 1819–1863*, University of Exeter, 1983.

17. Forsythe, *Reform of Prisoners*, p. 99.

18. McConville, *Prison Administration*, esp. chap. 9.

19. Sixteenth Report of the Inspectors of Prisons (Northern and Eastern District), *Parl. Papers*, 1851 (461), vol. xxvii, pp. xii–xiii, cited in McConville, *Prison Administration*, p. 261.

20. Forsythe, *Reform of Prisoners*, pp. 120–27.

21. M. H. Tomlinson, ' "Not an Instrument of Punishment": prison diet in the mid-nineteenth century', *Journal of Consumer Studies and Home Economics*, vol. 2, 1978, pp. 15–26; S. McConville, *English Local Prisons, 1860–1900: Next Only to Death*, London, Routledge, 1995, Table 7.2, p. 318.

22. McConville, *English Local Prisons*, p. 52. It should be noted that Carnarvon supported reformatory and industrial schools, believing that youthful offenders could be reformed, unlike the hardened adult criminal.

23. Equivalents for transportation and penal servitude, 1853:

Transportation	Penal servitude
Up to 7 years	4 years
7–10 years	4–6 years
10–15 years	6–8 years
15 years and above	8–10 years
Life	Life

McConville, *Prison Administration*, p. 397.

24. A prisoner serving three years' penal servitude could only have one-sixth of his sentence remitted, for those serving four or five years the fraction was one-fifth, rising to one-quarter for those serving between six and 12 years. For those sentenced to 15 years, or more, penal servitude, one-third of the sentence could be remitted.

25. There were dissenting views but these were neutralized through Carnarvon's careful handling of the select committee: McConville, *Local Prisons*, pp. 103ff.

26. This is not to say that he believed education and religion to be unimportant in all circumstances. Their role, he believed, was crucial before and outside prison.

27. E. Du Cane, *The Punishment and Prevention of Crime*, London, Macmillan, 1885, p. 159. In practice the majority of prisoners served short sentences in local prisons and there was no chance of moving through the various stages envisaged by Du Cane.

28. McConville is scathing on this point, arguing that the financial case for nationalization was erroneous to the point of being fraudulent: *Local Prisons*, p. 234.

29. Although it is common practice to identify late nineteenth-century prison regimes with Du Cane, he was putting into practice policies decided by others, many of which predated his term of office. In addition, there was a wide range of support for such an approach. For example, William Tallack, the secretary of the Howard Association, had no doubt that separation was 'an indispensable condition of success in penal treatment': W. Tallack, *Penological and Preventative Principles*, London, Wertheimer Lea, 1889, p. 107.

30. See especially McConville, *English Local Prisons*, chap. 10.

31. Ibid., chap. 12.

32. Ibid., p. 648.

33. Cited in W. R. Cornish *et al.*, *Crime and Law in Nineteenth Century Britain*, Shannon, Irish University Press, 1978, p. 40.

34. J. A. Stack, 'Deviance and Reformation in Early Victorian Social Policy: the Case of Parkhurst Prison, 1836–1864', *Historical Reflections*, vol. 6, 1979, pp. 387–404.

35. Mary Carpenter, *Reformatory Schools for the Children of the Perishing and Dangerous Classes, and for Juvenile Offenders*, 1851, and *Juvenile Delinquents, their condition and treatment*, 1853; Jo Manton, *Mary Carpenter and the children of the streets*, London, Heinemann, 1976.

36. Industrial School Act, 1866, 29 & 30 Vict. c.126.

37. S. Humphries, *Hooligans or Rebels? An Oral History of Working-class Childhood and Youth, 1889–1939*, Oxford, Blackwell, 1981: Chapter 8, Reformatories, is unambiguously sub-titled 'Resistance to Repression'. See also J. Hurt, 'Reformatory and Industrial Schools before 1933', *History of Education*, vol. 13, 1984.

38. Sue Maidens, 'The Linthorpe Industrial School: An Agency of Class Control?', unpublished dissertation, Teesside Polytechnic, 1991.

39. Cited in M. J. Weiner, *Reconstructing the Criminal: culture, law and policy in England, 1830–1914*, Cambridge University Press, 1990, p. 285.

40. T. Jeal, *Baden-Powell*, London, Pimlico, 1991; M. Rosenthal, *The Character Factory: Baden-Powell and the Origins of the Boy Scout Movement*, London, Collins, 1986; J. Springhall, *Youth, Empire and Society*, London, Croom Helm, 1977, and *Sure and Steadfast: A History of the Boys' Brigade, 1885–1983*, London, Collins, 1983.

41. Cited in L. Radzinowicz and R. Hood, *The Emergence of Penal Policy in Victorian and Edwardian England*, Oxford University Press, 1990, p. 385.

42. Gender roles were also mediated by considerations of class. As in education, the ideal working-class 'wife and mother' was a different creature, and thus required a different form of training, from the middle- and upper-class 'lady'. For the impact of class-based models of femininity on education, see J. Purvis, *Hard Lessons: The Lives and Education of Working-class Women in nineteenth-century England*, Oxford, Polity Press, 1989.

43. There is an extensive literature on gender roles but see particularly L. Davidoff and Catherine Hall, *Family Fortunes: Men and Women of the English Middle Class 1780–1850*, London, Hutchinson, 1987.

44. From the aims of the Association for the Improvement of Females at Newgate cited in R. P. Dobash, R. E. Dobash and S. Gutteridge, *The Imprisonment of Women*, Oxford, Blackwell, 1986, p. 44. This represents a marked change in attitude as there was an earlier belief that the Newgate women, 'lost as they were in every species of depravity', were beyond salvation.

45. L. Zedner, *Women, crime and custody in Victorian England*, Oxford University Press, 1994, p. 142.

46. Ibid., pp. 161–2. The situation was compounded by the fact that the social background of many prison warders was not that different from that of the prisoners in their charge.

47. Report of the Departmental Committee on Prisons [Gladstone Committee] *Parl. Papers*, 1895 (77020), vol. lvi, 1, Minutes of Evidence Q.5004.

48. Calculated from McConville, *English Local Prisons*, Table 8.1, p. 336.

49. The female convict prison system was later extended. In 1863–4, Parkhurst was used for Roman Catholic prisoners, and it was replaced by the new prison at Woking in 1869. In the same year, Brixton was closed as a female prison and Fulham Refuge became an ordinary female convict prison.

50. The average for women was almost identical to that for men.

51. According to Mayhew and Binney the women of Brixton prison produced 20 000 shirts, 10 000 flannel drawers and waistcoats, 1200 shifts, 3500 petticoats, 5700 sheets, 2000 caps, 3700 handkerchiefs, 2800 aprons, 2300 neckerchiefs, 1200 jackets and 3400 towels to the value of £1800 in 1854 H. Mayhew and J. Binney, *The Criminal Prisons of London and Scenes of Prison Life* 1862, reprinted London, Frank Cass & Co.,1968, p. 194.

52. Radzinowicz and Hood, *The Emergence of Penal Policy*, part 4, esp. chap. 9; Zedner, *Women, Crime and Custody*, chap. 6.

53. E. Showalter, *The Female Malady: Women, Madness and English Culture, 1830–1980*, London, Virago, 1987.

BIBLIOGRAPHY

Abel-Smith, B. and R. Stevens, *Lawyers and the Courts*, London, Heinemann, 1967.

Agar, N. E., *The Bedfordshire Farm Worker in the Nineteenth Century*, Bedfordshire Historical Record Society, vol. 60, 1981.

Archer, J. E., 'A Fiendish Outrage? A study of animal maiming in East Anglia', *Agricultural History Review*, vol. 33, 1985.

Archer, J. E., 'Poachers Abroad' in Mingay (ed.), *Unquiet Countryside*, 1989.

Archer, J. E., 'Under Cover of Night: Arson and Animal-Maiming', in Mingay (ed.), *Unquiet Countryside*, 1989.

Archer, J. E., *'By a Flash and a Scare': arson, animal-maiming and poaching in East Anglia, 1815–1870*, Oxford University Press, 1990.

Ascoli, D., *The Queen's Peace*, London, Hamish Hamilton, 1979.

Bailey, P. (ed.), *Policing and Punishment in the Nineteenth Century*, London, Croom Helm, 1981.

Bartrip, P. W. J., 'British Government Inspection, 1831–1875: some observations', *Historical Journal*, vol. 25, 1982.

Bartrip, P. W. J., 'Success or Failure?: the prosecution of the early factory acts', *Economic History Review*, 2nd ser., vol. 38, 1985.

Bartrip, P. W. J., 'Public opinion and law enforcement: the ticket of leave scares in mid-Victorian Britain', in Bailey (ed.), *Policing and Punishment*.

Bayley, D. H. (ed.), *Police and Society*, London, Sage, 1977.

Beattie, J. M., 'The Pattern of Crime in England 1660–1800', *Past & Present*, vol. 62, 1974.

Beattie, J. M., 'The Criminality of Women in the Eighteenth Century', *Journal of Social History*, vol. 8, 1975.

Beattie, J. M., *Crime and the Courts in England, 1660–1800*, Oxford University Press, 1986.

Beattie, J. M., 'Scales of Justice: defence counsel and the English criminal law trial in the eighteenth and nineteenth centuries', *Law and History Review*, vol. 9, 1991.

Beccaria, C., *On Crime and Punishment and other writings*, (ed.) R. Bellamy, Cambridge University Press, 1995.

Bohstedt, J., 'Women in English Riots', *Past & Present*, vol. 120, 1988.

Bottomly, K. and K. Pease, *Crime and Punishment: Interpreting the Data*, Milton Keynes, Open University Press, 1986.

Box, S., *Deviance, Reality and Society*, London, Holt, Rinehart & Winston, 1981.

Brewer, J. and J. Styles, *An Ungovernable People? The English and their law in the seventeenth and eighteenth centuries*, London, Hutchinson, 1980.

Brogden, M., *The Police: Autonomy and Consent*, London, Academic Press, 1982.

Brundage, A., 'Ministers, magistrates and reform: the genesis of the rural constabulary act of 1839', *Parliamentary History*, vol. 5, 1986.

Butcher, B. D., *A Movable Rambling Force: an official history of policing in Norfolk*, Norwich, Norfolk Constabulary, 1989.

Du Cane, E., *The Punishment and Prevention of Crime*, London, Macmillan, 1885.

Du Cane, E., 'The Unavoidable Uselessness of Prison Labour', *Nineteenth Century*, vol. 40, 1896.

Carpenter, M., *Reformatory Schools for the Children of the Perishing and Dangerous Classes, and for Juvenile Offenders*, London, Gilpin, 1851.

Carpenter, M., *Juvenile Delinquents: their condition and treatment*, London, W. & F. G. Cash, 1853.

Carpenter, M., *Our Criminals*, 1864, reprinted New Jersey, Patterson Smith, 1969.

Cavanagh, T., *Scotland Yard Past and Present: Experiences of Thirty Seven Years*, London, Chatto & Windus, 1893.

Charlesworth, A., *An Atlas of Rural Protest in Britain, 1548–1900*, London, Croom Helm, 1983.

Charlesworth, A. and A. J. Randall, 'Morals, markets and the crowd in 1776', *Past & Present*, vol. 114, 1987.

Chesney, K., *The Victorian Underworld*, London, Penguin, 1974.

Clark, A., *Women's Silence, Men's Violence: sexual assault in England, 1770–1845*, London, Pandora Press, 1987.

Clark, A., 'Humanity or Justice? Wifebeating and the law in the eighteenth and nineteenth centuries' in C. Smart (ed.), *Regulating Womanhood*, London, Routledge, 1992.

Clarke, A. A., *The Policemen of Hull*, Beverley, Hutton Press, 1992.

Clarke, A. A., *Country Coppers: the story of the East Riding Police*, Bridlington, Arton Books, 1993.

Clarkson, C. T. and J. H. Richardson, *Police!*, London, Leadenhall Press, 1888.

Clay, Rev. J., 'On the Effects of Good and Bad Times on Commitals to Prison', *Journal of the Statistical Society*, vol. 18, 1855.

Clay, Rev. J., 'On the Relation between Crime, Popular Instruction, Attendance on Religious Worship and Beerhouses', *Journal of the Statistical Society*, vol. 20, 1857.

Cobbe, F. P., 'Wife Torture in England', *Contemporary Review*, 1878.

Cockburn, J. S., 'Patterns of violence in English society: homicide in Kent, 1560–1985' *Past & Present*, vol. 130, 1991.

Cockcroft, W. R., 'The Liverpool Police', in S. P. Bell (ed.), *Victorian Lancashire*, Newton Abbott, David & Charles, 1974.

Cohen, S. & A. Scull (eds), *Social Control and the State*, Oxford, Martin Robertson, 1983.

Colquhoun, P., *Police of the Metropolis*, London, Bye & Law, 1806.

Conley, C., 'Rape and Justice in Victorian England', *Victorian Studies*, vol. 29, 1986.

Conley, C., *The Unwritten Law: criminal justice in Victorian Kent*, Oxford University Press, 1991.

Cooper, D. D., *The Lesson of the Scaffold: The Public Execution Controversy in Victorian England*, London, Allen Lane, 1974.

Cornish, W. R., 'Criminal Justice and Punishment', in Cornish *et al.* (eds), *Crime and Law*, 1978.

Cornish, W. R., *et al.* (eds), *Crime and Law in Nineteenth-Century Britain*, Shannon, Irish University Press, 1978.

Critchley, T. A., *A History of Police in England and Wales*, London, Constable, 1967.

Davey, B. J., *Lawless and Immoral: policing a county town, 1838–1857*, Leicester University Press, 1983.

Davey, B. J., *Rural Crime in the Eighteenth Century: North Lincolnshire, 1740–1780*, University of Hull Press, 1994.

Davidoff, L. and C. Hall, *Family Fortunes: Men and Women of the English Middle Class, 1780–1850*, London, Hutchinson, 1987.

Davies, A., 'The Police and the People: Gambling in Salford, 1900–1939', *Historical Journal*, vol. 34, 1991.

Davis, J., 'The London Garotting Panic of 1862: a moral panic and the creation of a criminal class in mid-Victorian England' in Gatrell, Lenman and Parker (eds), *Crime and the Law*, 1980.

Davis, J., 'A Poor Man's System of Justice: the London Police Courts in the second half of the nineteenth century', *Historical Journal*, vol. 27, 1984.

Davis, J., 'Prosecutions and their context: the use of the criminal law in later nineteenth-century London' in Hay and Snyder, *Policing and Prosecution*, 1989.

Davis, J., 'From "Rookeries" to "Communities": Race, Poverty and Policing in London, 1850–1985', *History Workshop Journal*, 1991.

Davis, J., 'Urban Policing and Its Objectives' in Weinberger and Emsley (eds), *Policing Western Europe*, 1991.

Dobash, R. P., R. E. Dobash and S. Gutteridge, *The Imprisonment of Women*, Oxford, Blackwell, 1986.

Dobson, Bob, *Policing in Lancashire, 1839–1989*, Staining, Landy, 1989.

Dobson, C. R., *Masters and Journeymen: a prehistory of industrial relations, 1717–1800*, London, Croom Helm, 1980.

Doggett, M. E., *Marriage, Wife-beating and the Law in Victorian England*, London, Weidenfeld & Nicolson, 1992.

Donajgrodski, A. P., 'Social Police and the Bureaucratic Elite: a vision of order in the age of reform', in A. P. Donajgrodksi (ed.), *Social Control in Nineteenth-Century Britain*, London, Croom Helm, 1977.

Dunbabin, J. P. D., *Rural Discontent in Nineteenth-Century Britain*, London, Faber & Faber, 1974.

Dunning, E., P. Murphy and J. Williams, *The Roots of Football Hooliganism: an historical and sociological study*, London, Routledge & Kegan Paul, 1988.

Eastwood, D., *Government and Community in the English Provinces, 1700–1870*, Basingstoke, Macmillan, 1997.

Elliot, D. J., *Policing Shropshire, 1836–1967*, Studley, Brewin Books, 1984.

Ellis, H., *The Criminal*, London, Walter Scott, 1890.

Emsley, C., *Policing and its context*, London, Macmillan, 1983.

Emsley, C., 'The thump of wood on a swede turnip: police violence in nineteenth-century England', *Criminal Justice History*, vol. 6, 1985.

Emsley, C., 'Detection and Prevention: the old English police and the new', *Historical social Research*, vol. 37, 1986.

Emsley, C., *Crime and Society in England*, London, Longmans, 1987.

Emsley, C., *The English Police: a political and social history*, Hemel Hempstead, Harvester Wheatsheaf, 1991.

Engels, F., *The Condition of the Working Class in England in 1844* translated by W. O. Henderson and W. H. Chaloner, London, Macmillan, 1973.

England, R. W., 'Investigating Homicides in Northern England, 1800–1824', *Criminal Justice History*, vol. 6, 1985.

Feeley, M. and D. Little, 'The Vanishing Female: the decline of women in the criminal process, 1687–1912', *Law & Society Review*, vol. 25, 1991.

Field, J., 'Police, Power and Community in a provincial English town', in Bailey (ed.), *Policing and Punishment*.

Fletcher, J., 'Moral and educational statistics of England and Wales', *Journal of the Statistical society*, vol. 12, 1849.

Foard, I., 'The Power of Heredity', *Westminster Review*, vol. 152, 1899.

Forsythe, W. J., *A System of Discipline: Exeter Borough Prison, 1819–1863*, University of Exeter, 1983.

Forsythe, W. J., *The Reform of Prisoners, 1830–1900*, London, Croom Helm, 1987.

Forsythe, W. J., *Penal Discipline, Reformatory Projects and the English prison Commission, 1895–1939*, University of Exeter, 1990.

Foster, D., *The Rural Constabulary Act, 1839*, London, Bedford Square Press, 1982.

Foster, D., 'The East Riding Constabulary in the nineteenth century', *Northern History*, vol. 21, 1985.

Foucault, M., *Discipline and Punish: the Birth of the Prison*, London, Penguin, 1991.

Garland, D., *Punishment and Welfare: a history of penal strategies*, Aldershot, Gower, 1985.

Garland, D., *Punishment and Modern Society: a study in social theory*, Oxford University Press, 1994.

Gatrell, V. A. C., 'The decline of theft and violence in Victorian and Edwardian England', in Gatrell, Lenman and Parker (eds), *Crime and the Law*, 1980.

Gatrell, V. A. C., 'Crime, authority and the policeman-state' in F. M. L. Thompson (ed.), *The Cambridge Social History*, vol. 3, Cambridge University Press, 1990.

Gatrell, V. A. C., *The Hanging Tree: Execution and the English People, 1770–1868*, Oxford University Press, 1994.

Gatrell, V. A. C. and T. B. Hadden, 'Criminal statistics and their interpretation' in E. A. Wrigley (ed.), *Nineteenth-Century Society: essays in the use of quantitative methods for the study of social data*, Cambridge University Press, 1972.

Gatrell, V. A. C., B. Lenman and G. Parker (eds), Crime *and the Law: a social history of crime in Western Europe since 1500*, London, Europa, 1980.

Geary, R., *Policing Industrial Disputes, 1893–1985*, Cambridge University Press, 1985.

Gillis, J. R., 'The Evolution of Juvenile Delinquency in England, 1890–1914', *Past & Present*, vol. 67, 1975.

Goring, C., *The English Convict: a statistical study*, London, HMSO, 1913.

Green, T. A., *Verdict According to Conscience: Perspectives on the English Criminal Trial Jury, 1200–1800*, University of Chicago Press, 1985.

Guy, J. A. and H. G. Beale (eds), *Law and Social Change in British History*, London, Royal Historical Society, 1984.

Hann, M., *Policing Victorian Dorset*, Wincanton, Dorset Publishing, 1987.

Harding, C., 'The Inevitable End of a Discredited System? The Origins of the Gladstone Committee Report on Prisons, 1895', *Historical Journal*, vol. 31, 1988.

Harding, C., 'The Dream of a Benevolent Mind: the late-Victorian response to the problem of inebriety', *Criminal Justice History*, vol. 9, 1988.

Harding, C., B. Hines, R. Freland and P. Rawlings, *Imprisonment in England and Wales*, London, Croom Helm, 1985.

Harris, P., *An Introduction to Law*, London, Weidenfeld & Nicolson, 1989.

Hart, J., 'Reform of the borough police, 1835–56', *English Historical Review*, vol. 70, 1955.

Hasting, P., 'Private law-enforcement associations', *Local Historian*, vol. 14, 1981.

Hay, D., 'Property, authority and the criminal law' in Hay *et al.*, *Albion's Fatal Tree*, 1975.

Hay, D., 'Poaching and the Game Laws on Cannock Chase', in Hay *et al.* (eds), *Albion's Fatal Tree*, 1975.

Hay, D., 'War, dearth and theft in the eighteenth century: the record of the English courts', *Past & Present*, vol. 95, 1982.

Hay, D., 'Controlling the English Prosecutor' *Osgoode Law Journal*, vol. 21, 1983.

Hay, D. and F. Snyder (eds), *Policing and Prosecution in Britain, 1750–1850*, Oxford University Press, 1989.

Hay, D., P. Linebaugh, J. G. Rule, E. P. Thompson and C. Winslow (eds), *Albion's Fatal Tree: crime and society in eighteenth-century England*, London, Allen Lane, 1975.

Hill, M. D., *Suggestions for the Repression of Crime*, London, Parker & Son, 1857.

Hobsbawm, E. J. and G. Rudé, *Captain Swing*, London, Penguin, 1973.

Holmes, T., *Pictures and Problems from London Police Courts*, London, Edward Arnold, 1900.

Holmes, T., *Known to the Police*, London, Edward Arnold, 1908.

Hopkins, H., *The Long Affray: the poaching wars in Britain*, London, Macmillan, 1986.

Howell, B., *The Police in Late Victorian Bristol*, Bristol Historical Association pamphlet, 1986.

Howkins, A., *Poor Labouring Men: Rural Radicalism in Norfolk, 1870–1923*, London, Routledge & Kegan Paul, 1985.

Hoyle, W., *Crime in England and Wales in the Nineteenth Century*, London, Effingham Wilson & Co., 1876.

Hughes, R., *The Fatal Shore: A History of Transportation of Convicts to Australia, 1787–1868*, London, Pan, 1988.

Humphries, S., *Hooligans or Rebels? An Oral History of Working-class Childhood and Youth, 1888–1939*, Oxford, Blackwell, 1981.

Hurt, J., 'Reformatory and Industrial Schools before 1933', *History of Education*, vol. 13, 1984.

Ignatieff, M., *A Just Measure of Pain: the Penitentiary in the Industrial Revolution, 1750–1850*, Columbia University Press, 1978.

Ignatieff, M., 'State, Civil Society and Total Institutions: a critique of recent social histories of punishment' in Cohen and Scull (eds), *Social Control*, 1983.

Jacobs, L. C., *Constables of Suffolk*, Ipswich, Suffolk Constabulary, 1992.

Jeal, T., *Baden-Powell*, London, Pimlico, 1991.

Jefferson, T. and R. Grimshaw, *Controlling the Constable: Police Accountability in England and Wales*, London, Academic Press, 1982.

Jervis, R., *Chronicles of a Victorian Detective*, 1907, reprinted Runcorn, P. & D. Riley, 1995.

Jones, D. J. V., 'Thomas Campbell Foster and the rural labourer: incendiarism in East Anglia in the 1840s', *Social History*, vol. 12, 1976.

Jones, D. J. V., *Crime, Protest, Community and Police in Nineteenth-Century Britain*, London, Routledge & Kegan Paul, 1982.

Jones, D. J. V., 'The New Police, Crime and People in England and Wales, 1829–1888', *Transactions of the Royal Historical Society*, 5th ser., vol. 33, 1983.

King, J. E., '"We could eat the police": popular violence in the north Lancashire cotton strike of 1875', *Victorian Studies*, vol. 28, 1985.

King, P., 'Decision-makers and Decision-making in the English Criminal Law, 1750–1800', *Historical Journal*, vol. 27, 1984.

King, P., 'Gleaners, farmers and the failure of legal sanctions in England, 1750–1850', *Past & Present*, vol. 125, 1989.

King, P., 'Prosecution Associations and their impact in eighteenth-century Essex', in Hay and Synder, *Policing and Prosecution*, 1989.

King, P. and J. Noel, 'The origins of "the problem of juvenile delinquency": the growth of juvenile prosecutions in London in the late eighteenth and early nineteenth centuries' *Criminal Justice History*, vol. 14, 1993.

de Lacey, M., 'Grinding Men Good? Lancashire's Prisons at mid-century' in Bailey (ed.), *Policing and Punishment*.

de Lacey, M., *Prison Reform in Lancashire, 1700–1850: a study in local administration*, Manchester, Chetham Society, 1986.

Landsman, S., 'From Gilbert to Bentham: the reconceptualization of evidence theory', *The Wayne Law Review*, vol. 36, 1990.

Langbein, J. H., 'The Criminal Trial before the Lawyers', *University of Chicago Law Review*, vol. 45, 1978.

Langbein, J. H., 'Albion's Fatal Flaws', *Past & Present*, vol. 98, 1983.

Langbein, J. H., 'Shaping the Eighteenth-Century Criminal Trial: a view from the Ryder sources', *University of Chicago Law Review*, vol. 50, 1983.

Lee, W. L. M., *A History of Police in England*, London, Methuen, 1901.

Lewis, F. D., 'The Cost of Convict Transportation from Britain to Australia, 1796–1810', *Economic History Review*, 2nd ser., vol. 41, 1988.

Lewis, J. R., *The Victorian Bar*, London, Robert Hale, 1982.

Linebaugh, P., *The London Hanged*, London, Allen Lane, 1991.

Lombroso, C., *On Criminal Man*, reprinted New Jersey, Patterson Smith, 1972.

Lombroso, C. and G. Ferrero, *The Female Offender*, Lava, Fisher Unwin, 1895; reprinted New York, 1955.

Lowe, W. J., 'The Lancashire Constabulary, 1845–70: the social and occupational function of a Victorian police force', *Criminal Justice History*, vol. 4, 1983.

Madigan, T. J., *The Men Who Wore Straw Hats: policing Luton, 1870–1974*, Dunstable, Book Castle, 1993.

Magarey, S., 'The Invention of Juvenile Delinquency in early-nineteenth century England', *Labour History*, vol. 43, 1978.

Maitland, F. W., *Justice and the Police*, London, Macmillan, 1985.

Malcolmson, R., *Popular Recreation in English Society, 1750–1850*, Cambridge University Press, 1981.

Manchester, A. H., *A Modern Legal History of England and Wales, 1750–1950*, London, Butterworths, 1980.

Manchester, A. H., *Sources of English Legal History: law, history and society in England and Wales, 1750–1950*, London, Butterworths, 1984.

Manton, J., *Mary Carpenter and the children of the street*, London, Heinemann, 1976.

Martin, J. P. and G. Wilson, *The Police: a study in manpower. The evolution of the service in England and Wales, 1829–1965*, London, Heinemann, 1969.

Mather, F. C., *Public Order in the Age of the Chartists*, Westport, Connecticut, Greenwood Press, 1959.

Maxim, P. S., 'An ecological analysis of crime in early-Victorian England', *The Howard Journal*, vol. 28, 1989.

May, M., 'Innocence and Experience: the evolution of the concept of juvenile delinquency in the mid-nineteenth century', *Victorian Studies*, vol. 17, 1973.

Mayhew, M. and J. Binney, *The Criminal Prisons of London and Scenes of Prison Life*, 1862, reprinted, London, Frank Cass & Co., 1986.

McConville, S., *A History of English Prison Administration, vol. 1, 1750–1877*, London, Routledge & Kegan Paul, 1981.

McConville, S., *English Local Prisons, 1860–1900: Next Only to Death*, London, Routledge, 1995.

McDonald, J., 'The Cost of Shipping Convicts to Australia', *International Journal of Maritime History*, vol. 2, 1990.

McGowen, R., 'He Beareth Not the Sword in Vain', *Eighteenth Century Studies*, vol. 21, 1981.

McGowen, R., 'The Image of Justice and Reform of the Criminal Law in early-nineteenth century England', *Buffalo Law Review*, vol. 32, 1983.

McGowen, R., 'The Body and Punishment in Eighteenth-century England', *Journal of Modern History*, vol. 59, 1987.

McGowen, R., 'The Changing face of God's Justice', *Criminal Justice History*, vol. 9, 1988.

McGowen, R., 'Civilizing Punishment: the end of the public execution in England', *Journal of British Studies*, vol. 33, 1994.

McLynn, F., *Crime and Punishment in Eighteenth-Century England*, Oxford University Press, 1991.

McWilliams, W., 'The Mission to the English Police Courts, 1876–1936', *The Howard Journal*, vol. 22, 1983.

Midwiner, E., *Law and Order in early-Victorian Lancashire*, York, St Anthony's Press, 1968.

Miller, W. R., *Cops and Bobbies: Police Authority in New York and London, 1830–1870*, University of Chicago, 1977.

Miller, W. R., 'Never on Sunday: Moralistic Reformers and the Police in London and New York' in Bayley (ed.), *Police and Society*, 1977.

Mingay, G. E., 'Rural War: the life and times of Captain Swing', in Mingay (ed.), *Unquiet Countryside*, 1989.

Mingay, G. E., (ed.), *The Unquiet Countryside*, London, Routledge, 1989.

Morgan, J., *Conflict and Order: the police and labour disputes in England and Wales, 1900–1939*, Oxford University Press, 1987.

Morrison, A., *A Child of the Jago*, London, Nelson, 1896.

Morrison, W. D., 'Are Our Prisons a Failure?' *Fortnightly Review*, vol. 61, 1894.

Morrison, W. D., 'Prisons and Prisoners' *Nineteenth Century*, vol. 69, 1898.

Munsche, P. B., *Gentleman and Poachers*, Cambridge University Press, 1981.

Muskett, P., 'The East Anglian Agrarian Riots of 1822', *Agricultural History Review*, vol. 32, 1984.

Muskett, P., 'The Suffolk Incendiaries, 1843–45', *Journal of Regional and Local Studies*, vol. 7, 1987.

Neeson, J. M., 'The opponents of enclosure in eighteenth-century Northampton-shire', *Past & Present*, vol. 105, 1984.

Oberwittker, D., 'Crime and Authority in Eighteenth-Century England: law enforce-ment on the local level', *Historical Social Research*, vol. 15, 1990.

Paley, R., ' "An Imperfect, Inadequate and Wretched System"?: Policing London before Peel', *Criminal Justice History*, vol. 10, 1989.

Paley, W., *The Principles of Moral and Political Philosophy*, London, R. Faulder, 1785.

Palmer, S. H., *Police and Protest in England and Ireland, 1780–1850*, Cambridge University Press, 1988.

Parker, G., 'The Prisoner in the Box – the making of the Criminal Evidence Act, 1898', in Guy and Beale (eds), *Law and Social Change*, 1984.

Pattenden, R., *English Criminal Appeals, 1844–1994*, Oxford University Press, 1996.

Peacock, A. E., 'The successful prosecution of the Factory Acts, 1833–55' *Economic History Review*, 2nd ser., vol. 37, 1984.

Peacock, A. J., 'Village Radicalism in East Anglia, 1800–1850' in Dunbabin (ed.), *Rural Discontent*, 1974.

Pearson, G., *Hooligan: a history of respectable fears*, London, Macmillan, 1985.

Perkin, H., *The Origins of Modern British Society, 1780–1880*, London, Routledge & Kegan Paul, 1969.

Petrow, S., *Policing Morals: the Metropolitan Police and the Home Office, 1870–1914*, Oxford University Press, 1994.

Philips, D., 'Riots and Public Order in the Black Country, 1835–60' in Stevenson & Quinault, *Popular Protest*, 1974.

Philips, D., 'The Black Country Magistracy, 1835–60: a changing elite and the exer-cise of its power', *Midland History*, vol. 3, 1976.

Philips, D., *Crime and Authority in Victorian England*, London, Croom Helm, 1977.

Philips, D., 'A new engine of power and authority: the institutionalization of law enforcement in England, 1780–1830', in Gatrell, Lenman and Parker (eds), *Crime and the Law*, 1980.

Philips, D., 'Crime and Punishment', in Cohen and Scull (eds), *Social Control*, 1983.

Philips, D., 'Good Men to Associate and Bad Men to Conspire: Associations for the Prosecution of Felons in England, 1760–1860' in Hay and Snyder (eds), *Policing and Prosecution*, 1989.

Philips, D. and R. D. Storch, 'Whigs and Coppers: the Grey Ministry's national police scheme, 1832', *Historical Research*, vol. 67, 1994.

Pick, D., *Faces of degeneration, a European disorder, c.1848–1918*, Cambridge University Press, 1989.

Plint, T., *Crime in England*, London, Charles Gilpin, 1851.

Priestley, P., *Victorian Prison Lives*, London, Methuen, 1985.

Pringle, N. and J. Treversh, *150 Years Policing in Watford District and Hertfordshire County*, Luton, Radley Shaw, 1991.

Potter, H., *Hanging in Judgment: Religion and the Death Penalty in England*, London, SCM Press, 1993.

Purvis, J., *Hard Lessons: The Lives and Education of Working-class Women in Nineteenth-cen-tury England*, Oxford, Polity Press, 1989.

Quinton, R. F., *Crime and Criminals, 1876–1910*, London, Longman, Green & Co., 1910.

Radzinowicz, L. and R. Hood, *The Emergence of Penal Policy in Victorian and Edwardian England*, Oxford University Press, 1990.

Reiner, R., *The Politics of the Police*, Hemel Hempstead, Harvester Wheatsheaf, 1992.

Reith, C., *The Police Idea*, Oxford University Press, 1938.

Reith, C., *The British Police and the Democratic Ideal*, Oxford University Press, 1943.

Reith, C., *A Short History of the Police*, Oxford University Press, 1948.

Reith, C., *A New Study of Police History*, London, Oliver & Boyd, 1956.

Reynolds, S., B. Woolley and T. Woolley, *Seems so! A Working-class View of Politics*, London, Macmillan, 1911.

Richardson, T. L., 'The Agricultural Labourers' Standard of Living in Lincolnshire, 1790–1840: social protest and public order', *Agricultural History Review*, vol. 41, 1993.

Richter, A. F., *Bedfordshire Police, 1840–1990*, Kempston, Hooley, 1990.

Richter, D., *Riotous Victorians*, Ohio University Press, 1981.

Robb, G., *White-Collar Crime in Modern England, 1845–1929*, Cambridge University Press, 1992.

Roberts, D., 'The Scandal of Birmingham Borough Gaol, 1853: a case for penal reform', *Journal of Legal History*, vol. 7, 1986.

Roberts, M. J. D., 'Public and private in early nineteenth-century London: the vagrant act of 1822 and its enforcement', *Social History*, vol. 13, 1988.

Roberts, R., *The Classic Slum*, London, Penguin, 1971.

Rosenthal, M., *The Character Factory: Baden-Powell and the Origins of the Boy Scout Movement*, London, Collins, 1986.

Ross, E., '"Fierce Questions and Taunts": married life in working-class London, 1840–1914', *Feminist Studies*, vol. 8, 1983.

Ross, E., *Love and Toil*, Oxford University Press, 1993.

Rudé, G., *Protest and Punishment*, Oxford University Press, 1978.

Rudé, G., *Criminal and Victim: crime and society in early nineteenth-century England*, Oxford University Press, 1985.

Rule, J., *The Experience of Labour in Eighteenth-Century Industry*, London, Croom Helm, 1981.

Schapiro, B., '"To a Moral Certainty": theories of knowledge and Anglo-American juries, 1600–1850', *The Hastings Law Review*, vol. 38, 1986.

Schubert, A., 'Private Initiative in Law Enforcement: Associations for the Prosecution of Felons, 1744–1856', in Bailey, *Policing and Punishment*.

Scollan, M., *Sworn to Serve: Police in Essex*, Chichester, Phillmore, 1993.

Selleck, R. W. J., 'Mary Carpenter: a confident and contradictory reformer', *History of Education*, vol. 14, 1985.

Shaw, A. G. L., *Convicts and the Colonies*, London, Faber & Faber, 1996; reprinted Melbourne University Press, 1981.

Showalter, E., *The Female Malady: Women, Madness and English Culture, 1830–1980*, London, Virago, 1987.

Shpayer-Makov, H., 'The making of a police labour force', *Criminal Justice History*, vol. 24, 1990.

Shpayer-Makov, H., 'A portrait of a novice constable in the London Metropolitan Police, c.1900', *Criminal Justice History*, vol. 12, 1991.

Shpayer-Makov, H., 'Career prospects in the London Metropolitan Police in the early twentieth century', *Journal of Historical Sociology*, vol. 4, 1991.

Sindall, R. S., 'Middle-class crime in nineteenth century England', *Criminal Justice History*, 1983.

Sindall, R. S., 'The London Garotting Panics of 1856 and 1862', *Social History*, vol. 12, 1987.

Sindall, R. S., *Street Violence in the Nineteenth Century: media panic or real danger?*, Leicester University Press, 1990.

Smith, D., 'The demise of transportation in mid-Victorian penal policy', *Criminal Justice History*, vol. 3, 1982.

Smith, P. T., *Policing Victorian London*, Westport, Connecticut, Greenwood Press, 1985.

Smith, R., *Trial by Medicine: insanity and responsibility in Victorian trials*, Edinburgh University Press, 1981.

Springhall, J., *Youth, Empire and Society*, London, Croom Helm, 1977.

Springhall, J., *Sure and Steadfast: A History of the Boys' Brigade, 1885–1983*, London, Collins, 1983.

Stack, J. A., 'Deviance and reformation in early-Victorian social policy: the case of Parkhurst prison, 1836–1864', *Historical Reflections*, vol. 6, 1979.

Stead, P. J., 'The New Police' in Bayley (ed.), *Police and Society*, 1977.

Stead, P. J., *The Police of Britain*, London, Macmillan, 1985.

Steedman, C., *Policing the Victorian Community: the formation of the English provincial police from 1856 to 1880*, London, Routledge, 1984.

Stephen, J. F., 'Capital Punishment', *Fraser's Magazine*, vol. 69, 1864.

Stevenson, J. and R. Quinault (eds), *Popular Protest and Public Order*, London, Allen & Unwin, 1974.

Stevenson, J., *Popular Disturbances in England*, London, Longmans, 1992.

Stevenson, S., 'The "habitual criminal" in nineteenth-century England: some observations on the figures', *Urban History Yearbook*, vol. 14, 1986.

Stockdale, E., *A Study of Bedford Prison, 1660–1877*, London, Phillimore, 1977.

Stockdale, E., 'A Short History of Prison Inspection in England', *British Journal of Criminology*, vol. 23, 1983.

Storch, R. D., 'The Plague of Blue Locusts: police reform and popular resistance in northern England, 1840–57' *International Review of Social History*, vol. 20, 1975.

Storch, R. D., 'The policeman as domestic missionary', *Journal of Social History*, vol. 9, 1976.

Storch, R. D., 'Police Control of Street Prostitution in Victorian London' in Bayley (ed.), *Police and Society*, 1977.

Storch, R. D. (ed.), *Popular Culture and Custom in Nineteenth-Century England*, London, Croom Helm, 1980.

Storch, R. D., 'Policing rural southern England before the police: opinions and practice, 1830–1856', in Hay and Snyder (eds), *Policing and Prosecution*, 1989.

Streib, V. L., 'Capital Punishment History', *Criminal Justice History*, vol. 10, 1989.

Sturt, G., *Change in the Village*, London 1912, reprinted London, Caliban Books, 1984.

Swift, R., 'Another Stafford Street Row', *Immigrants and Minorities*, vol. 3, 1984.

Swift, R., *Police Reform in Early-Victorian York*, University of York, Borthwick Papers, vol. 73, 1987.

Swift, R., 'Urban Policing in Early-Victorian England, 1835–1856: a reappraisal', *History*, 73, 1988.

Swift, R., 'The English Urban Magistracy and the Administration of Justice during the early nineteenth century: Wolverhampton 1815–60', *Midland History*, vol. 17, 1992.

Styles, J., 'The Emergence of the Police – Explaining Police Reform in eighteenth and nineteenth century England', *British Journal of Criminology*, vol. 27, 1987.

Taithe, B., *The Essential Mayhew*, London, Rivers Oram Press, 1996.

Taylor, D., *999 And All That*, Oldham Corporation, 1968.

Taylor, D., 'The Antipodean Arrest: or how to be a successful policeman in nineteenth-century Middlesbrough' *Bulletin of the Cleveland and Teesside Local History Society*, vol. 58, 1990.

Taylor, D., 'Crime and Policing in early-Victorian Middlesbrough, 1835–55', *Journal of Regional and Local Studies*, vol. 11, 1991.

Taylor, D., 'The standard of living of career policemen in Victorian England: the evidence of a provincial borough force', *Criminal Justice History*, vol. 12, 1991.

Taylor, D., '*A Well-chosen, effective body of men': the Middlesbrough police force c.1841–1914*, University of Teeside, 1995.

Taylor, D., 'Policing and the Community: late twentieth-century myths and late nineteenth-century realities', in K. Laybourn (ed.), *Social Conditions, Status and Community*, Stroud, Sutton, 1997.

Taylor, D., *The new police in the nineteenth century: crime, conflict and control*, Manchester University Press, 1997.

Thackeray, W., 'Going to see a Man hanged', *Fraser's Magazine*, vol. 22, 1840.

Thompson, E. P., 'Crimes of Anonymity' in Hay *et al.*, *Albion's Fatal Tree*, 1975.

Tobias, J. J., *Crime and Industrial Society in the Nineteenth Century*, London, Penguin, 1972.

Tomes, N., '"A Torrent of Abuse": crimes of violence between working-class men and women in London', *Journal of Social History*, vol. 11, 1978.

Tomlinson, M. H., '"Not an Instrument of Punishment": prison diet in the mid-nineteenth century', *Journal of Consumer Studies and Home Economics*, vol. 2, 1978.

Vickery, A., 'Golden Age to Separate Spheres?', *Historical Journal*, vol. 36, 1993.

Vogler, R., *Reading the Riot Act*, Milton Keynes, Open University Press, 1991.

Wakefield, E. G., *The Punishment of Death*, London, James Ridgway, 1831.

Walkowitz, J., *Prostitution and Victorian Society: Women, Class and the State*, Cambridge University Press, 1980.

Walton, J. K. and R. Poole, 'The Lancashire Wakes in the Nineteenth Century', in Storch (ed.), *Popular Culture*, 1980.

Weaver, M., 'The new science of policing: crime and the Birmingham Police Force, 1839–1842', *Albion*, vol. 26, 1994.

Weeks, J., *Sex, Politics and Society: the regulation of sexuality since 1800*, London, Longman, 1989.

Weinberger, B., 'The police and the public in mid-nineteenth-century Warwickshire', in Bailey, *Policing and Punishment*.

Weinberger, B., 'Are the Police Professionals? An Historical Account of the British Police Institution', in Weinberger and Emsley (eds), *Policing Western Europe*, 1991.

Weinberger, B., *Keeping the Peace: Policing Strikes in England, 1906–1926*, Oxford, Berg, 1991.

Weinberger, B. and C. Emsley (eds), *Policing Western Europe*, Westport, Connecticut, Greenwood Press, 1991.

Weiner, M. J., 'The March of Penal Progress?', *Journal of British Studies*, vol. 26, 1987.

Weiner, M. J., *Reconstructing the Criminal: culture, law and policy in England, 1830–1914*, Cambridge University Press, 1990.

Wells, R., 'Sheep rustling in Yorkshire in the age of the industrial and agrarian revolutions', *Northern History*, vol. 20, 1981.

Wells, R., 'Rural rebels in southern England in the 1830s', in C. Emsley and J. Walvin (eds), *Artisans, Peasants, Proletarians*, London, Croom Helm, 1985.

Williams, K. S., *A Textbook of Criminology*, London, Blackstone Press, 1991.

Wilson, S. R., 'The Court of Quarter Sessions and Larceny in Sussex, 1775–1820', *Criminal Justice History*, vol. 7, 1986.

Woodgate, J., *The Essex Police*, Lavenham, Dalton, 1983.

Woods, D. C., 'The Operation of the Master and Servant Act in the Black Country, 1858–75', *Midland History*, vol. 7, 1982.

Zedner, L., *Women, crime and custody in Victorian England*, Oxford University Press, 1994.

INDEX